COMBAT COPS

Nigel Allsopp

COMBAT COPS

THE PAST, THE PRESENT AND THEIR STORIES

CONTENTS

ACKNOWLEDGEMENT

This book was written over several years as the process included contacting over 40 nations embassy's where Military Attachés provided either information or contacts of their respective countries' military police. I would also like to thank the dozens of serving and ex-military policemen and women from across the world who were keen to provide information on a subject dear to their hearts but also elusive to many. I would also like to thank several military police experts whom I interviewed in person, their knowledge and insight was invaluable. Finally, I would like to acknowledge all the current serving military police across the globe in harm's way. There were maybe days where you may feel like all law enforcement officers occasionally do – unloved, unneeded, and not respected by politicians or the higher echelons of command. Know one thing. History has shown no army in the world can operate without the military police.

This book on military police history although extensive in its own right is still the tip of the iceberg of what various units do in numerous countries. It would be impossible to cover all the worlds' military police history in one book. I would like to bring to the attention of readers the numerous military police museum and websites around the world if you seek further information on a particular country.

ABSTRACT

We know your name and where you live.

Try turning on the TV – scan all the channels and you will see at least a police show, documentary, or drama on most channels. People are interested in crime and police work.

But what do you know about the closed world of the military police? Maybe you have seen TV Cop shows – but what are Military Cops.

No detailed book like this has been written on the subject – this one is written by an ex-MP with more than 20 years' experience plus an additional 18 years as a Civilian Police Officer.

Smartly dressed one day – arresting drunken soldiers – then in combat gear clearing a house full of terrorists in a far-off land.

The military policeman must be one of the least appreciated yet most indispensable military figures in modern history. In the mobile warfare of the 21st century no army could keep its vital supply routes open without the military policeman. This book documents the organisation of many of the Worlds military police units. Their duties included VIP Close Personnel Protection, traffic control; maintaining military order and discipline; collection and escorting prisoners of war; prevention of looting; disarming civilians; checking captured enemy soldiers for documents; training local police forces and providing street patrols in occupied areas. They are also one of the Military's least known organizations, now come inside their world.

I will take you behind the scenes; it's a sometimes scary, sometimes humorous world.

Facts have been gathered from MP units across the world, plus I use a few short stories from real MPs to back up real time missions and operations. It would be impossible to cover the history of every military police force, so I have concentrated in the first part of the book on the UK and America whose tradition either go back hundreds of years or have been the major integrators of the changing role and employment of these forces.

The book is suited to Military historians, anyone interested in law enforcement, servicemen and civilian alike. It is not however a complete history of each country's military police rather an insight into that nation's MP force. There are several books which I mention throughout the chapters that specialize in a specific country or time period on military police.

The first half of the book tells you who the MP is and how he is made – their roles and missions from ancient times to today.

The second half of the book talks about several of the world's MP units country by country.

Sometimes hated by their own side, sometimes loved as saviours – always feared, but respected. No military in the world today can function without them.

They are the Military Police.

PREFACE

The Provost must have a horse allowed him and some soldiers to attend him, and all the rest commanded to obey and assist, or else the Service will suffer, for he is but one man and must correct many, and therefore he cannot be beloved. And he must be riding from one garrison to another to see the soldiers do no outrage nor scathe the country.

– Extract from Clode's Military and Martial Law.

This was written almost four hundred years ago during the English Civil War and serves as an early example of correction to any errant soldier's behaviour. As a consequence, fear of the military amongst the civilian population was greatly reduced as a result of this measure. Today the various service police disciplines provide a vital role in ensuring orderly behaviour within the military ranks. In contrast the civilian police slowly evolved from the military model almost two hundred years ago and has provided a continuous and essential community service ever since.

The military footprint was strong initially with the civilian police, as many of the early recruits were former military personnel and most of the Chiefs of Police had held high military rank.

However, as policing evolved, they quickly became an essential and respected community service. Sadly, unlike its companion fire and ambulance emergency services, the civilian police service is forever destined to be merely respected rather than loved by the people it serves.

Consequently, the service and civilian police services are forever destined to be uniquely linked together as sharing the burden of never being 'beloved' by its clients while still resolutely providing a professional and essential service.

Nigel has brought his unique experience as a service policeman with both the Royal New Zealand and Royal Australian police services, coupled with his lengthy service with the Queensland Police Force, in providing a balanced view of the trials and tribulations of the military and civilian police services. As a former member of civilian and military police forces, I am very aware of the vital role both supply to the communities they serve and strongly recommend this book as a true and balanced account.

Richard Coulthard

Squadron Leader (Retired) – Royal Australian Air Force Police 1989–2003)

Detective – Peel Regional Police Force Ontario Canada 1976–89

Detective Constable – Bermuda Police Bermuda 1970–76

Police Constable – Newcastle City Police England 1967–70

FOREWORD

The Provost

> *A man with great judgement and experience of martial discipline.... well versed in all laws and ordinances of a military camp and in all matters essential to the smooth running of an army... the* Provost Marshal *should love justice, be impartial with his dealings and have an eye that could gaze on all objects without winking and while having a heart filled with discreet compassion was not touched by foolish or melting pity.*

Articles of War 1662

The qualities that make a good service policeman or woman include trust, integrity, compassion, determination, and intelligence. Many in the armed forces over the years have looked down upon those who are in service police trades. Yet while every officer and non-commissioned officer is required to maintain discipline at all times, it is the service police who are tasked with dealing with the more unpleasant aspects of human behaviour that can be found in any society, including the armed forces. To allow such behaviours to go unchecked not only adversely impacts upon the victim, but has a deleterious effect on the efficiency, operational ability and professionalism of the armed forces concerned.

As society has evolved over the centuries, so have policing methods and service police organisations have not always been allowed to keep up with the latest methods and technology. Fortunately, that now seems to be changing in these ever-increasing troubled times.

Nigel's research and writing of this book combines his experiences and passion for this subject. His exemplary service as an RNZAF Police Dog Handler and subsequently service in the RAAF and Queensland Police show the esteem in which he is held in both Australia and New Zealand. His dedication to Purple Poppy Day and remembering those animals that have also served lends extra weight to a book, carefully researched, well written and which I strongly recommend.

Roger Parton
Flight Lieutenant (Retired)
Royal New Zealand Air Force Police (1966–1984)
Deputy Provost Marshal, Air Staff (1978–1984)

INTRODUCTION

Crimes can happen anywhere, and the Military is no exception. Fortunately, the Military has their own law enforcement and security specialists to handle crimes committed on Defence property or that involve Defence personnel. Military Police protect lives and property on Defence establishments by enforcing military laws and regulations, as well as controlling traffic, preventing crime, and responding to emergencies.

Military Police are primarily responsible for providing support to the battlefield by conducting area security, police intelligence operations, internment and resettlement, manoeuvre and mobility support, and law & order operations. In peace and war operations duties of the Military Police team may include patrolling areas on foot, by car or by vessel. They interview witnesses, victims, and suspects in the course of investigating crimes. They collect fingerprints and other forensic evidence, to enable the arrest and charging criminal suspects. They train and work with police dogs. Testifying in court. Guarding entrances and conducting traffic control. It's not just a sense of authority that attracts men and women to the MP Corps, recruits want to help and serve others. An MP's job can be stressful with so much responsibility entrusted to them they must make decisions on an independent basis, and not rely on being steered by others.

Particularly in today's war on terrorism, both internationally in places such as Iraq and Afghanistan as well as homeland security, much public attention has focused on the role of conventional Army units, and Special Forces. However, a disproportionate share of the warfighting has been done, under the media radar by Military Police units. These squad and platoon-sized units patrol dangerous urban streets, train local police units to improve neighborhood stability, and conduct civic action missions. On many occasions they have been rushed into a vicious fire fight to come to the assistance of infantry units in desperate straits.

In Afghanistan they keep villages terrorist free, monitor balloting sites, and interdict drug shipments. In detention centres at Camp Bucca, Iraq, Bagram, Afghanistan, and Guantanamo, Cuba they guard some of the most dangerous terrorists in history.

The fact that an Army will not conduct operations without military police formations and defines the role of the MP in support of joint, multinational, and interagency operations as essential. The capabilities and organization of the Military Police demonstrates their flexibility and diversity able to adapt to any mission throughout the full spectrum of army operations and characterizes the MP as a combat-force multiplier. They can also be a less threatening presence than tanks and infantry. It is their subdued yet persuasive presence most military planners' value on the battlefield.

This book shows how the Military Police patrol in harm's way, whether in the bloody streets of Iraq, the dangerous backcountry of Afghanistan, too domestic emergency situations or wherever they are needed. Skilled at switching between roles in public order and war, military police have become leading players in many militaries' wars on terrorism. So essential are MPs on today's battlefield that according to its Commanding Officer any recruits attending the Military Police School at Fort Leonard Wood, in the USA are almost certain to deploy overseas as their first duty once qualified.

By far the Army have the largest military police formations, to the extent that some people do not rely on the fact that other services have them. Within the armed forces Military Police are known by many names, whether Army, Air Force, Marines or Navy they all have similar functions. In most Navies, Shore Patrols of Commonwealth and US Navies, usually formed only for patrols of naval facilities or in the country they are visiting rather than full time Police formations. Whereas Master of Arms are full time professionals.

A Master-at-arms (MA) is the Naval version of the military Police responsible for discipline and law enforcement.

The Master-at-arms is a ship's senior rating, normally carrying the rank of chief petty officer or warrant officer, the MAA is in charge of discipline and is addressed as 'Master' if holding the rank of chief petty officer, even if the rating in question is a woman, she is still addressed as 'Master' and known as the master-at-arms. The MAA is assisted by regulators of the Royal Navy Police, of which he is himself a member. He is nicknamed the 'jaunty', a corruption of the French Gendarme. The non-substantive (trade) badge of an MAA is a crown within a wreath.

The post of master-at-arms was introduced to the Royal Navy during the reign of King Charles I; their original duties were to be responsible for the ship's small arms and edged weapons, and to drill the ship's company in their use. This was not an onerous task, and masters-at-arms came to made responsible for 'regulating duties'. Their role as weapons instructors was eventually taken over by the chief gunner.

Air Force Police protect assets associated with that service as well as having a law enforcement capability. Both Air Force and Naval Police frequently train together and in many countries at army military police schools.

In the Air Force some police functions have been combined with that of airfield security. Such units as the British RAF Regiment, the Australian Air Defence Guards, New Zealand Airfield Protection Squadron or USAF Security Police have a combination of both.

Military police may refer to a section of the military solely responsible for policing the armed forces (referred to as Provosts) or a section of the military responsible for policing in both the armed forces and in the civilian population such as the French Gendarmerie, or the Italian Carabinieri, or a section of the military solely responsible for policing the civilian population such as the Romanian Gendarmerie or Brazilian State Police (Policia Militar).

For ease of the reader to understand I will, where possible, refer to them all as Military Police (MP) or Service Police (SP). Throughout the chapters if known by other names I will highlight it there.

The Military policeman must be one of the least appreciated yet most indispensable military figures in modern history. In the mobile warfare of the 21st century no army could keep its vital supply routes open without the military policeman. This book documents the organisation, and roles of the many and varied military police units of the World.

"You cannot have a good army without a police force within."
– Napoleon Bonaparte

Supporting The Three

"I am the Infantry, follow me
Not a foot soldier, we're much more you see
We'll take the fight to the enemy
I am the Infantry, first of THE THREE"

"I am the Cavalry, follow me
A Modern horse soldier in an APC
Charging straight forward to the enemy
I am the Cav, most daring of THE THREE"

"I am the armour, follow me
The arm of decision I'll always be
When the going gets rough, call on me
I am Armour, the best of THE THREE"

"Armour, Cav and Infantry
Rush headlong into the melee
Breaking the lines like an angry sea
Deep into enemy territory"

"Approaching a cross-road, what do we see
the area secured by two lonely MP's
Directing us forward, how can this be
How long has he been here waiting for me"

"What a crazy person an MP must be
He has no firepower or armour like me
And I thought everyone followed THE THREE
Armour, Cav and Infantry"

"I am the MP; don't follow me
You don't want to be where I will be

Guarding a crossroad, waiting for THE THREE
Just my partner, an M-sixteen and me"

"With the objective taken, wait and see
No one will remember the lonely MP
Who held this ground so they could run free
But that's my job, supporting THE THREE"

– Written by SGT Allan Perkins, 1982 (an MP)

PART ONE

Carabinier

1812.

Gendarme d'Élite

GARDE IMPÉRIALE

MILITARY POLICE EARLY HISTORY

Since the creation of time there has existed some form of Law Enforcement. In any ancient army there has always been someone to take the job of the Provost Marshal. There had been an office of the Provost Marshal with the ability to arrest and punish soldiers for desertion, plundering or outrage stretching back centuries.

Each Country throughout the world has its own Military Police history and I will discuss several countries histography on Military Police roles in part two of this book, however they have all to some extent been influenced by ancient armies' employment and development of such forces.

There may have been some form of ad hoc military police function performed by individuals in ancient armies, and indeed up until the establishment of permanent armies in Western Countries the Military Police or Provost function was carried out by formations usually raised for a particular campaign then disbanded. However, it is within the Roman Army that we first find official recorded information on soldiers carrying out this function full time. The Romans had a three *Urban Cohorts* stationed in Rome itself created by Augustus.[1]

Tacitus clearly stated their duties, "to control the slaves and those citizens whose natural boldness gives way to disorderly conduct, unless

---

1 Christopher J. Fuhrmann, *Policing the Roman Empire: Soldiers, Administration, and Public Order* (Oxford University Press, 2012), pp. 202, 211.

they are overawed by force". The cohorts were regarded part of the Imperial Army and had considerable power; in effect they were one of the first Military Police Forces in history. To carry out their function they used large clubs and employed large fierce attack dogs and it is said 'hounds to track down runaway slaves'.

Augustus further created in AD 6 the *Vigiles* of 7000 men within the fourteen regions of Rome they were in effect a cross between fireman and policeman. Amongst their duties were the task of putting down riots. In the Rome Legions themselves, there were specialist staff in the Head Quarters known as *tabularium legionis*. One Officer post was the *questionarii* (Police and investigation staff) this officer had several *Immunes* under his command. The Rome army had no specialist branches but instead had the important privilege – immunity from heavy fatigues for soldiers required to undertake special duties. Of interest to this book were the *legati pro praetor* for the *immunes* (Police officers). A Centurion was not only a leader of men but that formations disciplinarian and would award and give out punishment, so they too preformed a type of Military Police role.[2]

Precursors of the modern military police force can also be traced back to the Chinese dynasty eras. According to ancient Chinese records, armed forces akin to the modern MP served from the Chou dynasty (approximately 3000 B.C), through Han, Wei, Tang, all the way to the Qing dynasty. These forces were elite guards who were responsible for the safeguard of the emperor and his surroundings, but also for enforcement of proper military conduct. It was not until the late Qing dynasty, in light of the invasion of the Eight Nations Alliance and Japanese influence, did the emperor finally decide to create the nation's first Military Police units.

The Egyptians had a militarized police force in the earliest historical times whose duty it was to protect and serve, prevent crimes, and catch

---

2 Edward Echols, *The Roman City Police: Origin and Development.* The Classical Journal Vol. 53, No. 8 1958, pp. 377–385

criminals, and patrol the land, ensuring the safety of the citizens and their property. There were doorkeepers who controlled the traffic at the city gates and temple doors and guards who supervised the goings-on in the marketplaces, where they apprehended thieves. So effective were they that foreign conquerors left the Egyptian police organizations mostly intact and used them for their own purposes. Under the Roman occupation the police became an arm of the military, being locally supervised by centurions. The office of the *strategos* examined the evidence gathered by the police and prepared the court case which would be presented to the viceroy or one of his deputies for judgment. During the Middle and New Kingdoms, a nationwide police force grew out of the semi-military units securing the borders, which consisted to a large part of Nubian Medjay, who had been employed during the late Old Kingdom in accompanying expeditions into the South and policing the frontier region of the country. These Medjay became identified in this role to such an extent that in the New Kingdom their ethnonym was synonymous with 'police'[3].

The Anglo-Saxon system of maintaining public order since the Norman conquest was a militarized system led by a Constable, which was based on a social obligation for the good conduct of the others; more common was that local lords and nobles were responsible to maintain order in their

---

3 Roger S. Bagnall. Army and Police in Roman Upper Egypt. *Journal of the American Research Center in Egypt*, Vol. 14 (1977), pp. 67–86.

lands, and often appointed a Constable, sometimes unpaid, to enforce the aw.[4] During medieval times dog handlers were called *Fewterers.* These men were responsible for the Kings or his Lords war dogs and hunting dogs. They were true military dogs as selected large mastiff type breeds were trained to attack humans in peace and war (perhaps the first military police dogs). The Fewterers also trained Hound breeds that were used as tracker dogs.

Henry the Fifth, most famous for the battle of Agincourt, had six thousand men at arms, mainly consisting of five thousand-foot archers fought against some 30,000 French nobility. This battle perhaps overshadows his professional military approach overall. This professional conduct to military campaigning saw one of the first recorded standing orders being laid down that the English Army would not rape, steal or loot the towns and countryside they were marching by.

The first modern record of a person conducting the duties of a Provost Marshal stem from 28 May 1241, when Henry II appointed William of Cassingham as a Military 'Sergeant of the Peace'. He and his Under-Provosts were the ancestors of the modern Royal Military Police.[5]

The first recorded Provost Marshal in English history of whom there is a personal record is Sir Henry Guldeford (or Guylford) appointed in 1511. The Provost Marshal was responsible for maintaining discipline within the English armies together with the King's personal security and was also described as the 'first and greatest gaoler of the Army'. As the Provost Marshal's office gradually assumed more and more duties of a policing nature within the Army, he was provided with State-paid troops, referred to in Henry VIII's day as Provost Companies.[6] Articles of War of 1591, during the reign of Queen Elizabeth laid down that:

"No man shall resist the Provost Marshal, or other of his officers, in apprehending any malfactor, but if need be shall aid and assist him…"

---

4 Loyn, H. R., *The Governance of Anglo-Saxon England, 500–1087* (1984).
5 https://www.britishmilitaryhistory.co.uk/docs-services-corps-military-police/
6 https://rhqrmp.org/rmp_history.html

The office of the Provost Marshal (PM) is one of the most ancient in Britain and the Commonwealth and it is difficult to establish its origins with any certainty. The word provost originated from the French word *prevot*, which means 'Military Sense'. The appointment of Provost Marshal within the United Kingdom dates back to the 13th century when they were appointed by the King to keep order in the rabble armies raised by his barons.

Queen Elizabeth I created provost marshals in the English counties to apprehend lawless disbanded soldiery. Offenders arrested were hanged on the spot. These provost marshals were the first County Chief Constables.

The fact remains that someone did the job because it was vital to the effectiveness of the army. Francis Markham's *Five Decades of Epistles of Warre*, published in 1622, states that the 'Provost Marshal would be a Soldier of great judgment and experience in all martial discipline, well seen in the laws and ordinances of the Post or Camp'. Even today the senior Military Police officer at the Theatre, Corps, Division, and Brigade Level and for each garrison, is known as a Provost Marshal.

The need for military police has been evident to military commanders since the first wars evolving masses of troops. Whenever a nation engaged in warfare, some form of police element emerged to assist its leaders in maintaining various aspects of discipline. Surfacing when necessity dictated, the military police evolved through several phases, each meeting the needs of a particular period in history. Eventually germinating into the birth of the modern military police assuming increased responsibilities, military police established their place as combat soldiers who have the professional knowledge and flexibility needed to perform a variety of missions in war and peace.

Had every soldier over the centuries been an obedient and dutiful soul, there would have been no need for military police. Sadly, armies particularly in historical times have often been the home for the criminal, and all had their share of thieves and cut-throats, as well as its drunken and licentious element. How these were contained, or dealt with, and the men who tamed the lawless are the main subject of this book. The Military Police have had to process extreme power to be able to control the masses. In fact, right up to the 20th Century often Military Police had the power of field execution without trial. Military Police were often associated with hanging offenders, in fact when I first became a Military Policeman in the Air Force, I was amused to find that the Defence Regulations had not be revised since the 17th century and as a Provost it stated I was entitled to pick up a horse, saddle and hangman's rope from the quartermaster's store. Unfortunately, the quartermaster did have a sense of humour when I tried.

In a latter Article of War in 1629 King Charles I, described the role of his Provost Marshal in the following terms:

> *"The provost must have a horse allowed him and some soldiers to attend him and all the rest commanded to obey him and assist him, or else the service will suffer. For he is one man and must correct many and therefore he cannot be beloved. And he must be riding from one garrison to another, to see that the soldiers do not outrage nor scathe about the country."*

There were no permanent police in the army and only during war would a provost marshal, an officer of field rank, be charged to "secure deserters, and all other criminals." The provost marshal, or his subordinates, were to "go round the army, hinder the soldiers from pillaging, indict offenders, execute the sentence pronounced, and regulate the weights and measures used by the army in the field." In the Iberian Peninsula, a provost marshal served at Wellington's headquarters, and each of the British divisions had an assistant-provost marshal and several men.[7]

During the Peninsula War of 1813–14, Duke of Wellington asked for a Provost Marshal to be appointed to hang looters; by the end of the Peninsular War the Provost Marshal controlled 24 Assistant Provost Marshals. The Assistants were also authorised to hang offenders and eventually each division had its own Assistant Provost Marshal. The Duke of Wellington took a great interest in his Provost Service, issuing comprehensive orders laying down Provost duties and those of his Provost Marshals and their assistants: his 'Bloody Provosts'. In 1810,

---

7 *Canadian Military History* Volume 16 | Issue 4 Article 3 4-26-2012 'Bloody Provost': Discipline During the War of 1812 John R. Grodzinski Royal Military College of Canada.

Wellington complained that the Provost service was not large enough, so he raised the Staff Corps of Cavalry *(This must be distinguished from both the Royal Staff Corps: an organization of field engineers and craftsman that had existed throughout the Peninsula War and the Allied occupation of France; and the Corps of Mounted Guides, also established by Scovell, and employed as couriers; to conduct reconnaissance; and to act as guides.)* (SCC) consisting of volunteer cavalrymen – 144 in the UK, and 142 in Spain and Portugal, under the command of Brevet Lieutenant-Colonel (and Major Commandant of the Corps) George Scovell. Until their new uniforms were issued, they wore a red scarf tied around their right shoulder to distinguish them as serving with the Staff Corps rather than their own regiments. While Scovell had seen his new command as an embryonic unit of special troops able to undertake a variety of duties, Wellington saw them undertaking one task above all others namely to police his notoriously ill-disciplined Army. Disbanded following Napoleon's abdication in 1814, it was re-formed a year later just after the Battle of Waterloo, providing Provost duties for the Allied armies occupying France, before its final disbandment in 1819. During the 'Long Peace' after Waterloo, the Provost Services dropped shapely in number, and the appointment of Provost Marshal General reverted to the earlier form of 'Provost Marshal', at the same time dropping in rank to Captain. Following the outbreak of the Crimean War (1853–56), the Mounted Staff Corps (MSC) was formed to assist the Provost Marshal with the majority of recruits coming from the Irish Constabulary and some from the Metropolitan Police. The MSC was disbanded at War's end.

Normandy after all was his own land so he claimed and therefore he wanted to win hearts and minds of its people. The aim of the overall invasion was to make Henry King of England and France. During the campaign several towns were spared being ransacked if they supplied food for Henry's soldiers. only bread and wine were frequently available at many of these sieges. He ordered his troops not to consume wine as it would cause the English troops, so he thought to go crazy with a belly fall of wine and get up to no good. To achieve this Henry selected foot men at arms to enforce his discipline and orders, any soldier who disobeyed were hanged.

Oliver Cromwell instigated the first truly professional army in England, set down with four basic principles, in the parliamentarian army you had to obey roles, believe in the course, have standing orders and work as a team. To achieve at least two of these principal guidelines he had to employ '*enforcers*' in his army. These selected men ensured that orders were obeyed and men at arms behaved in accordance with the political values of the parliamentarian forces. Although not referenced as such they sound to me like military police.

There has been an office of the Provost Marshal with the ability to arrest and punish soldiers for desertion, plundering or outrage, stretching back centuries in all European Armies. Duke of Wellington asked for a Provost Marshal to be appointed to hang looters and by the end of the Peninsular War the Provost Marshal controlled 24 Assistant Provost Marshals. The assistants were also authorised to hang offenders and eventually each division had its own Assistant Provost Marshal.

In the early 1800s Duke of Wellington raised the Staff Corps of Cavalry as a Military Police Corps. Until a uniform was approved members of the Staff Corps of Cavalry were identified by a red scarf tied around the right shoulder of their original uniform which could well be the origins of the red cap which identifies the modern Military Policeman.[8]

In 1855 the Provost Marshal recommended that the additional manpower he required be of a certain calibre. They must have at least 5 years' service of sober habits, intelligent, active and discreet. This development was the beginning of the existing organization of the Corps of Military Police. On 1 August 1877 this small unit raised in 1855 was formerly established as a distinct corps for service both at home and abroad.

The duties of the Provost Marshal seem essentially the same today as they were in the 17th century – the maintenance of discipline, the prevention of crime within the military and the arrest and bringing to trial of soldiers

---

8 DE Graves, *British Military Discipline in the Napoleonic Period: Gleanings from the Inquiry into the System of Military Punishments in the Army, 1836.* In 1835, King William IV created a commission "for the purpose of inquiring into the several modes of Punishment now authorized and in use for the maintenance of discipline and the prevention of crime" in the British army. The thrust of the commission's work was to ascertain whether or not the punishment of flogging should be retained or abandoned in favour of other means of discipline.

committing offences against military law. The Provost Marshal has evolved into an essential figure on the modern battlefield guiding Commanders at all levels on their duties and responsibilities reference the behaviour and standards of their troops either in battle, at home or abroad.

These were usually formed on an ad hoc basis and were disbanded when campaigns and wars were over. Duke of Wellington somewhat formalised the system into a staff corps with responsibility of keeping order in the ranks during the Napoleonic War. This force was technically disbanded at the end of the war, although it did continue for a while to police the occupied territories of France until Bourbon rule could be re-established.

During the Napoleonic period Military Police were known by several names, they were usually mounted Light Cavalry. The dislike of the Military Police (or hatred in some cases) resulted from horror stories about some harsh treatment being handed out. Perhaps the greatest underlying reason was the feeling MPs were an extension of the military that reached out of the camps where men were and infringed on their free time. They were, as today, in the main not there to stop fun but to ensure the soldiers did not abuse and rob the local population.

The Gendarmerie is the direct descendant of the *Marshalcy of the Ancien Reime*, more commonly known by its French title, the *Maréchaussée* which were the French provost marshal units dating back to the twelfth century. Likewise, in the Continental Army of George Washington the term *Marechaussee* was adopted from the French term Marecheaux (Marshow).

During the Middle Ages there were two Grand Officers of the Kingdom of France with police responsibilities: The Marshal of France and the Constable of France. The military policing responsibilities of the Marshal of France were delegated to the Marshal's provost, whose force was known as the Marshalcy because its authority ultimately derived from the Marshal. The Marshalcy dates back to the Hundred Years War, and some historians trace it back to the early twelfth century. The constabulary was regularised as a military body in 1337. Under King Francis I (who reigned 1515–1547), the *Maréchaussée* was merged with the Constabulary.

During the revolutionary period, Marshalcy commanders generally placed themselves under the local constitutional authorities. As a result, the *Maréchaussée*, whose title was associated with the king, was not disbanded but simply renamed *Gendarmerie Nationale* in February 1791. Its personnel remained unchanged, and the role remained much as it was. However, from this point, the gendarmerie, unlike the Marshalcy, was a fully military force.

Like other German states, Bavaria had also set up in 1812 after a French model Gendarmerie Corps, which was subordinate to the War Department, maintaining public order and security of the Interior. In 1813 for military service outside of Bavaria Lieutenant Colonel Count von Tauffkirchen was named the first commander of the gendarmerie force. Part of the gendarmerie, he used for backup tasks at the command post and in the local neighbourhoods in law-and-order roles. Additionally, a Captain and 40 policemen were used for the personal protection of General Wrede. The bulk of the "gendarmerie in the field was used to protect the baggage (replenishment), keeping the supply routes, collecting and forwarding of stragglers, requisitions, provision of accommodation, security service in the quarter and, patrolling of the battlefield to prevent looting.

Many South America countries were influenced by European powers, in 1566, the first police investigator of Rio de Janeiro was recruited. By the seventeenth century, most 'capitanias' already had local units with law enforcement functions. On the 9th of July 1775 a Cavalry Regiment was created in Minas Gerais for maintaining law and order. In 1808, the Portuguese royal family relocated to Brazil, due to the French invasion of Portugal. When there, King João VI established the *Intendência Geral de Polícia* (General Police Intendancy) for investigations. He also created a Royal Police Guard for Rio de Janeiro in 1809. In 1831, after independence, each province started organizing its local 'military police', tasked to maintain order.

The value of the mounted soldier in Australia was first shown in 1804 when redcoats of the New South Wales Corps set out in pursuit of a large force of rebel convicts who had broken out of the Castle Hill Prison Farm. Strangely some of the mounted troops used in this police role were in fact convicts. Riding with the commanding officer of the Corps was a trooper called Thomas Anelzark, a member of Governor King's mounted convict bodyguard. Anelzark scouted the rebels' movements, helped capture their leaders and was slightly wounded in the Battle of Vinegar Hill that followed. He won a pardon and a land grant. After this, men of the 'bodyguard', already described as 'light horsemen', played an increasingly important role and were fore runners of the Australian military mounted police force.

Many of the roles Military Police perform today can be traced back to the earliest times. Such roles as personnel bodyguards are reflected in today's Close Protection operatives, likewise the movement and flow of a marching army governed by Napoleonic Troops can be seen in today's traffic Military Policeman's duties.

Today's military police personnel provide commanders with an essential element of command and control through the application of several main Military Police functions of Law Enforcement – Mobility and Manoeuvre Support; Security; and Internment and Detention operations. Due to the varied roles a Military Policeman may find themselves during their careers personnel are encouraged to specialise by undertaking further military and category courses, as well as tertiary studies, during their initial engagement. Military Police personnel may specialise in the following areas after serving for a period of time in the area of general police duties such as Dog handlers, Investigators, Correctional staff, and Close Protection Operators to name a few.

In more modern times the military police have developed specializations after serving a number of years as a general duty's role. These are Special Investigation Branch (SIB) and Close Protection (CP). The SIB take on serious and protracted investigations and provide specialist support to investigations such as Scenes of Crime. They provide this service both in garrison and on operations. The Close Protection operatives from within the MP services of the world for senior military personnel on operations and provide a number of on call trained operatives for the Foreign and commonwealth Office.

Boer War

Mounted Military police. Photo courtesy of ALHA.

On the outbreak of war with the Boer republics in 1899, nearly all Britain's 300 military policemen were dispatched to South Africa. They went from MP units in the United Kingdom, Malta, and Egypt, to be employed under the Provost Marshal on a wide range of duties over and above their peace time tasks. These included the supervision of civil police forces; the care of prisoners of war in transit to prisons and camps; the provision of guards for important places; the issue of permits and passes, and the confiscation of arms and ammunition. All this is still done by MPs today.[9]

Prior to WW I camp security and military law enforcement was just an extra detail in the United States army. As such, military police duties were carried out by ordinary troops without any special training or supervision, with varying degrees of efficiency. During the Philippine Insurrection, a special Provost Brigade was organized, which successfully handled all military police activities in that region. Soon after, Army leadership began to realize the emerging importance of well-trained provost troops. This of course, eventually led to the formation of the Military Police as a branch of service in the Army in July of 1918. To aid the soldiers selected to act as Military Police (MP), a symbol of authority in the form of a brassard bearing the initials 'MP' was devised

Image courtesy of Yves Potard, France.

---

9 Captain H. Bullock F.R.Hist.S., I.A. (1929) The Provost Services from 1809 to the Present Day, *Royal United Services Institution Journal*, 74:494, 296–304, DOI: 10.1080/03071842909422558

and issued to the troops detailed to perform the duties of the MP.[10]

Although the US Military Police had an historical background dating back to the American Revolution, it was not until General John J Pershing recognized the need for a unit to carry out police duties which led to the modern identity of the Military Police Corps. The War Department approved a divisional table of organization in 1917, authorizing a headquarters section and two Military Police Companies, marking the first use of a unit officially called Military Police.

World War I marked a significant step in the military police's journey toward permanent branch status within the Army. Once again, the Army organized units both at the War Department level and in the field to carry out military police duties. Following America's entry into the war in 1917, the War Department appointed General Enoch Herbert Crowder the Provost Marshal of the United States Army.

The AEF, the War Department approved a divisional table of organization in May 1917 that included authorisation of a headquarters and two military police companies, a total of 316 officers and men in each division. As the war progressed so did the need for MPs.

The new corps was to consist of the Provost Marshal General Department, AEF, all military police units in the AEF, and 'additional personnel.' The basic organizational unit remained the military police company, which as of October 1918 consisted of 205 officers and men.

Equipment for the AEF military police company was listed in the new legislation. Including 50 horses, 6 mules, 1 wagon, 18 motorcycles, and 105 bicycles, it was one of the most mobile organizations in the Army.

Military Police duties were initially established to supplement the direct support units controlling supply trains to and from the front. Units quickly adapted to the ever-changing needs of the Army and began controlling traffic in the rear area, caring for prisoners of war (POW), and the prevention of unauthorized individuals entering zones of operation. Theses assignments proved to be critical and would eventually shape modern policing functions during wartime operations. The American Expeditionary Force (AEF) established the Provost Marshal General

10 Wright, R. K. (1992). *Army Lineage Series: Military Police.* Washington, D.C.: U.S. Army Centre of Military History.

which had central authority to supervise Military Police or related POW activities. World War I created massive numbers of prisoners of war, and unlike previous conflicts where POWs would be held temporarily until an exchange occurred, MP units were charged with caring for POWs for longer periods of time, transitioning most of them to the rear area over the course of the war. Over 48,000 POWs were transferred from temporary cages to central POW enclosures during the 10-month period the United States was involved in the conflict. As hostilities came to an end in 1918, Europe saw a large number of American Troops begin to occupy sights like Paris, often on unauthorized leave. Military Police units were called upon once again to assist Commanders in enforcing law and order while the Armistice was signed, and troops began transitioning back to America. Even though Brigadier General Harry A. Bandholtz, the Provost Marshal General of the AEF, lobbied the War Department to maintain a dedicated Military Police Corps after the War, the Military Police Corps was abolished due to the reduction of forces. Congress ratified the permanent organization of Military Police units in the Army in the National Defence Act of 1920; organizing a Military Police Branch in the Officers' Reserve Corps.[11]

The British Military Police began the First World War as a tiny corps of 508 Regulars, boosted by 253 former Military Police soldiers who had been 're-called to the Colours'. By the end of the conflict, they numbered over 18,000 and had been deployed on every front. Some 375 lost their lives and the corps won 477 decorations including 13 DSO's (Distinguished Service Order). Their duties included traffic control and enabling manoeuvre on the battlefield, the handling of prisoners of war, the prevention and investigation of crime, and conducted close protection duties a role that would expand as the years and wars went by.[12]

The Battle of Neuve Chapelle (1915) was the first major battle when military police of various divisions and brigades worked to a common plan to serve the Army as a whole, rather than their own particular formations to which they were attached. All Military Police from

---

11 https://history.army.mil/html/bookshelves/resmat/wwi/historical_resources/default/sec09/Over_There/Over_There_ 05.pdf

12 Director of the Royal Military Police Museum, Colonel Jeremy Green OBE,

Brigades and rearwards were coordinated on an organized road network in order to control traffic, and for the first time in mechanized warfare demonstrated their indispensability if order rather than chaos, was to reign in the battlefield. Indeed, not only in traffic control, but also in the new methods for handling stragglers, prisoners-of-war, the recovery of weapons and many other tasks made possible by the coordination of Provost on the battlefield at the highest level, was Neuve Chapelle an outstanding date in Military Police history, since when their essential role in modern warfare has been recognised. Nor was the need for Military Police over with the signing of the Armistice as no Unit or Corps was called upon to play so big and important a part as the Military Police in the Army of Occupation on the Rhine.[13]

Always the first in and last out it was fitting that a British military motorcycle policeman was the first to cross the Rhine during the occupation of Cologne.

At War's end the first Colonels-Commandant of the Corps (and the former Commander of 2nd Army during the liberation of Europe); General Sir Myles Dempsey KCB, KBE, DSO, MS, paid the following tribute:

> *"The military policeman became so well known a figure on every road to the battlefield that his presence became taken for granted. Few soldiers as they hurried over a bridge, which was a regular target for the enemy, gave much thought to the man whose duty it was to be there for hours on end, directing the traffic and ensuring its rapid passage."*

> In the battle zone, where frequently they had to do duty in exposed positions under heavy fire and suffered severe casualties, the military police solved an important part of the problem of traffic control. In back areas the vigilance and zeal have largely contributed to the good relations maintained between our troops and the civilian population.
>
> – Field Marshal Sir Douglas Haig, Commander-in-Chief of the BEF

---

13 https://rhqrmp.org/rmp_history.html

World War II

At the start of World War II, there was a MP platoon organic assigned to each US army divisions. By the end of the war, there was a MP company organic to the division. The evolution of this increase was in response to challenges in the European Theatre.

Infantrymen often have described the Corps of Military Police as the soldiers who posted 'Off Limits' signs even before towns were liberated. But there's one place where soldiers found no signs; there were no complaints about the early presence of MPs. That was the Normandy beaches.[14]

MPs crossed those narrow belts of sand at H-Hour, D-Day, and began clearing vehicles from the beaches, evacuating wounded, guarding prisoners in an improvised cage, and assisting in beach head logistics. In the pre-dawn air invasion, Airborne MPs had come in fighting with allied paratroopers.

They were not immune. The same murderous fire caught them as well as their infantry comrades. In some ways it was even tougher for the MP. Once posted, he had to stand up and remain in place. Their duty didn't allow him to duck into a foxhole. If he became, a casualty, another MP replaced him.[15]

In the early morning of June 6, 1944, 16,000 American and 8,000 British paratroopers jumped into southern France under heavy German anti-aircraft fire. Concurrently, 125,000 Allied Soldiers loaded onto 4,000 landing vessels in preparation for the largest amphibious landing in history. D-Day of Operation Overlord had commenced. Overlord is an example of how the military police supported the largest-scale combat operation of that war. Once the allied forces executed a forcible entry

---

14 Max Hastings, *Overlord: D-Day and the Battle for Normandy* (New York: Simon and Schuster, 1984), 73–74.

15 MAJ Christopher A. Evans. *School of Advanced Military Studies* US Army. 2018

operation against heavy German opposition on the beaches of Normandy in the summer of 1944. The Military police extended the division's operational reach by getting them off the beach. Can you imagine the traffic jams a road accident causes in the city of New York, London, or Sydney at a major intersection? Well, that's a bit what it was like when tens of thousands of men and vehicles in a small beachhead have to get off and onto roads whilst under intense fire. It was the MPs that got the show moving, often well ahead of the Infantry working side by side with engineers making road access and route marking.

Military police braved enemy fire and directed traffic to keep the beach landing areas clear. Traffic control on the 'Red Ball Express' enabled commanders to maintain momentum and retain the initiative. Military police were on the front lines to guard and escort German prisoners to the rear area to preserve combat power.[16]

The 1st Military Police (MP) Platoon crossed the channel with two officers and fifty enlisted. When the traffic section was about to land on Omaha beach, an enemy shell exploded on the landing craft deck wounding fifteen military policemen. Lieutenant Charles M. Conover, although wounded by indirect fire, immediately established traffic control points on the beach. Afterward, he personally conducted a reconnaissance of vehicle routes off the beach until he collapsed from blood loss. Lieutenant Conover received the Silver Star for his valour on Omaha Beach. Individual military policemen directed traffic under enemy fire and were critical to First Army's success.

Military Police in World War II kept the Army Rolling Along
Division cannot function efficiently with less if you have less. You cannot take untrained men from combat elements to do the same work as military policemen as GI cannot handle traffic. – Colonel H. J. P. Harding, Infantry Observer.[17]

---

16 'MP: The Story of the Corps of Military Police' *Stars & Stripes* 1944.
17 US Army, FM 3-0 (2017), 5–20.

Throughout the Second World War, men of the Corps of Military Police served wherever the British Army served. They were on the front line, landing soon after the initial wave at Sicily, Salerno, Anzio, and Normandy for example. In addition, they had to deal with issues of behaviour of British troops, such as the riot in Cairo by men of the 78th Infantry Division following their arrival from Italy in 1944. They served in Burma, Hong Kong, Malaya, and Singapore, alongside men of the Corps of Military Police (India). By Victory Day some 40,000 men had passed through MP school.

The Korean War also introduced a new duty for military police. The war witnessed a dramatic increase in black market activities associated with an army fighting in a third world nation. They again found themselves all weather directing transport along an extensive network of roads. In fact, both the United States and Commonwealth MPs found this task was so great that over 80% of MP staff were attached to this duty. They also found themselves conducting battlefield close protection for various UN Officials and VIPs that visited the country.

In ensuing decades America's involvement in Southeast Asia brought about yet another significant expansion in military police responsibilities, underscoring new and varied uses for military police in a war without defined rear areas. In addition to their usual wartime functions, military police units served in a direct combat support role. They provided convoy security, often escorting supplies and equipment through districts subject to direct enemy attack. They controlled traffic throughout the four combat zones, where front lines had ceased to exist in the usual sense of the word. They secured highways and bridges against both local subversives and North Vietnamese regulars. They joined combat troops in the hazardous task of locating and destroying enemy tunnels.

During 1968 the Army Chief of Staff, acknowledging the Military Police Corps' active involvement in support of military operations in Vietnam, approved changing the branch's identification from combat service support to combat support. This change was clearly justified by the responsibilities assumed by the corps in Vietnam where military police units were organized, trained, and equipped to perform operations in a combat support role.

Left to right, Cpl Brian Marfleet Australian MP, ARVN MP, unidentified, unidentified SP/4 member of A Company, 720th MP Battalion, and CPL Bruce Duncan, New Zealand MP. Courtesy of CPL Bruce Duncan, New Zealand Military Police, 1 Australian Provost Corps, Vietnam, 1970.

It was 8am on June 15, 1982, and the Argentine forces in and around the town had surrendered to the British only hours before. But the Royal Marines and the Parachute Regiment had been kept on the outskirts of Port Stanley. This made sense as it avoided any potential reaction from the Argentines if the British troops had moved into the town too soon. So initially, for a short period, apart from Major-General Moore's surrender party, the RMP were the only British military personnel in the town.

The RMP team worked in shifts, day and night, for a week, in their efforts to get the prisoners processed so they could be sent home as quickly as possible. In some parts of the islands, prisoners had to be kept in sheep-shearing sheds before they could be repatriated. The MPs dealt with around 11,500 Argentines POW.

Already in charge of policing all task force personnel, the seventeen MPs were sworn in as special constables and oversaw civilians as well as servicemen on the Island. Once the fighting was over and the troops settled to a more normal life, perhaps with a few beers now and then, the 'normal problems' police deal with could result, and the RMP needed to have authority over everyone in case soldiers and civilians clashed.

THE MILITARY POLICE TODAY

One of the smallest Corps in any military is usually the Military Police or more commonly known as MPs. So vital are they to an army's operations that during my research I have not found a defence force in the world that did not have MPs in its organizational structure.

Military Police are commonly overlooked by their own Defence Departments or senior staff officers as a small but necessary unit. They perform however well above their size in terms of numbers and operational effectiveness. In many cases if there is a requirement for a special task that does not fall into any particular area of responsibility it is usually done by the MPs.

Recruitment into Military Police units is not straight forward, with a lot of allocated power assigned to the individual a high degree of maturity and intelligence is expected of a MP even at their lowest rank. Even a MP lance Corporal one of the lowest junior non-commissioned ranks in the army will be called on to brief senior Officers on his specialist subject knowledge.

I have worked as a MP Junior Non-Commissioned Officer (JNCO) in charge of a large team of MPs assigned to provide close personnel protection to various Heads of State. A junior MP may also find themselves on a motorbike many kilometres ahead of an Armoured formation signposting the route it is to take. As such Military Police are usually recruited from within the defence force, many requiring a candidate to have served several years in another branch of the services. For example, being in the Infantry for two years prior to an application as an MP.

MPs are therefore experienced soldiers as well as law enforcement specialists, twice the volunteer, once as a soldier then as an MP. Many recruiters also target ex-civilian Police officers as candidates and many Army Reserve formations are filled with personnel who in their regular jobs are sheriffs or constables in the local police force.

The functions of the Military Police are as varied as they are challenging, an MP can find themselves checking the identity of a person entering a base facility one day, the next route marking and escorting a large traffic convoy. The next day protecting a high threat VIP dignitary in a foreign land or investigating a murder at a military facility.

That however is just some of the tasks that fall within their law enforcement role. MPs are also soldiers and conduct patrols and guard functions in the field. MPs are often called upon to clear urban buildings and patrol dangerous streets in occupied lands.

Military Police are unique within the battlefield environment, often being either miles in front of the main battle, route marking the advance or patrolling miles behind front lines looking for deserters. This unique ability to go anywhere has been exploited by various Special Forces units who often disguised themselves as MPs to avoid challenge and suspicion.

Some notable occasions during WWII were during the successful capture and kidnapping of General Heinrich Kreipe on crete when commandos dressed as German MPs conducted a road bloke, the only way they could get close to the heavily guarded officer. Another during the battle of the Bulge saw elite German saboteurs parachute behind allied lines dressed as American MPs. Their role was to change road signs, conduct sabotage and spread general confusion within US Forces which they did for a considerable time, before being captured and executed. Again, both these daring plans worked due to the authority and sheer presence that Military Police have in the Military. These same principals would work today.

MPs are not the Hollywood stereo typical image of a large soldiers welding batons to break up a drunken bar fight, although they can and if required do that. They are much more, they are highly trained soldiers with a law enforcement specialty, many very well educated and motivated for the mission they are assigned.

The military police can change roles at a moment's notice, one day dressed in camouflage in the thick of action, the next day dressed in your smart dress uniform patrolling the occupied or liberated territory you were just fighting over. MPs have performed this role for many centuries. Here is one story of the 160 Provost Company Royal Military Police, located in Aldershot who sent a detachment with the task force for the Falklands conflict. After the Argentine forces surrendered, the 5 Infantry Brigade Provost Unit Royal Military Police remained on the islands, sworn in as Special Constables carrying out civilian police duties until the Falkland Islands Police Force were able to become operational again. This included conducting patrols at night, taking statements of complaint from residence, looking for local farmers missing stock and even attending a domestic violence incident. On occasions they would have to revert to the Military role to detain isolated prisoners of war who had been hiding. Such as after the re-capture of South Georgia when the Argentine commander Lieutenant-Commander Alfredo Astiz was taken to the UK and questioned by the Royal Military Police and Sussex Police Detectives in the United Kingdom about the murder of Swedish and French nationals several years before. As there was no jurisdiction for extradition to Sweden or France, he was repatriated to Argentina by the Red Cross.

Military Policewomen are equal in all respects to their male counterparts and are deployed in all roles and operational areas.

In an organization like the Army that actively promotes teamwork and unit solidarity, it takes a special type of person to be able to be an individual when required. These are qualities often looked for in the selection Special Forces and is true of the military policeman as well.

MPs have to have the ability to work in cohesion with the Army but at the same time often find themselves in small teams carrying out specialist functions or acting like their civilian counterparts on their own usually heavily outnumbered.

By this I could use the example of a drunken crowd or mob content to cause trouble, in a restricted area or outstaying their curfew at the local bar, it takes a special breed of person with immense personnel bravery to confront them alone or with just a single partner as backup and order their dispersal. This is the type of tasks MPs or civilian Police do every day. Would you have the metal to do such a job.

You cannot be a military policeman in most armies by walking into a recruiting office and asking to become one. Usually, it requires the selection into another branch of the service, in many cases a combat branch such as the Infantry, where several years' service is required prior to a request to become an MP.

There are several reasons for this, MPs are required to be conversant in tactical operations in the field often working in small combat groups behind enemy lines. MPs have to address senior officers making recommendations as subject matter experts on highly detailed operations such as the route a convoy will take. The lives of many are in the hands of a MP during this type of situation.

MPs by virtue of instilling law and order enforcement require to be at least junior non-commissioned officers (JNCOs) a rank that usually takes several years to obtain.

Maturity is a requirement that goes along with credibility when dealing with other soldiers, simply put a young wet behind the ears kid is not going to have the physical presence a military policeman requires to effectively do their job. This can also be said for their physical stature, like their civilian counterparts many MP units have height and fitness requirements for the job. You cannot wrestle a drunken 100 kg soldier to the ground and hand cuff him if your five foot nothing and weigh 45 kg dripping wet.

However, I must state it's not about gender, there is an old saying: "It's not the size of the dog in the fight it's the size of the fight in the dog". I have come across several petite female MPs in my time and would hate to pick a fight with them – I would lose. While on the subject I do use the wording Military Policeman, it is excepted terminology in the military for both genders, thus I use it for simplicity in the book. Recently for gallantry in action in the Salman Pak region in Iraq, Sgt Leigh Ann Hester of the Kentucky National Guard 617th Military Police Company became the first woman since WWII to be awarded the silver star and the first in history for actions in combat. Other members of her squad including other female MPs received Bronze Stars, Army Commendation medals and Purple Hearts that day. Despite the media attention given to the female MPs at the time, their Commander summed it up, MP women had been in combat for a long time, "They shouldn't be held up as a show piece for why there should be women in combat", he commented. "They should be held up as examples of why it's irrelevant".

Sergeant Leigh A. Hester is cited for conspicuous gallantry in action against an armed enemy of the United States while engaged in military operations involving conflict with anti-Iraq forces (AIF) as a team leader for Raven 42B, 617th Military Police Company, 503rd Military Police

Battalion (Airborne) stationed at Camp Liberty, Iraq on 20 March 2005, in support of Operation IRAQI FREEDOM. The team's mission was to assist Raven 42 in searching the Eastern Convoy Route for improvised explosive devices (IEDs) and provide additional security to sustainment convoys traveling through their area of responsibility. While patrolling Alternate Supply Route (ASR) Detroit, Raven 42B was shadowing a sustainment convoy consisting of 30 third country national (TCN) semi-tractor trailers with a three-vehicle squad size escort, call sign Stallion 33, traveling from LSA (logistics support area) Anaconda to CSC (convoy support centre) Scania. The weather for this ASR patrol was 75 degrees and sunny with a 10-knot breeze from the southwest. While traveling on ASR Detroit approximately 50 AIF ambushed the convoy with heavy AK47 fire, RPK heavy machine gun fire, and rocket propelled grenades (RPGs) from the southwest side of the road at 1140 hours. The AIF were utilizing irrigation ditches and an orchard for the well-planned complex attack. The AIF had cars combat parked along a road perpendicular to the ASR with all doors and trunks open. The AIF intent was to destroy the convoy, to inflict numerous casualties, and to kidnap several TCN drivers or U.S. Soldiers. The initial ambush disabled and set on fire the lead TCN vehicle, which effectively blocked the southbound lanes of ASR Detroit, stopping the convoy in the kill zone. The squad leader, Staff Sergeant Timothy Nein, directed the squad to move forward, traveling on the right shoulder and passing through the engagement area between the enemy and the convoy. Sergeant Hester directed her gunner to provide heavy volumes of MK 19 and M240B fires into the field where an overwhelming number of insurgents were executing a well-coordinated ambush on the convoy. Raven 42 elements were outnumbered five to one. Staff Sergeant Nein ordered the squad to flank the insurgents on their right side.

The squad continued to come under heavy machine gun fire and rocket propelled grenade fire when Sergeant Hester stopped her vehicle, the middle vehicle, at a flanking position enfilading the trench line and the orchard field where over a dozen insurgents were engaging the squad and convoy. She then directed her gunner to focus fires in the trench line and the orchard field. Sergeant Hester dismounted and moved to what was thought to be the non-contact side of the vehicle. She ordered her gunner to continue to fire on the orchard field as she and her driver engaged insurgents in the orchard field with small arms. Sergeant Hester began engaging the insurgents with her M203 in order to suppress the heavy AIF fire. Sergeant Hester followed Staff Sergeant Nein to the right-side berm and threw two well placed fragmentation grenades into the trench eliminating the AIF threat. Sergeant Hester and Staff Sergeant Nein went over the berm into the trench and began clearing the trench with their M4s. Sergeant Hester engaged and eliminated three AIF to her front with her M4. They then made their way to the front trench and cleared that as well. After clearing the front trench cease fire was called and she began securing the ambush site. The final result of the ambush was 27 AIF KIA (killed in action), 6 AIF WIA (wounded in action), and one AIF captured.

The many roles a junior military policeman has to undertake is still only the top of the iceberg, after several years as a MP he can then specialize in areas such as Special Investigation or Close Protection of personnel. Both these field are extremely challenging, one requires a high degree of law knowledge and analytical skills, where the other requires intense physical fitness and clear mind of thought.

Korean Military Police conducting convoy escort duties.

For example, as part of a Close Protection team an MP can expect to be deployed anywhere in the world where the Military is operating and in some cases were, they are not. The Close Protection Unit deploys service personnel in small teams around the world for operational Close Protection support to military operations and other Government Departments missions in order to protect high ranking individuals in high threat environments.

Not only do MPs learn specialist soldiering skills for the role in close protection, they also develop strong communication skills as an MP will be speaking to and assisting senior officers and diplomats on a daily basis when deployed. They learn to work as part of a team and also on their own, and to be responsible, dependable, and quick-thinking under pressure. Most courses around the world are at least eight weeklong, successful students may then be assigned to any one of a number of teams for a further theatre specific training. Prior to any operation pre-deployment training takes place to introduce advanced weapons and tactics and prepare the team for the job at hand. This could be preparing to embed them into an embassy or to be on the front line protecting senior commanders. Challenging and rewarding, Close Protection is but one of the many exciting opportunities in Military Police perform.

As a member of the Special Investigation team, an MP learns how to investigate serious and complex crimes, domestically and in adverse conditions on international operations. They will be required to make important decisions on their own and communicate with soldiers and officers of all ranks, as well as a diverse cross section of society. Investigators learn forensics, photography, advanced interviewing techniques and Information Communication Technology. This role is comparable to Civilian Police Detectives.

All of these jobs will be explained in detail in the Chapter Roles of the Military Police.

THE MPS ROLE

German MPs stack-up prior to a forced entry to a barricaded residence.

On the battlefield the Military Police provide commanders with an essential element of mobility and manoeuvre support, conducting route reconnaissance, route signing, controlling and monitoring traffic, enforcing traffic regulations and movement priority, controlling military stragglers and the movement of the civilian population. Military Police provide support to logistic operations and provide physical and personal security. Military Police are responsible for the internment and detention of captured persons including their collection, processing and registration in accordance with international, host nation, national and command conventions and requirements.

In combat, military police have much the same duties as the regular soldier: accomplishing assigned missions in the face of possible enemy aggression. Military police may also be tasked with seeking out and eliminating any enemy special forces, terrorists, and other small unit opposition across the battlefield. Providing defence for military operations, assets and strategic locations also fall under the job duties of an MP. Military police combat tasks also include actions to secure the environment, remove organized resistance and set conditions for the other lines of operation. It may include close combat under contemporary conditions in complex, particularly urban, terrain. Military police maintain a capacity to provide combat policing support to combat forces operating in a medium to high threat environment.

Area security is a big element in the duties of military police. They help guard vital military supplies, especially all-important ones like food and ammunition. They are also primarily responsible for the care of prisoners-of-war, including their security and transportation.

Military police are specifically responsible for regulating and enforcing military laws in both peacetime and wartime. Military law enforcement is also a predominant duty for military police. They assist commanders in keeping military discipline on military installations, and work with civilian authorities outside of military jurisdiction when necessary.

When domestic disturbances arise in and around a military installation, the military police may be called on to help restore order. Civil disturbances for which the military police may be assigned include natural and man-made disasters.

Military police are of prime importance when it comes to crime prevention and investigation on military grounds. In this capacity, they help to ensure that military personnel and locations are safe, secure, and ready to handle the needs of the Army.

Military police work in the Army's correctional functions and facilities, such as at Fort Leavenworth, Abu Ghraib or Guantanamo Bay. They help oversee the treatment and rehabilitation of both uniformed inmates with the mission of returning them back to a quality military or civilian life and supervision of terrorists.

Recent US Military Police Experience, The United States 18th Military

Police Brigade supporting Operation Iraqi Freedom indicated that the MP contributed to the success of operations were due to the diversity and flexibility of military police functions by conducting over 24,000 combat patrols; processed over 3,600 enemy prisoners of war, detainees, and insurgents; confiscated over 7,500 weapons; and trained over 10,000 Iraqi police officers.

Military Police patrols came under direct or indirect attack over 300 times throughout the operation. MPs as a combat support force multiplier, provide essential operational assistance to combat elements and commanders through the provision of varied MP effects which contribute to providing the tactical freedom that the Land Force needs to achieve its mission. The restoration and maintenance of law and order within a population facilitates dominance of the Army narrative and enhances decision superiority over the Land Forces opponents. In these ways MP contributes to the dislocation and denial of the enemy and/or non-traditional adversary and prevents them from imposing such effects on our own forces.

Another example of this type of employment occurred in May 2003, Lieutenant Colonel John Hammond, commander of the 211th Military Police Battalion, Massachusetts Army National Guard, was ordered by V Corps to stand up a unique task force (TF). Designated TF Enforcer, it was composed of military police units and counterintelligence and psychological operations teams. They were tasked to establish afoot hold in Fallujah and to identify, locate, and capture or kill enemy forces operating in the area. TF Enforcer conducted patrols designed to gather actionable intelligence, then executed raids based on this intelligence. Lieutenant Colonel Hammond's main effort was a military police company. In an article in the April 2005 issue of Military Police, he argued that military police soldiers can perform this type of mission with more precision than many combat arms organizations. He compared the two types of units to the difference between using a scalpel and a bayonet. The military police technique reduced collateral damage and often yielded greater cooperation from local citizens. Lieutenant Colonel Hammond stated that, "Precision, speed, and stealth are critical components that are the calling cards of the military police platoon. By the time the TF was dismantled in late 2003, tons of explosives and ammunition had been seized and the overall goals had been accomplished.

Lieutenant Colonel Hammond said that the success of the TF was a direct result of the unique military police skill sets. In order to gain intelligence in this environment, it was critical to balance war fighting skills with a more diplomatic approach. Platoon leaders were required to develop relationships and operate within the existing infrastructure to achieve results and gain actionable intelligence. For several reasons, military police Soldiers are better at this than most other Soldiers.

There are many roles an MP must be conversant with on a daily basis, outlined in this chapter are but a few.

Traffic movement on the Battlefield is perhaps the most vital role the Military Police play. It enables operational reach which is the distance and duration a unit can manoeuvre away from their base of operations. Military police aid the commander in balancing the tension between endurance, momentum, and protection. Traffic control maximizes the flow of vehicles to the front lines and enables the commander to maintain momentum. Momentum is the seizure of initiative and the high tempo of operations that overwhelm the enemy's ability to react.[18]

Without the flow logistics any army is crippled. It is the MPs who enable convoys of supplies and war equipment to travel via the safest and most direct route to wear they are most needed on the battlefield. MPs are always seen at intersections directing traffic often under fire, standing upright, wearing or using a fluorescent device to control the convoys.

Once posted, the traffic MP accepts a tremendous responsibility. Proper movement of traffic demands that he never once neglect his duty. Rain, snow, mud, enemy patrol, tank fire, strafing, artillery bursts, mortar, nothing must budge him. His post is sacred ground which he must preserve, even if he must give his life.

---

18 US Department of the Army, Field Manual (FM) 3-0, Operations (Washington, DC: Government Printing Office, 2017), 1-22.

Traffic control is not a new concept as early as 1879 in the British Army Mounted Military Police, Provost duties are listed as enforcing discipline, lines of communication duties and traffic control an aspect that was to burgeon in the wars of the 20th century, especially with the mechanization of armies. Tactical success often hinges on keeping traffic moving.

One recorded example comes from the 9th Infantry Division MP platoon on March 1, 1945, around 0200 hours who were charged with the responsibility of traffic control at the Ludendorff Bridge, Remagen, Germany. Remagen has become famous not only by the Hollywood movie of the same name but because its taking and movement across the Rhine was so vital. MPs were stationed at the approaches and out on the uncertain bridge span itself. Intense artillery fire from aroused Germans rained down. Posts were maintained 24 hours a day as MPs evacuated wounded, laid communication lines, removed knocked-out vehicles. Traffic had to keep flowing fast. One MP raced to a blazing tank, climbed inside, rescued a trapped crew member. Four days later, the platoon, relieved of its task, had a slight breathing spell. It counted its casualties a total of 14 wounded, two killed. They were not immune. The same murderous fire caught them as well as their infantry buddies.

A time-honoured role

Leading up to First World War trench systems and the front line was a mile's deep labyrinth of dirt and gravel roads, narrow gauge railway lines, muddy lanes and winding pathways circling around or through flooded shell craters, flattened forests, and rubble towns. Maintaining a (relatively) smooth flow of traffic to and from the front lines was of the highest priority. This was the responsibility of Movement Control Officers and Military Police.

At an intersection, a Traffic Control Military Policeman operates a traffic control signal. The white 'STOP' and 'GO' signs were painted over respective red and green backgrounds.

Traffic duty is also far more than the role of a points man in peace or war time the MP must investigate traffic accidents similar to their civilian counterparts. This includes having a skill set which includes investigative and forensic skills to calculate culpability, a knowledge of traffic law and regulations and often forgotten, as MP are frequently the initial responder at any scene. They must possess lifesaving first aid skills to render victims safe. In operational areas such as Iraq and Afghanistan today the MP is often the local law enforcement agency or is training the local traffic force up.

Two other areas linked firmly with traffic duty are route reconnaissance and convoy escort, often the same MP that reconnoitred the route a convoy will take will be the same MP who is leading it on his motorcycle Leaping ahead from intersection to intersection, often dismounting to conduct traffic control to ensure the convoy does not stop, he then again remounts, overtakes the convoy leader and resumes the task all over again at the next vital traffic point. MP if always under manned are at least always multi-skilled. These skill sets alone are frequently, in a civilian police force, the area of a specialist unit such as Traffic Branch or Highway Patrol. In the military police this is just one of many skill sets required.

The view of the importance of this role in war was stated below.

> *The battle of Normandy and subsequent battles would never have been won but for the work and co-operation of Provost on the traffic routes"*
> Field Marshal B. L. Montgomery 1945.

The middle East has seen the MP perform many acts of bravery on the battlefront. At the battle of El Alamein in 1942 Lance Corporal J. Eeles of the 10th Armoured Division Provost Company won the Distinguished Conduct Medal for clearing mine fields under fire. Again, during the Gulf War as the main ground assault phase began on 24 February 1991 a mixed force of Royal Engineers and Military Police led the British Battle Groups forward, the Sappers clearing obstacles and the MPs signing the way and controlling Traffic. An MP Staff Sergeant K. M. Davis having discovered the death of one soldier and wounding of three others by bomblets led a retrieval group by using a shovel to clear the devices, for this he was awarded the Distinguished Conduct Medal.

During the Gulf War MPs were early on the scene in Saudi Arabia, traffic control and patrolling the base area was followed by preparation for offensive operations. Upon the Desert Storm phase began US General Norman Schwarzkopf feint attack towards Kuwait while the main body of forces attacked Iraqi in the rear. These manoeuvres involved large numbers of vehicles, men and munitions under the direct control of MPs from coalition forces, several MPs lost their lives during this time.

Even the Naval police, conduct traffic control on naval bases to ensure the safety of servicemen, contractors or civilian that are on base.

Defence staff travelling to work are under threat of attack by extremists as are the personnel who travel in and out of them to do their job of defending Britain. Air Force stations in the UK have proven particularly vulnerable because they are by their nature remote and vast – making their security open to lapses and more difficult to impose.

RAF Policeman at a base entrance conducting traffic control and vehicle inspections.

Several attempts have taken place in the UK and USA where service personnel have been attacked off duty. Terrorist groups such as ISIS have been responsible for the killing of a UK soldier in 2018 and several attempts. Garrison policing especially traffic control of base roads, married quarters and along roadway approaches to bases have seen US and UK service police conducting traffic control well away from their usual jurisdictional areas of responsibility.

Photo courtesy of RMP Museum.

Garrison duties encompass the day-to-day police activities, such as: Law Enforcement Criminal Investigations, Running the Military Detention Barracks, Base Policing and Community Relations. The role of garrison policing encapsulates the same law enforcement duties as their Civilian Police counterparts in addition to guarding restricted areas, conducting patrols of the base, dealing with any security issues, traffic control, and speeding enforcement on the installation. Garrison Policing is also known as domestic policing is the role when the general public most often observe the MP at work, as they are seen controlling the entrance to Military establishments. They are seen as immaculately dressed and disciplined.

There is however much more under the surface to this role. Garrison Policing has many aspects and is perhaps the absolute front line to counterterrorism and counterintelligence operations. Military police have always played an important role in Anti-Terrorist awareness as, as the police force for military communities, they are responsible for the safety and security of installations and facilities against criminal and terrorist threats. They achieve this by providing leadership, guidance, and advice to commanders and managers who are responsible for the security of those installations and facilities. For many years, the military police have acted as the bulwark against attacks on Military installations. Military police units have adjusted to the terrorist threats of today and continue to serve at the leading edge of current security efforts. But the building and sustaining of security is only a small part of the value of military police to the Military community for which terrorism protection is designed.

Due to their status and experience with communities, military police have the lead role in expanding and enhancing criminal and terrorist threat awareness among local communities. By working together, the police and citizens of the community form the first line of defence against terrorist activities. Through their daily interaction with community members, the Military police educate and inform the community about potential threats. A knowledgeable and empowered community, in turn, extends the reach of police and security forces by serving as additional 'eyes and ears.' Soldiers, civilians. Army contractors, and family members can add tremendous value to Army AT prevention and detection capabilities by serving as 'sensors' in the fight against extremists and terrorists.

The Military Police law enforcement role is a critical component of the Military Justice System whose purpose is to maintain military effectiveness and to maintain the reputation of the Army. This law enforcement function is provided in both domestic and international operations. The day of the heavy-handed MP has gone. In his stead is a specially trained MP, an expert in verbal communication, common sense, and diplomacy. Minimum force is used to carry out his task; his club today is a last resort.

One example of the importance of the garrison role was in WWII when more than 10,000 US MPs, stationed in Germany, Belgium, France and the United Kingdom, guarded runways, hangars, bomb dumps and aircraft at all Air Corps installations. The almost complete absence of theft, tampering and sabotage testify to effective security methods. At the end of the Second World War saw the British Military Police force total 50,000 men (this is more than many standing armies today) another indication of the important role MPs have in war.

In modern armies the guarding of installations is no less important, in fact the terrorist threat to facilities and personnel have increased. Likewise, a large role in Garrison policing is directly post a conflict, after WWII thousands of MPs were required to oversee the axis countries as no formal government or civilian police forces existed. Today the same garrison role is being carried out by coalition MPs in Iraq. It is the MPs that oversee the transition from a conquered government under martial law to the restoration of its own juridical system.

Several countries have enhanced garrison security by either supplementing the military police with civilian police such as the US Department of Defence Police or Britain's Ministry of Defence Police or many Countries use civilian contracted security guards.

In the case of the United Kingdom changes to the structure of the Army and the increased threat of terrorist attack have resulted in the creation of the Military Provost Guard Service (MPGS). This is a newly formed area of service and lies within the Provost Branch of the Adjutant General's Corps under the direction of Provost Marshal (Army), who is the Director and Head of Service. The aim of the MPGS is to rationalize guarding arrangements at sites where soldiers normally live and work. The MPGS replaces previously civilian held duties with highly trained, experienced and armed soldiers.

MPGS provide armed guard protection of units, responsible for control of entry, foot and mobile patrols and armed response to attacks on their unit. The MPGS was formed using the model of the Vulnerable Points Wing of the Corp of Military Police. At the onset of World War II, the Corp of Military Police (CMP) fulfilled normal policing duties. As the war progressed the CMP divided into three distinct parts:

- Provost Wing – Known as 'The Red Caps'. These were employed on both general and specialist policing duties.
- Traffic Control Wing (TCW) – Formed solely to deal with the Traffic Control of formations in both frontal and rear echelon areas. TCW personnel were organized into armed companies each responsible for

a specific geographical area. Although they belonged to the CMP, they carried out all instructions issued by Movement Control.

- Vulnerable Points Wing (VPW) – It was the task of the VPW to provide guards for installations and buildings that were seen as vulnerable points, such as ammunition and petrol dumps, docks, locks, bridges, and power stations. They were organized into sections, each of 7 privates, under command of an NCO. They were armed with SMGs and batons and used guard dogs during the night. Their primary task was anti-sabotage, and this was undertaken by a mixture of static guards and patrolling.

All MPGS Soldiers are trained at the Defence College of Policing and Guarding, Southwick Park, Hampshire. The MPGS course takes 5 days and is designed to provide you with the knowledge and understanding required of a professional armed security guard. The course takes account of your previous service history and, therefore, does not replicate many of the areas of Phase 1 Basic Training, such as foot drill, room inspections and parades.

The current MPGS cap badge incorporates the Royal Crest in gold with beneath, the scroll inscribed 'Military Provost Guard Service', all superimposed on crossed keys in silver. The design follows that of the Military Foot Police, who were raised in 1882 and disbanded in 1926, but with the addition of the crossed 19th century government keys, a traditional symbol of the custodian representing a function of the Military Provost Guard Service. The Royal Crest forms part of the badge of the Adjutant General's Corps and was worn until 1900 by the Adjutant General's Department, the Provost Marshal, and Officers of the Military Police.

Regimental police or regimental provost (RP) are soldiers responsible for regimental discipline enforcement and unit custody in armies especially those armed forces structured in the British military tradition. They belong to the regiment in which they enforce discipline rather than the Military Police function serving a none policing function. Army Regimental Policemen usually work office-hours (8am–5pm). The responsibility of night security is usually assigned to the unit's guard

duty personnel, although a Duty RP may stay on in a supervisory role. Depending on the individual soldier's medical and combat rating, an Army RP may be allowed to guard the gate with rifle and live ammunition, or with just a baton and shield. Army RP training is usually held at the Military Police Training School.[19]

The term Regimental Police was causing quite a bit of confusion and has been retired in some countries. They are now called Regimental Duty Staff and tend to be NCOs who are trusted by their chain of command to exercise the CO's authority to maintain discipline within their own unit. Despite wearing a flash brassard, they have no exceptional powers of arrest conferred upon them by the Armed Forces Act, whereas Military Police do.

Fijian RP on guard duty, he is part of an Infantry battalion performing policing duties as required.

The roles of the Regimental Policemen in the Singapore Armed Forces are similar, in that they too enforce discipline and are responsible for the security of the base they are assigned to. RPs are usually full-time National Servicemen and are to be broadly divided into two different groups.

Air Force and Navy RPs are called Field Defence Troopers in the Air Force, and Sea Soldiers in the Navy; and are organized at the squadron level. In contrast to Army Regimental Policemen, Field Defence Squadron troopers have much higher appointments and responsibilities. Trainees undertake the twelve weeks Field Defence Course, which includes rigorous physical and mental training, as well as teaching advanced security and fighting techniques. They are trained in small arms, less-lethal weaponry, and crew-served weapons. In the final theory exam in FDC, trainees must pass the Military Security Knowledge Exam in order to pass out. Field Defence Squadrons are organized at the battalion level during wartime, and normally field reinforced company-sized units. Unlike their Army

---

19 Mike Chappell, *Elite series 65 redcaps Britain's military police*. Osprey.1997.

counterparts, Air Force and Navy RPs are stationed at their base 24/7. In both cases, military installations with higher security requirements are normally assisted by Military Policemen seconded from the Singapore Armed Forces Military Police Command, who have greater powers of arrest and detention. These MPs operate in a manner dependent on the local base security, carrying out normal duties within the unit according to their rank, or deployed solely to perform access control into the base at key entry points. Members of the Regimental police are always dressed in battle fatigues when on official duty and wear a brassard, with the letters 'RP' in orange. [20]

One role Regimental Police can often find themselves doing is looking after the Regiments mascot. In this case the Royal Regiment of Fusiliers traditional mascot the Blackbuck was replaced by a canine due to political interference claiming due to conservation of the species the Regiment should not have one.

Romanian MPs conduct patrols on UN mission, note they use a mixture of equipment from Soviet rifles to US helmets to British 4X4.

Convoy Escort is a highly dangerous occupation the media is full stories of roadside bombings and they carnage that occurs. A role that finds MPs conducting frequently. This seems logical as the Military Police are also responsible for route marking of convoys.

In many instances it falls under MP taskings to escort logistical vehicles heading forward to operational areas from secure bases. These convoys are often seen by terrorist groups as soft targets, as they usually have to proceed along set roads and are therefore semi predictable targets of opportunity.

Very often many of the vehicles are soft skinned that is to say have little or no ballistic protection against small arms fire or improvised explosive devices. For many years' MPs have conducted convoy escort details without the aid of a specialist armoured vehicle.

---

20 https://www.mindef.gov.sg/oms/arc/our-formation-military-police.html

When I was posted to Mogadishu, Somalia in 1993 one of my many jobs as the Security Police Detachment Commander was to conduct the daily 'Milk Run' from the Airport to the US Embassy in downtown Mogadishu. This sound simple enough, the Milk Run in fact was a requirement to take the United Nations Intelligence Officer for daily briefings, alas there were only three ways of getting there, so to vary a route and routine was difficult, thus making us vulnerable to any planned attack.

We had a Mercedes Unimog truck which we had decked out with sandbag flooring, inserted additional bullet proof jackets under the driver's seat and door to aid protection. We also made it look as threatening as we could to deter would be attackers by placing a Minnimi Light Machine Gun (LMG) front and rear, adjusting the seating sideways to allow two security staff per side to face outward, one with a shotgun the other with a Steyr rifle. Our fellow ANZACs from the Australian Military Police detachment had even less protection having to drive Landrover LR110 4WD vehicle. These vehicles were also employed during VCP and mobile check points throughout the city. In addition, they were used as escort vehicles for food aid convoys throughout the region. On several occasions UN Forces were ambushed whilst conducting these operations. Luckily other MP Forces during UNSOM had armoured vehicles to conduct duties such as M117 Armoured Humvee, LAV II, Panhard, Fahad and Cougar APCs.

We had a secret weapon on board in case of ambush or if hostile crowds surrounded the vehicle, that was *Minties* – a kids' mint-flavoured candy, which we would throw out like chaff. It would cause the kids to gather up the sweets and calm most situations down.

We worked closely with MPs from the 1st Marine Division, within the Headquarters Battalion is a Military Police Company. During operation

Restore Hope USMC Military Police units conducted daily, around-the-clock patrols throughout the port city resulted in the seizure of nearly 5,000 weapons and pieces of equipment over a five-month span. Meanwhile, over 15,000 metric tons of food was successfully distributed from 38 different food sites during the operation. The final phase of the operation involved the transition from U.S. peacekeeping force to a U.N. peace keeping Force, this also included MPs training local Somali Police Officers. The U.S. Marine MPs involvement in Operation Restore Hope officially ended May 4, 1993, when operations were turned over to United Nations.

Although some Foreign Forces MPs were injured during the UNSOM mission regardless of the extra protection the results would have been greater if they had happened in unarmoured vehicles. Alas it would take the death of many more soldiers in the next major conflict, the Iraqi War to learn these lessons.

In current operations with a greater increase in roadside bombings and suicide incidents the need for armoured protection has increased. It makes scene to provide MPs who on many occasions operate well into the front lines are provided with armoured protection. Also, the terrorist modus-operandi in current conflicts has shown that support and rear echelon forces are equally vulnerable to attack.

The current role of the MPs includes CCP, VCP and high-risk convoy and security details which require better protection than soft skin vehicles. Military Police worldwide are finding an ever-increasing role in protecting facilities, VIPs and support structures as terrorists see these as weak and easy targets. Increasingly MPs are placed in harm's way to protect them and must be likewise protected with armoured vehicles. A look at current operations shows that personnel deployed in rear areas are no longer safe. The war concept and the complex operating environment, with its risk of regular, irregular, or insurgent forces acting throughout the theatre, implies increased risk to what would have been traditionally classified as rear areas. As the elements tasked with maintaining protection for commanders and primarily being located in the so-called rear areas MP are high value targets for irregular forces in order to disrupt command and control.

Military Police are also tasked with the handling of Prisoners of War (POW) in the rear areas. Once a POW comes under control of Military Police it becomes a responsibly and requirement to adequately protect and care for that person. Transporting POW in a soft skin vehicle does not provide any protection for occupants, both guards and detainees.

The US Military Police in Iraq currently use the M1117 an updated version of the Commando which saw service in the Vietnam War with the USAF Security Police on Base protection duties. Today its armament consists of an Mk 19 grenade launcher and M2 Browning Machine Gun, mounted in a turret similar to that used on the US Marine Corps' Amphibious Assault Vehicle; and a M240H Medium Machine Gun mounted outside the gunner's hatch. The vehicle has become very popular with U.S. Military Police Units and Convoy Security Units in Iraq. It is a more heavily protected and heavily armed alternative to the armoured Humvee which was not originally designed to be a protected fighting vehicle.

The requirement for harden vehicles has seen the Army concept has seen the commencement of many new projects and the acquisition of many new pieces of equipment in many Armed Forces throughout the world, especially ones operating its forces in mission in Afghanistan and Iraq. There is a requirement for the Military Police to have a mobility platform with a cupola or organic means of defending itself that is a good mobility platform with improve crew protection, plus an off-road capability to keep up with and support tracked or other armoured vehicles.

In Iraq the M1114 Armoured Humvee was used in the convoy escort role and rapid reaction force roles. Both USAF Security Police and US Army MPs and local Iraq forces use them extensively.

The Australian built Bushmaster enables a section of MPs to deploy under protection during convoy escort or VIP transportation missions. Unlike a tracked APC the Bushmaster gives a capability in a less threatening manner and can use existing road structure during any internal security function such as Aid to Civil power.

One of the most important requirements for a combat vehicle's protection is counter-mine design. Traditionally, guerrilla forces used standard mines to hit enemy patrols and military vehicles.

Such mines included small (anti-personnel) or larger anti-tank mines, as well as armour penetrating and self-forged fragmentation (SFF) mines.

The rise of the global terror, assisted by the proliferation of modern communications technology, introduced a dangerous shift from the familiar standard issue weapons to the use of improvised explosive devices (IEDs). The introduction of such makeshift weapons proliferated in Ireland, Chechnya, Iraq and Afghanistan, Bosnia, Lebanon and by the Palestinians in the occupied territories. As evidently proved in Iraq and Chechnya, the use of such explosive devices is not adopted from lack of basic, standard issue weapons, but due to the tactical advantages of such systems, when employed by loosely organized urban guerrilla cells. Unlike the mine which is triggered by pressure or magnetic influence, IEDs do not necessarily require physical contact or pressure for activation but can be activated by remote control, including wire, electronic signals, or cellular phone. This mode of operation can be employed against selective targets, even on busy urban traffic lanes, as repeatedly demonstrated in Iraq. In fact, the IED has become the symbol of the modern urban guerrilla.

Standard mine protected vehicles do not always provide the optimal protection against IED. But they can provide the first of defence when an army encounters IED environment. Since operation of IED is characteristic of urban guerrilla warfare, rapid response against IED is imperative for survival. Unarmoured vehicles must be fitted with armoured cabins, providing reasonable blast protection, on top of standard bullet-proof defence. Large windows, firing ports and access doors on both sides of the vehicle, are required for rapid and safe dismounting of the crew, enabling them to regroup and respond quickly with effective fire. Such concepts are provided for both Humvee tactical utility and transportation vehicles, such as the MTVR truck and Remote-controlled firing stations, mounting light machine guns, Automatic Grenade Launchers (AGL), observation systems and ranging devices (target markers, laser rangefinders etc), are required for effective counter-IED action in an urban environment. Such equipment is of course vulnerable, but mutual cover by precision firepower from adjacent vehicles in the combat patrol denies the enemy further damage, provided that the engagement is quick, decisive, and accurate.

USAF Policeman training Iraqi MP on the range.

MPs already train alongside their civilian counterparts to aid civil power and improve interoperation skill exchanges. One task Military Police inevitably find themselves doing in combat zones is training up a new or reformed civilian police force. Many military police soldiers in Iraq and Afghanistan have found themselves training, coaching, and mentoring the national police forces. Whilst Australian MPs assisted training civilian police in East Timor and British Red Caps continue to train and exercise with several African and Commonwealth countries to enhance their capabilities.

During North Atlantic Treaty Organization offensive operations in Helmand Province, Afghanistan, provincial residents asked International Security Assistance Force (ISAF) troops not to turn their area responsibilities over to the Afghan National Police (ANP) because of a fear of police corruption. The residents were so fearful of the ANP that they actually preferred Taliban rule. NATO Military Police from Britain, USA, Croatia, Poland, and Germany have all been heavily involved in retraining the ANP to restore their professionalism and community trust.

In a collapsed state the multinational coalition force may be charged with the responsibility of re-establishing police services, courts, and prisons. Supporting the police is essential. Police are instrumental in supporting the community by identifying problems at the most local level possible. In essence, the police become the conduit by which other government agencies address quality-of-life issues throughout the community.

Police provide civil security while also assisting with the delivery of other essential services, as determined by the community. The people engage in continuous, positive interaction with the government through the police. This leads to economic development and the legitimacy of government.

As ISAF develops the ANP capability to secure Afghanistan, defeat terrorism, and neutralize the insurgency, an effective police force is critical to the security line of operation. ISAF are assisting Afghan National Security Forces to clear areas of enemy control, hold areas free from enemy control by ensuring that they remain under the control of a peaceful Afghan government with adequate security presence, and build the ANP and capacity of local institutions. The ANP role is to concentrate on solving community problems and becoming a conduit between the people and the government.

Police are not low-cost trigger pullers; they are part of the development of governance and criminal justice. Social control in Afghan society resides at the local level, and policing is a local issue. Local police departments can be tied to a national system through legal and training standards.

The Military Police Corps should be the proponent for police transition team training certification requirements. After all many US and British Reserve Military Police units consist of civilian police officers who have been deployed for this specific mission. Simply put, Police should train police.

Iraqi Federal Police members assigned to 3rd Battalion, 4th Brigade, take part in a class in urban warfare training from Spanish Guardia Civil trainers, at the Besmaya

Range Complex, Iraq, Feb. 8, 2018. Since 2014, Operation Inherent Resolve members have built baseline capacity of more than 130,000 Iraqi security forces trained to defeat ISIS within the Iraqi Security Forces, it is time to enhance those capabilities to prevent resurgence of ISIS and create stability within their nation. U.S. Army - Image ID: M63332.

Multinational Military Police training over 2019 and 2020 has increased due to the Covid-virus as many countries release their military police will be a vital asset to civilian law enforcement in case social breakdown.

MPs from Denmark train with US MPs in joint exercises to perfect skills that can be used when units work together on operations in 2019.

In 2019, the 220th Military Police Company of the Colorado National Guard, cross-trained with Slovenian forces near Divaca, Slovenia for protective services training and advanced rifle marksmanship training. They worked on firearms techniques such as assuming a good firing stance and performing tactical reloads. Part of a multinational exercise (Response 19) the 220th MPs' training was designed to improve the Slovenia mission readiness and involved the rapid transportation of equipment around Slovenia, Hungary, and the Republic of Croatia.

The 2019 exercise Redcap Pegasus has seen 156 Provost Company, 4th Regiment Royal Military Police training on

the windswept STANTA Ranges in Norfolk to be ready to provide military policing support to 16 Air Assault Brigade, the British Army's Rapid Reaction Force. Airborne operations - where troops could find themselves operating in hostile territory with limited reinforcement and resupply - demand soldiers on top of their specialist skills, but also able to show initiative and flexibility to meet the needs of the mission.

The Redcaps started the two-week training with an infantry masterclass from 3rd Battalion the Parachute Regiment to develop their infantry and patrolling skills, before focussing on their core policing skills of detainee handling, evidence gathering and route reconnaissance and signing.

Major Mike Boyd, Officer Commanding 156 Pro Coy RMP, described the training as 'a building block' to confirm the unit's skills ahead of larger exercises alongside 16 Air Assault Brigade.

"Airborne operations demand soldiers working at a higher mental and physical standard," he said. "We all need to be physically robust and able to live, manoeuvre and fight alongside paratroopers. While doing that, a junior soldier may find themselves working as the sole policing specialist with little ability to receive direction. Soldiers have to demonstrate that they're on top of their skills to be able to carry the responsibility of making the right policing decisions on their own."

USMPs with MP K9 team about to patrol the streets of Iraq.

For the foreseeable future, the coalition military forces can expect be employed in irregular warfare operations involving stability and peacekeeping missions, humanitarian assistance, and counterinsurgency (COIN). military leaders continue to struggle with fully understanding the policing nature of security operations in COIN. To successfully put down an indigenous rebellion, security must first be established. Criminals and guerrilla leaders, often indiscernible, must be patiently identified and dealt with so that native populations can come to know justice. This effort can only be accomplished by working closely with the local population, ensuring they have a stake in the successful outcome of COIN operations. Only after an acceptable level of security has been established will the legitimacy of a western backed government be accepted by the local population.

Military Police offer a unique contribution to support counterinsurgency operations. Traditionally, civilian police forces are optimized for law enforcement operations and would only be deployed in a low threat environment. In contrast, military combined arms teams whilst able to operate through the threat spectrum, are optimized for combat operations in a medium to high environment. Civil police may be initially unable to restore law and order without the aid of the military, however the military is not trained as police officers. Both elements must complement each other in the initial stages, with the military taking responsibility for putting down the insurgency but not assuming the responsibility of being the police force. MP however provide a force element with the skills, equipment and communications which will assist commanders in providing options and effects to fill the capability gap across the threat spectrums.The initial aim to any counterinsurgency is to restore law and order and allow the local government to take control. MPs can also train the local Police Force if its infrastructure requires. MP provide a vast array of specialist support able to operate in any environment including mobility capabilities, lethality in weapons mix, and trained communications skill to support the of restoring and maintaining law and order.

ISAF counterinsurgency (COIN) Policing operations in Afghanistan can be an effective tool. According to the US Army Field Manual

(FM) 3–24, police are the most visible institution of the government's response to an insurgency. Police are or at least should be able to determine the individual needs of a community and address each constituency's concerns. In theory, this enhances the government's legitimacy.

Families, tribes, and ethnic identities are the cornerstone of Afghan society. This is due to the rugged geography that results in the presence of autonomous villages throughout the country. "Afghans identify themselves by *Qawm* – the basic sub-national identity based on kinship, residence, and sometimes occupation. This instinctive social cohesiveness includes tribal clans, ethnic subgroups, religious sects, locality-based groups, and groups united by interests." 'In Afghan culture, social control mechanisms are organized at the local level. The real Afghan social and political powers also reside at the local level. Therefore, policing is a local issue for Afghans, and police development should occur at that level. The central government should establish the conditions necessary to allow the concerns of the populace to be addressed within the communities. Community-oriented policing (COP) is a policing philosophy that is compatible with COIN theory and ISAF strategy. The COP model can assist the Government of the Islamic Republic of Afghanistan in establishing the conditions necessary for local communities to address local problems. The legitimacy of the Afghan government depends upon its ability to accomplish that objective. The legitimacy of the central government facilitates the accomplishment of ISAF and U.S. strategic objectives in Afghanistan. Therefore, ISAF should place the highest priority on police training and development. Police are members of the government agency that is closest to the people, and they can serve as a communication conduit between the people, local government, and central government. Under the COP philosophy, the community is placed at the centre of crime prevention. The components of COP are Strategic-oriented policing (SOP). Police surge and use directed, aggressive, and saturation patrols to *clear* the criminal element from the community. They then *hold* that effort as they transition to the next phase.

Neighbourhood-oriented policing which can be considered the second phase of implementation, can actually occur simultaneously with SOP. This is the heart of Community-oriented policing. For neighbourhood-oriented policing to work, the community must be more than an ally or partner in the fight against crime; it must be at the head of the organization to which police are responsible and accountable. Communities with police *build* mechanisms to identify and prioritize problems. Examples of neighbourhood-oriented policing programs include communication programs, community social control programs, community patrols, and community crime prevention.

Problem-oriented policing (POP) is a concept of effectiveness in policing. "Problem-oriented policing addresses a particular problem, analyses the problem, determines a course of action, implements the program, then follows up in an evaluative manner. If the problem is resolved, the police and community must only keep the problem in check. If it is not resolved, alternative solutions are generated and implemented."

Sadly, not all the training missions go without danger the mob killing of six Royal Military police soldiers in the eastern Iraqi town of Majar Kabir, is one example. The detachment of Red Caps had been sent north of Basra on 24 June 2003, barely two months after George Bush had declared a formal end to hostilities, to liaise with Iraqi police officers. Equipped with only 50 rounds of ammunition each and carrying an antiquated radio transmitter, the Royal Military Police unit arrived in the dusty police compound on a ferociously hot summer's morning. They were not aware that British colleagues from the First Battalion the Parachute Regiment were operating at the other end of town. That patrol became involved in a protracted street battle and was forced to withdraw after shooting dead five Iraqi insurgents.

An infuriated crowd surged through Majar Kabir craving retribution. The Red Caps, standing beside their army Land Rovers, were caught by surprise. Corporal Simon Miller, 21, was the first man to be hit, and they all retreated into the police station. Trapped, heavily outnumbered and with inadequate reserves of ammunition, the six men were unable to defend themselves for long. There was no mast for their radio equipment, so they could not summon help.

One of those killed was 20-year-old Thomas Keys. When his body was recovered from a storeroom in the police compound, it had 12 gunshot wounds and the marks of repeated beatings. In a subsequent inquiry,

Major-General Peter Wall revealed that the town had been "swimming with weapons" and was an "incredibly unhealthy and unsafe place". The deaths of the men have since become a symbol of Britain's misadventure in Iraq, a painful reminder of the poor intelligence and equipment shortages that undermined what was supposed to have been an era of peaceful reconstruction.

The U.S, military relies on strong partnerships with other militaries to successfully complete the mission in Afghanistan. In 2010 Macedonia's Military Police and the United States National Guard MPs of the 230th Military Police Company, 95th Military Police Battalion held joint military manoeuvres recently. Macedonia was part of a ten-month small unit exchange project. The thirty-six Soldiers from1st Platoon, 230th Military Police Company, deployed to Krivolak, to take the lead in a crew-served, weapon training exercise designed to prepare Macedonian military police, ranger, and special forces soldiers for their upcoming Special Operations Regiment deployment to Afghanistan with the 86th Brigade Combat Team from the Vermont National Guard. Macedonia already has a military contingent in Iraqi Freedom, and also participates in the NATO mission in Afghanistan and the EU-Althea mission in Bosnia and Herzegovina.

Again in 2011 two platoons of the Macedonian Army (ARM) Military Police Battalion and a military and police platoon of the Vermont National Guard participated in the manoeuvres, practicing urban environment operations. The United States and Macedonia have already had 11 years of cooperation in the area of security. The goal of these exchanges with instructors from Vermont is to train Macedonian Army (ARM) military police platoons to take part in international peacekeeping missions. The involvement of the Vermont National Guard 230th Military Police Company in Macedonia was a testament when US Defence Secretary Donald Rumsfeld decorated three Macedonian soldiers for heroism during the most recent mission in Iraq.

Another area where Military Police conduct joint training is with civilian law enforcement agencies in peace time. This has several main functions, firstly many civilian agencies have access to equipment and training materials that MP units do not have. Civilian Police Forces often have years of ongoing up to date experience in major investigations something the military environment does not have on a regular basis. Many MP units throughout the world send staff on Investigative and Forensic courses for example. Some benefits are common procedures when the Military have to aid Civil power during emergency situations. It is vital in today's terrorist environment that homeland security also be considered as a role for Military Police units in times of National emergency.

Getting the army from one place to the next is a vital task of the MPs.

When a transport driver starts up his engine and conducts his routine vehicle checks prior to the start of his dangerous convoy mission into the heart of enemy territory or up to the front lines, does he think of the MPs who for many hours prior have reconnoitred his route ensuring it is useable and safe, or how it has taken them several hours to sign post it for him so he does not get lost and the fact that all the markers need retrieval after the operation. Probably not, he only remembers the time when the MPs stopped him drinking too much in the pub.

The basic concept of manoeuvre and mobility support operations is the swift and uninterrupted movement of combat power and logistics forward, laterally, and across the battlefield in support of the battlefield commander's intent. This is achieved by clearly marking the way, this done by the MPs. It is however not only a vital role it requires a great deal of skill and knowledge. Before you drive off in any direction you must ensure several things, the enemy are not there, the logistical transporters you are leading can get over, under or across the roads, this is done by careful route reconnaissance.

A route is the road or roads, including tracks and bridges, used when moving from one place to another. It includes those roads, bridges, tunnels, fords, and ferries selected from a networking a given area for the movement of troops, equipment, and supplies. Although a route may also include the use of navigable waters, rail transportation facilities, and aircraft landing facilities, the MPs can do it all. The nature of the terrain. Existing roads and their physical characteristics, including lengths and load-bearing capabilities and obstructions which may create bottlenecks or slow down movement. They are classified as natural or artificial. Natural obstructions include such features as watercourses, terrain compartments, wooded and jungle areas, swamp and inundated areas and mountains. Artificial obstructions include such factors as nuclear radiation, built-up areas, tactical obstacles (minefields, barbed wire), communication wire, low underpasses, narrow tunnels, narrow bridges, and other physical features. Bridges and other stream-crossing means tunnels must be able to support the weight of a convoy or such things as a tank.

The purpose of route reconnaissance is to gain information which will aid in the selection of a route or routes to be used for the movement of troops, troop equipment, and supplies in military operations. A MP must plan several routes for the one move as the flow of a fluid battlefield may cause immediate alterations to an existing plan. This is where many commanders have been impressed with an MPs quick reaction and decision-making processes at what to many is a relatively lowly rank. It is the norm for a Junior Non Commissioned Officer of the Military Police to make decisions effecting millions of dollars' worth of logistics and human lives on the move.

General Pattern stated: *"without his Military Police he would not have been able to move his Corps to join the battle of the Bulge and to achieve this in a limited time frame and in adverse winter conditions shows the professionalism of this Corps".*

While planning a route an MP must have knowledge of the specific route requirements include the maximum weight, maximum width, maximum height, and classification of the vehicles to be moved; the approximate number of each class to be moved per hour; and the approximate length of time the route is to be used.

Road reconnaissance is performed to obtain the information about existing roads upon which to base road classifications, primarily in support of the establishment of a route. It is concerned with the conditions of existing roads for immediate use and not for maintenance operations. The information obtained is used to estimate the quantity and kind of traffic and loads that a road can accommodate in its present condition. Road reconnaissance may also include estimates of the practicability of improvement and of the engineer work involved in conditioning a route to accommodate specified traffic and loads. A road reconnaissance carried out by an officer or NCO other than an engineer may require supplementation by an engineer reconnaissance to provide additional data necessary for complete classification of the road. It not just on the roads, MPs ensure the vital flow of equipment, on D-Day in WW2 MPs were amongst the first troops on the beach.

Motor bikes are still used on by MP's on the battlefieldby MPs. They are often the quickest way to conduct route signage and act as quick liaison means between headquarters and front lines.

Infantrymen often have described the military police as the soldiers who posted 'Off Limits' signs even before towns were liberated. But there's one place where soldiers found directional signs and there were no complaints about the early presence of MPs then. That was on the WWII Normandy beaches. MPs crossed those narrow belts of sand at H-Hour, D-Day, and began clearing vehicles from the beaches, evacuating wounded, guarding prisoners in an improvised cage, unloading shells. In the pre-dawn air invasion, USMPs had come in fighting with the 82nd and 101st and British MPs from the 6th Airborne Division Provost Company on D-Day were among the first to set foot on French soil. Things do not change that much over time as I can recall when I was in Mogadishu, Somalia having a small chuckle to myself seeing the USMC "invade Somalia. Yes, I guess the SEALs had done their thing perhaps several days before, but on the beach awaiting the mass of amphibious air cushioned vessels and landing craft was several USMC Military Policemen giving directions to the grunts and hurrying them off the beach. By all accounts they had been there several days.

On February 26, 1991, the Commander of the Allied Forces, General Norman Schwarzkopf directed "Send in the First Team. Destroy the Republican Guard. Let's go home." And like General MacArthur before him, he requested that the 545th MP's lead the way. The division charged west pausing only to refuel before passing through breeches in the enemy obstacle belt. Racing north and then east, the division moved in a vast armada of armour, stretching from horizon to horizon. Within 24 hours, the First Team had gone 300 kilometres, slicing deep into the enemy's rear. As the division prepared to destroy a Republican Guard Division, the cease fire halted it.

During all this activity, the 1st, 2nd, and 3rd platoons of Americas 545th MP Co. were with their respective Brigades while the 4th Platoon provided security for the Division Main Command Post and the 5th Platoon remained with the Division Tactical Operations Centre. Each of the platoons with the Brigades operated the POW Forward Collecting Point for that brigade and these facilities were never static for too long as the division kept constantly on the move. The 4th Platoon maintained and operated the Division Central POW Collection Point as well as security for the 545th MP Co headquarters and the office of the Provost Marshals.

In this war that was a monumental task as the Iraqi soldiers surrendered as fast as the 545th MPs could transport them. In 100 hours, the Iraqi Army went from being the 4th largest Army in the world to the 2nd largest Army in Iraq!

The 545th MP Company set up defensive positions where the cease fire had stopped their forward movement and attack, then expanded north to Highway 8, clearing bunkers, and looking for enemy equipment and soldiers.

Within two weeks the 545th MP Company moved south into Saudi Arabia and its new assembly area (AA) Killeen. There, on the plain of the Wadi al Batin, the 545th MPs began to prepare for their redeployment home.

Addressing the division and the 545th MP Co at AA Killeen on Palm Sunday, VII (US) Corps Commander, Lt. Gen. Frederick Franks emphasized the division's major role in the allied victory. *"You were leading the corps – you were the major combat power VII Corps had. You were the First Team. You led us into combat. You began the fight; you led the way ....”*

Austrian MPs prepare to assist civilian Police during a recent world summit meeting.

Riot control, Crowd control, Public Safety Response are just a few names given to police or military squads controlling a large group of demonstrators. As a Military Working Dog handler especially military police members will encounter this task at some point. It can be so controversial that high ranking Commissioned Officers are usually required to authorize the use of MWDs at a riot.

Within riot control and public disorder operations the service dog can be employed to attack armed aggressors that try to hide in the crowd. In such cases the employment of a service dog provides the on-site commander with an additional step in the escalation of force that ranges from the use of batons to the use of firearms.

There are many reasons riots start, during United Nations operations in Kosovo and Bosnia demonstrations took place due to racial tensions and many UN troops found themselves in the middle of decade old conflicts.

With 2,000 soldiers deployed in Kosovo, France contributes a lot to KFOR (Kosovo Force) and represents the 3rd largest strength contingent after Germany and Italy. French forces are mainly deployed within the MNTF-N (Multinational Task Force-North). KFOR is the 2nd most important NATO-led operation after Afghanistan. France took command for a year in September 2007. French MWD teams in Kosovo man vehicle check points searching for explosives and arms. A secondary role of dog teams is to support KFOR Civilian Police Forces in crowd control operations.

Recently in Iraq and Afghanistan many demonstrations can be incited by religious attacks from one group against another or simply high spirits after an intense football game between two rival towns or clans.

German MPs in Afghanistan recently assisted other ISAF Forces with rioters during a Soccer Match in Kabul which got out of control. Afghani soccer supports like soccer supporters the world over can be passionate about the game and this spilled over between two rival clubs. The MPs had to be deployed to prevent both an escalation of violence and to prevent some crowd members being crushed.

In Somalia and other African Countries demonstrations often started due to the way food rations were or were not distributed. In East Timor demonstrations occurred due to election fraud allegations.

One thing all riot control operations have in common is their high media profile and the often-negative attention they encounter. Journalists seem often in a position to take a photograph of a snarling military police dog or baton holding MP in an aggressive stance but seem to never capture the spitting, verbal abuse, rock throwing, firebomb-wielding mass of agitators outnumbering them hundreds to one.

The other major use of Police dogs has been as a force multiplier, one Police dog in a riot control incident is worth twenty men as a physiological deterrent to would be agitators. Police officers themselves often call on Police dog teams to back them up at dangerous situations.

The International Stabilisation Force QRF were assessed on PPC by members of the ISF Military Police. Under a United Nations Agreement, the ISF is requested to provide PPC when a situation escalates beyond the capabilities of the East Timor National Police (PNTL) and the United Nations. The New Zealand Defence Force provided a realistic protest and rioting group, with the QRF passing the assessment with flying colours. Deep caption: Operation ASTUTE is the ADF contribution to the Australian Government's response to a request from the Government

'Diesel' the Military Police Dog and handler Corporal Ben Liston send rioting protesters running during a Quick Response Force (QRF) Population Protection and Control (PPC) training exercise in Dili, East Timor. Photography by LSPH Paul Berry.

of East Timor to assist in restoring peace and stability to their country. The ADF has deployed to East Timor with a mission to assist the East Timorese government and the United Nations to bring stability, security, and confidence to the Timorese people to allow them to resolve their differences peacefully. The New Zealand Defence Force (NZDF) is working alongside the ADF to assist with this mission. Together, the ADF and NZDF personnel form the International Stabilisation Force (ISF) in East Timor. International police from Australia and 20 other nations provide security in Dili as part of the United Nations Police Force. The ISF provides support to these police operations as required.

MPs in a joint exercise with other NATO MPs contain illegal immigrates protesting in detention camps. The Croatian-Slovenian border in particular has several such camps.

In 2020 Military Police are being used by several governments in boarder protection. Normal police and customs patrols in countries such as Austria are being overwhelmed by over 8,000 refugees and illegal migrates arriving per day from Africa Eastern Europe and via Greece. With riot control training and a soldier's self-discipline needed in a very controversial area. The MP seems an ideal fit between a soldier and law enforcement officer, whose training and ideology of a civilian police officer gives them compassion yet a disciplined body of troops to do what is for many a necessary but distasteful job.

These same skills can be used to back up civilian law enforcement during large national security events such as World Summit leaders' conferences. Australian MPs for example were deployed during the G20 summit in various roles from Vehicle check point control, Close Protection and standby for public disorder duties.

Serbian MPs conduct a roadblock.

There are two types of check points – vehicle and personnel – both have their own characteristics. Added to this, there are two ways of conducting them, permanent checkpoints or snap or random checkpoints. Military Police Vehicle Checkpoints (VCPs) are set up during emergencies both to apprehend wanted persons and to prevent the smuggling of arms and equipment. Checkpoints also enhance the visibility of the forces of law and order, acting as a deterrent.

During emergency periods, the most effective means of checking vehicles and individuals is the roadblock. Identification of personnel is of utmost importance. Acting in valve terms an efficiently operated roadblock regulates the flow of authorized traffic and personnel.

The Provost has often been charged with rear area security. During emergencies his principal concern was enemy agents disguised as Army personnel or as civilians, or saboteurs. Today the same principals apply but the world has changed to prevent terrorist attack.

VCPs can come in two forms mobile and static. Static VCPs are currently in places such as at the entrance of Kandahar Airfield. Its aim is not only to establish who and what gains entry to base but the prevention of vehicle suicide attack. Mobile VCPs are a weapon of surprise, an MP unit can position them anywhere and at any time and are an effective deterrent to contraband smugglers and terrorists alike.

Roadblocks are usually mounted in an internal security (IS) or counter-insurgency situation. They are in the form of either snap or permanent roadblocks; the purpose of both is to check traffic going through a particular point or to completely block a road to prevent its further use.

The sighting of the roadblock is important. Preferably, it should be around a corner or behind the crest of a hill so as to take the driver by surprise and should be flanked by hedgerows or ditches so that it is difficult or impossible for a car to turn round.

Terrorists have to usually use (in Afghanistan there is a growing number of donkey-mounted suicide bombs) wheeled transports to move weapons, explosives, supplies and other equipment to safe hiding-places, from which they will have to move them again when they intend to use them. The best way to counter this threat is to create a permanent infrastructure of roadblocks, or vehicle checkpoints (VCPs) upon which you can superimpose as many extra snap or temporary roadblocks as the operational situation demands.

However as stated it's not just people or vehicles that require vigilance at VCPs. In 2009, the Taliban strapped an improvised explosive device to a donkey. The gate guard noticed something suspicious when a group of men let the donkey go a short way from the camp and then hurried off. The donkey was stopped with a rifle shot. One soldier set fire to the hay with a flare provoking a "considerable explosion".

May 25 2010 – A small Syrian-backed militant group in the Gaza Strip blew up a donkey cart laden with explosives close to the border with Israel. According to a spokesman for the group, more than 200 kilograms of dynamite were heaped on the animal-drawn cart. The explosives were detonated several dozen meters from the border fence with Israel. The animal was killed in the blast, but no human injuries or damage were reported.

The basic, permanent VCP will impose restrictions on the terrorist. Even though he knows it is there, and the surprise element is lacking, it forces him to use other routes, thereby reducing his options; it also reduces the number of routes upon which you need mount snap or temporary VCPs.

Permanent roadblocks or VCPs must be well defended, permanently manned, and well equipped. Your perimeter should be well defended with wire to prevent attack or fire, and with concrete bollards to prevent terrorists leaving a car bomb alongside your position. By searching people and vehicles at checkpoints, weapons or other items that may be used to undermine the unit's mission can be discovered and confiscated. Check points allow the area of operations to remain immune from outside influence and to keep the ratio of enemy to friendly forces unchanged.

They also deny the enemy intelligence gathering opportunities. Check points make a large contribution to the security of military personnel and units and to the local population within the area of operations. To be effective check points must be set up in such a way so that they cannot be 'by passed'. When there is host nation or local police or military personnel available it is usually useful to have them present and to make any necessary arrests. Many times, this can aid in avoiding incidents or an escalation in tensions at the VCP.

Random checkpoints are a common tactic used by many military police forces and have been recently used by UN forces in Kosovo, Lebanon, Israeli Army in the West Bank, US forces in Kurdistan and Iraq in search of insurgents, fugitives, and other law breakers. In some war zones these checkpoints can heave lethal consequences. This is especially true in the case of suicide blasts which produce casualties regardless of political or cultural affiliation.

Random checkpoints are usually established for no more than a few hours, in order to decrease the possibility of insurgent attacks on them, as well as to maintain their effectiveness as a surprising, unexpected obstacle. They can be set up by foot patrols, by vehicle patrols or by patrols dropped from a helicopter. This latter technique is known by

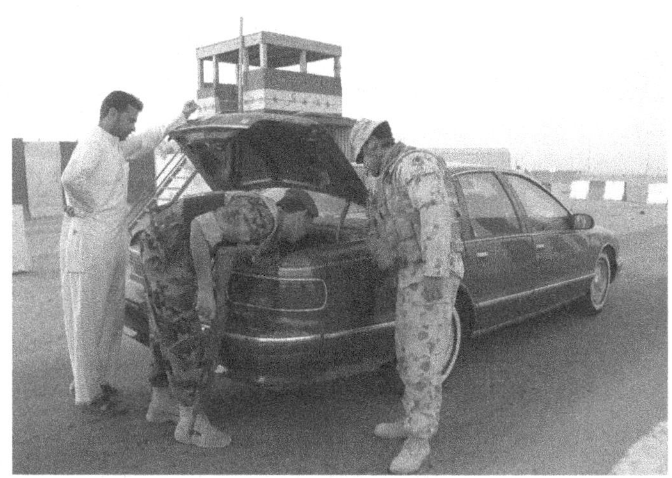

Australian MP overseas an Afghan MP conducting a vehicle inspection prior to entry to a coalition base.

the British Army in Northern Ireland as an Eagle Patrol.

The aims of roadblocks and VCPs are to dominate the area, deterring terrorist activity and movement. Prevent reinforcements of enemy or terrorists reaching sensitive areas or riotous gatherings. Deny contacts between terrorists and local inhabitants. Prevent supply of arms, ammo, food, and medical supplies to the enemy. Win public confidence and impress the local inhabitants. Facilitate other operations against the enemy or terrorists. Gain information and intelligence.

In many of the conflicts military police will find themselves operating in, the location of vehicle checkpoints will often be between two or more ethnic, political, or religious factions. In these cases, check points will have to be erected along the existing boundaries between the warring factions. If given a choice in selecting a check point location, MPs, if possible, set up VCP on the upward slope or on the crest of high ground. This aids in negating the problem associated with vehicle brake failure and having an uncontrolled vehicle crashing into the check point. By setting up a VCP at crossroads it will deny enemy freedom of movement or to bypass the VCP.

An example of the need to be flexible conducting VCPs is in Kosovo where they are used in an attempt to catch smuggled weapons or cargo. However, after 20 minutes of standing up a vehicle checkpoint, the VCP is no longer effective. Smugglers today in Kosovo are much smarter than in 1999, and over the years have developed multiple tactics to avoid the Kosovo Force (KFOR).

This is mainly due to the flood of cell phones used by Kosovars living or traveling in the area of operation. Two distinct tactics, techniques, and procedures are used for vehicle smuggling in Kosovo. One is using a small nondescript car driven by one passenger carrying a cell phone driving ahead of the cargo truck actively looking for any KFOR MP, United Nations or Kosovo Police Service (KPS) checkpoints in the area. This vehicle is typically able to spot the VCP, move through it, and then call back to the truck carrying cargo alerting them not to continue moving along the current route. The cargo truck will take one of two actions, either stop movement along that route altogether by halting at a local cafe and hiding the truck, or it will move to an alternate route, if available, to bypass this VCP. The second method used by smugglers in Kosovo is to pay people living on or around smuggling routes to call the smugglers the moment KFOR, or KPS enters the town or sector. This is relatively easy in some areas since the road networks are relatively limited, and in many border areas there are only one or two routes into the border crossing areas. With these methods, it is very difficult for military and law enforcement forces to capture large amounts of smuggled goods moving into Kosovo. To combat this, military police conduct mobile random VCPs. aimed at surprising smugglers. This has worked and MPs were able to seize large amounts of smuggled goods attempting to come into Kosovo illegally.

Another example of how heavy the workload is for MP on VCPs is at Camp Bastion at the Main Entry Point where, on average, 300 vehicles of all shapes and sizes enter the camp gates daily. In more recent times during the Commonwealth Games in Australia in 2016 saw Australian MPs from the Air Force and Army man vehicle check points at both the main transport hub and Games facilities, processing some 400 plus vehicles daily.

USAF MP K9 team searches for explosive during the first gulf war in 1991.

Military workind dogs are perhaps at their most valuable when they are trained to detect explosives at a VCP, in fact the British army employ dogs whose speciality role is just that, explosive detection of vehicles. Explosive Detection Dogs (EDD) can detect minuscule amounts of a wide range of explosives, making them an invaluable addition both to entry points and in a mobile VCP team. A well-trained EDD team can conduct a significantly more effective search of vehicle in a much shorter time than a number of people can. Using MP EDD teams helps reduce the potential risk to persons who would otherwise have to do the search without the benefit of the dog's superior sense of smell. Unlike specialist explosive search dogs from the Corps of Engineers, Military Police dog teams are frequently dual trained in attack or 'bite' work enabling them to search and detain suspects.

Elite MP armed teams respond to a hostile situation on Base.

Throughout the last few decades of the twentieth century a wave of violent protest and vicious terrorist attacks swept across the western world. Many of these incidents were specifically directed at Military personnel and installations. These attacks, coupled with the increased number of violent crimes being encountered by military police personnel, caused great concern amongst many military law enforcement agencies.

Highly trained teams have been established in many military police forces throughout the world including the United States, called Special Reaction Team, or SRT. SRTs are the Army's version of a civilian Police SWAT team.

In the USA this new threat was recognised by the Air Force who have been conducting tactical team training for its Security Police (SP) units Emergency Services Teams (EST) at Lackland Air Force Base for a number of years. The US Army sent a small team of MP's to Lackland, to attend their course. The results were deemed so successful that the Department of the Army who have mandated that all Army MP units, assigned to a major installation, form specially trained teams to respond to potential crisis situations. As a result, of this directive, all major Army posts now maintain the ability to deploy a MP Special Reaction Team to be deployed in the event that a situation develops that is beyond the scope of the regular MP units, assigned to that installation. Possible scenarios that may call for the deployment of a Special Reaction Team include hostage situations, counterterrorist operations, barricaded criminals, sniper incidents, VIP protection duties, high risk searches threatened suicide or barricaded mentally disturbed persons.

In the event that a Special Reaction Team is deployed, the teams primary focus would be to ensure the safety of all parties involved. Teams would also try to apprehend any offenders and secure the area for investigators. A scenario maybe a SRT Teams may be confronted with a situation where a suspect is hiding or barricading themselves within a building and a dynamic and quick entry may jeopardize the safety of officers, the suspect, and innocent parties.

In situations such as these, a slow and deliberate entry/search would be employed. This requires a team to move slowly and quietly through a building, entering and stealthily clearing each room until the suspect is located, at which point negotiations can start, the suspect can be called out, or a dynamic entry can be employed to surprise and take the suspect into custody.

Potential SRT members are selected from the ranks of experienced MPs. After passing an initial selection which includes a physical fitness test, a psychological screening, and a records review; candidates then attend a two week long Special Reaction Team One course at the US Army Military Police School. During the 160 hours course of instruction students receive instruction in selective firing, physical training, rappelling, breaching techniques, and tactics. Students must successfully complete eight scenarios, including some conducted at night, to graduate. SRT marksman-observers (snipers) attend a separate one week long SRT 2 course. Team members receive additional training at US Army, civilian, and military training courses.

A standard Special Reaction Team consists of at least 9 members lead by a team leader; 5–6 men comprise the entry team with the remaining four men making up two – 2-man marksman/observer teams. MP Canine teams are assigned to SRT as required. Military police canines use all of their senses to locate their quarry. The most powerful sense they use is their nose, which is thousands of times more sensitive than a human's. The next most powerful sense a dog possesses is their hearing, which far exceeds human capabilities. And lastly, dogs use their eyesight to help them in confirming what their eyes and ears have told them-there's a person hiding in the immediate vicinity. Canine searches can be completed much quicker than human searches, regardless of lighting and environmental conditions, and greatly reduce the risk to human officers. When using the canine in a SRT environment the dog is used to clear areas of concern for the SRT team. The dog is sent forward of the team off lead, to clear hallways, rooms, or blind corners.

The US Marine Corps use similar teams, one such team is based in Okinawa. Ten Marines from the Provost Marshal's Office there make-up such a team. The Special Reaction Team is specially trained to handle missions beyond the call of duty for basically trained military policemen. "We're a S.W.A.T. team for the Marine Corps," said Staff Sgt. Steven Rowe, commander, Special Reaction Team, Provost Marshal's Office, Marine Corps Base. "Our mission is to train, practice and rehearse for any situation, such as hostages, barricaded suspects and felony arrests."

"Today we're going over basic entry and room clearing," Rowe said. "These guys do this a thousand times and they know how to do it, but as a team you're not a really well-rounded team until you do it a thousand times together."

Once the Marines get into their building, either by kicking it in, or using one of their many sophisticated breeching methods, they wait for the commands from the 'shield. "The shield is the 'hall boss' who runs the team," Rowe said. "He's the man up-front in ballistics from head-to-toe and can take a couple of rounds."

A military policeman is selected to be a member of Special Reaction Team after he completes an indoctrination, which is an evaluation of how quickly he can learn the unit's special tactics, once they become Special Reaction Team, they are sent SRT School at Fort Leonard Wood, Mo. After Special Reaction Team School, their training is endless as the only military SRT on the base constantly trains to hone the tightly knit team's skills, often training six or seven days a week.

After receiving the command to enter a room, two or more Marines buttonhook or cross into the room to either locate their objective or ensure it's clear. With danger around every corner, many men may not be fearless enough to be a member of such an elite squad. Though this SRT has not had a real-world situation to respond to for many years, that hasn't stagnated their training the team considers themselves a group of elite Marines.

SRTs are typically no smaller than 9 men. In order to cover all contingencies, an installation may train enough men for 2 9-man SRTs. A typical 9-man Special Reaction Team is made up of:

- The Entry Team – Consists of a minimum of Team leader, point man, first and second defenseman, and rear security
- Team Leader – organizes and supervises the SRT during training and operations. Coordinates training, mission planning, logistics. Certifies SRT and responsible for maintenance of that certification for each team member. Accountable for SRT weapons. Prepares after-action reports.
- Point man – Conducts recon and recommends primary and alternate routes of approach to target. Leads entry team throughout the phases of the mission. Carries special equipment such as concussion grenades and other pyrotechnics needed for the mission.
- 1st and 2nd Defence-man – Provides security for the point man during movement. Acts as a point man when team splits or when necessary. Covers the entry element during exfiltration.
- Rear Security – Provides rear security during movement to and from target. Cover the entry element during exfiltration. Assists EOD with placement of explosive breaching charges.

- Cover Element / 2nd Entry Element – Each cover element is made up of a marksman and spotter (observer). Two pairs of cover elements can also be deployed if available.
- Marksmen – Maintains surveillance on the target area from a fixed position. Provides information to team leader. Neutralizes hostile fire acting as a sniper if needed. Provides cover for the entry element.
- Observers / Recorders – Also known as spotters for the marksmen. Records all events prior to, during, and after incident for law enforcement evidence. Provides security for the marksman. Helps locate hostile personnel for the marksman. Relieves Marksman as needed.[21]

In many other Countries similar teams of Military Police perform the same function as US SRTs, all be they known by different names however the same underlying role is the same. They are used as civilian police forces elite armed squads are to conduct high police work that ordinary first responder officers cannot or deal with.

In the New Zealand and Australian Air Forces (RNZAF & RAAF) the SRT role is conducted by Airfield Defence Squadrons, similar to Britain's RAF Regiment. All work in conjunction with the service police however as part of overall force protection elements.

Military discipline was maintained through the laws and practices established by royal and parliamentary authorities. The Rules and Articles for the Better Government of all His Majesty's Forces, better known as the Articles of War, formed the basis of military law and were first promulgated in 1663. These are distinct from the Articles of War used

21 https://www.thebalancecareers.com/marine-corps-enlisted-job-descriptions-3345573

by the Royal Navy, which appeared in 1661. The Rules and Articles provided general instructions on the procedures should an officer or soldier be arrested or placed in custody. The mechanism for dealing with them was the court martial.[22]

MPs are responsible for keeping the world's most dangerous terrorist secure. Photo courtesy of USAF.

The Articles of War were applicable in Great Britain and Ireland, the dominions beyond the seas and foreign places dependent upon Britain. They were applicable to every officer, non-commissioned officer, soldier, volunteer, and, in some cases, civilian attached to an army. They were read once in every two months – often monthly – to the officers and men, along with "whatever parts of the present or future general orders are meant to regulate the conduct of officers and men." If an officer, NCO, or soldier was caught red-handed in the act of a crime, the Provost could issue and carry out an immediate sentence, otherwise a matter of evidence went to court martial. Hence the term, "bloody Provost."[23]

Today there are two types of custodial environments military police are involved in. Firstly peace time or garrison prisoner management, where a soldier commits a crime whilst serving in the Defence Forces and has been found guilty of that crime, they then may face a period of incarceration in a military correctional facility. The second, in war

---

[22] James, *Military Dictionary*, entry for Articles of War; Rules and Article for the Better Government of All His Majesty's Forces (London, 1826), p.53.

[23] Arthur Swinson, *A Register of the Regiments and Corps of the British Army* – Appendix, 'The Mutiny Act, 1689' (London: The Archive Press, 1972), pp.315–317.

operations, is the handling of enemy prisoners of war (POWs).

MPs specializing in corrections branch learn skills they'll need for running correctional and confinement facilities, topics include prisoner administration, handling and safeguarding prisoners of war, refugees, or evacuees; conducting small unit offensive and defensive combat operations; guarding military prisoners and absentees/deserters returned to military control; and supervising correctional custody units.

Alas MP correctional staff gained adverse media attention when a limited number of staff became the focus of the media's spotlight on the abuse of enemy prisoners of war at the U.S.-controlled Abu Ghraib prison in Iraq. Most MPs I know were shocked that this incident happened. The US Army's focus on the treatment of POWs has not changed since the Abu Ghraib controversy, "The doctrine has not changed. The mission has not changed, and training has not changed". Showing that there is nothing wrong with the Modis-operandi – just some bad apples in the barrel. Future plans for many MP Corps include the creation of entire companies that specialize in detainee operations. In several countries' MPs are trained in dealing with prisoners of war and other detainees, with special training in restraining, searching, and transporting prisoners to detainee camps. MPs can also be used as prison guards in detainee camps, although that responsibility usually falls on Internment/Resettlement Specialists.

Captured soldiers are trained to believe that escape from captivity is their duty; therefore, they must be closely guarded. While the initial encounter between MPs and POWs can be hostile, as one of the basic principles of gaining control over enemy prisoners after capture is to retain the shock of the event. This will enable enemy prisoners to be interviewed by Military Intelligence Officers (MI) to find out vital information to determine if captives, their equipment, and their weapons have intelligence value which may save our forces lives.

MPs are taught to let up on force once prisoners are seized and under control. They learn to treat prisoners respectfully; the same way MPs are expected to treat military members apprehended in garrison environments. However firm control must be used as most POWs are taken to the rear if they escape, they could do great harm. In the middle

East the Commonwealth MPs often were called on to deal with large numbers of POWs, especially after the surrender of 275,000 Axis troops in May 1943.

Another example of MPs dealing with large numbers of prisoners is at the conclusion of WWII. By V-E Day, 1945 WWII the transfer of prisoners from front lines to rear was a mission of great significance. These bedraggled, beaten members of the German Army POWs had mounted to the gigantic count of nearly 3,000,000 a total that exceeded the size of many armies. An amazing feat accomplished by MPs was moving POWs en masse. Pre-invasion plans established a safe, sound ratio of one guard to every ten prisoners in transit. Nine months later on the Continent, the accepted ratio was one to 50, and one to 150 was not unusual. MPs met with success in handling POWs because, while strictly observing Geneva Convention rules, they punished without compassion and in accordance with approved methods any German overstepping the bounds.

Nothing has changed today, MPs are also responsible for feeding and clothing POWs and in the case of an attack, they must also defend prisoners.[24]

One specialist POW guarding force is part of the British Military Police who have created a specialist arm, it is called The Military Provost Staff who are the Army's specialists in Custody and Detention, providing advice inspection and surety within custodial establishments. They are under direct command of Provost Marshal (Army) and are based primarily at the Military Corrective Training Centre (MCTC) at Colchester from where they deploy regularly in support of British Military operations.

The Military Provost Staff are manned wholly by volunteer transfers from within the Armed Services, their main task is to provide rehabilitation training within a secure environment for service personnel who are either to be retained in the service or be dismissed.

Critically the Military Provost Staff also provide operational support through the provision of advice on Prisoner of War handling through the Provost staffs. They provide the technical advice required to the POW Guard Force and monitor the POWs in custody. The Military Provost

---

24 Kathy West, Historian Assistant, *U.S. Army Military Police Corps Bulletin*, 11 August 2010.

Staffs operational role in Peace Support Operations has historically sent them to deal with the myriad of custodial issues that affect host nations in the event of the collapse of Law and Order.

Prior to the specialist arm any MP could find themselves dealing with POWs. During the Falklands War in 1982, RMPs initially worked on beach logistic control, marshalling helicopters manning information posts and conducting VIP protection of Brigade Headquarters staff.

However soon Argentineans POWs were flooding in and some 11,000 were disarmed, searched, documentation lodged and guarded, much of this work was done or supervised by the RMPs.

In recent history the Military Provost Staff have been responsible for the provision of custodial facilities for indigenous criminals and internees. In Iraq they were responsible for the regeneration of the Iraqi Custodial System.

As seen with great effect in the Military the use of dog teams to guard POWs is highly effective, likewise it did not take civilian Corrective Service Agencies long to use this potent force multiplier to guard prisoners in the civilian prison system. Many countries do not see dogs in the same way as Western people many are intimidated or revile dogs due to cultural or religious beliefs. This can be taken advantage of by deploying military working Dogs in guarding masses of prisoners that would otherwise require high manpower levels. In the First Gulf War the coalition ground offensive into Kuwait began and after only four days, the territory was liberated, and the Iraqi forces swiftly defeated. As the overall operation was completed in a very short space of time, a huge number of Iraqi prisoners of war were suddenly captured by, or surrendered to, the coalition forces, making the task of guarding them a momentous commitment. To assist in overcoming the problem, RAF police dog handlers were instantaneously deployed to the prisoner of war (POW) compounds, known as the 'Mary Hill Camp'. the number quickly rose to around four thousand prisoners. The RAF Police dog teams were used on a variety of tasks, providing twenty-four-hour coverage at the camp. Apart from being used to patrol the perimeter wire of the enclosures containing the captured Iraqi troops they were also used for escorting prisoners from the Chinook helicopters, which brought them into the camp.

On 14 November 2001, the 5th Platoon, 545th Military Police Company deployed to Camp Doha, Kuwait in support of Task Force BLACKJACK THUNDER, Operation DESERT SPRING 03–01. While undergoing their training exercises, on 15 December they were redeployed and assigned to HQ-ARCENT located at Bagram, Afghanistan in support of Operation Enduring Freedom. The Afghan Military Forces were holding up to 4,500 detainees throughout the Coalition Joint Operational area, Afghanistan who required interrogation and documentation of Personal Identification Data.

The purpose of collecting Personal Identification Data is to create a better database for identifying potential enemy threats and to screen these individuals to determine if they meet the criteria to be treated as detainees. If an individual meets the specified criteria, they are taken into custody in a detainee status and secured for further processing.

In their new assignment in Afghanistan, the 545th Military Police Platoon collected Personal Identification Data (PID) on potential Taliban and al-Qaeda members in an effort to identify America's newest enemies. In their role that covered the collection of personnel data, the security of detainees during the operations, and subsequent aerial escort missions back to the collection points, the 545th Military Police Platoon proved to be a true combat multiplier in Afghanistan. On 11 February, the Platoon, their operations in Afghanistan completed, returned to Kuwait and continued their training and support of Task Force Blackjack and then returned in April 2002 to the United States.[25]

These forensic MPs are in uniform, often MP investigators dress in plain clothes.

The level of responsibility placed on military Investigators is immense due to the nature of their work, little information concerning ongoing military investigations and

25 Military Police Internment Resettlement Operations FM 3-19.40

techniques is ever released. They often work independently, with little or no supervision. They may be assigned missions that have a significant impact on the local command or even the entire Army. Unlike many other major civilian law enforcement organizations, Military Investigators do not always specialize in any singular discipline, so they could find themselves conducting a murder investigation one week and an arson investigation the next.

They can be some of the most highly trained criminal investigators in law enforcement. American Army CID agents for example have the opportunity to attend advanced training at some of the most prestigious law enforcement programs in the world, such as the Federal Bureau of Investigation (FBI) National Academy, Metropolitan Police Crime Academy at Scotland Yard, Department of Defence (DOD) Polygraph Institute, and the Canadian Police Academy.

Military Investigators work predominantly in plain clothes similar to civilian police Detectives. They are known by several acronyms such as CID – Criminal Investigation Branch, SIB – Special Investigation Branch, NCIS – Naval Criminal Investigation Service and ADFIS – Australian Defence Force Investigation Service to name just a few.

In some Countries Military Investigators have the right to investigate matters concerning not only their own Servicemen but their dependents or even foreign persons who are connected to that military in some capacity. For example, On the 8th of May 1945 the German High Command signed the Military Act of Surrender. This Act was followed by the Assumption of Supreme Authority over Germany by the United Kingdom, the United States of America, the then Union of Soviet Socialist Republics and the Provisional Government of the French Republic. In simple terms this assumption made the Military Police forces of these nations responsible for the investigation of crime and the reforming of what today is the German Civil Police under the auspices of the United Nations. The signing of the Status of Forces Agreement on the 19th of June 1951 and the Supplementary Agreement between the UK and Germany on 3rd August 1959 laid the foundation for the role, function, and duty which the RMP carry out in Germany to this day. The Agreements formally relinquished jurisdiction by Germany over members of UK forces, dependents, and UK Based Civilians.

Some of these units have vast resources the US Air Force Office of Special Investigations (AFOSI), is a Field Operating Agency (FOA) of the USAF that provides professional investigative services to commanders throughout the Air Force. AFOSI manages offensive and defensive activities to detect, counter and destroy the effectiveness of hostile intelligence services and terrorist groups that target the Air Force. These efforts include investigating the crimes of espionage, terrorism, technology transfer and computer infiltration. This mission aspect also includes providing personal protection to senior Air Force leaders and other officials, as well as supervising an extensive antiterrorism program in geographic areas of heightened terrorist activity.

The vast majority of AFOSI's investigative activities pertain to felony crimes including murder, robbery, rape, assault, major burglaries, drug use and trafficking, sex offenses, arson, compromise of Air Force test materials, black-market activities, and other criminal activities.

A significant amount of AFOSI investigative resources is assigned to fraud (or economic crime) investigations. These include violations of the public trust involving Air Force contracting matters, appropriated and no appropriated funds activities, computer systems, pay and allowance matters, environmental matters, acquiring and disposing of Air Force property, and major administrative irregularities. AFOSI uses fraud surveys to determine the existence, location, and extent of fraud in Air Force operations or programs. It also provides briefings to base and command-level resource managers to help identify and prevent fraud involving Air Force or DOD resources.

The Air Force is now countering a global security threat to our information systems. Our role in support of Information Operations recognizes future threats to the Air Force, and our response to these threats, will occur in cyberspace. AFOSI's support to Information Operations comes in many facets. AFOSI's computer crime investigators provide rapid worldwide response to intrusions into Air Force systems.

The desires of potential adversaries to acquire or mimic the technological advances of the U.S. Air Force have heightened the need to protect critical Air Force technologies and collateral data. The

AFOSI Research and Technology Protection Program provides focused, comprehensive counterintelligence and core mission investigative services to safeguard Air Force technologies, programs, critical program information, personnel, and facilities.

AFOSI has numerous specialists who are invaluable in the successful resolution of investigations. They include technical specialists, polygraphists, behavioural scientists, computer experts and forensic advisers.

AFOSI is the DOD executive agent for both the defence Computer Forensics Laboratory and the Defence Computer Investigations Training Program, which together comprise the defence Cyber Crime Centre. The forensics laboratory provides counterintelligence, criminal, and fraud computer-evidence processing, analysis, and diagnosis to DOD investigations. The investigations training program provides training in computer investigations and computer forensics to DOD investigators and examiners.

In Australia the Australian Defence Force Investigation Service (ADFIS) is a Tri-Service Defence investigation unit staffed by Service Police investigators from all three Services with Army's contribution coming from the Military Police. Trained and experienced Military Police Investigators are posted to ADFIS. ADFIS conducts investigations and enquiries into the more serious criminal and complex/disciplinary military matters involving personnel from all three services within the Australian Defence Force. To become an ADFIS Investigator (MP) you must first be a trained MP with at least 18 months experience. You then apply for a posting to ADFIS and a place on the next Service Police Investigators Qualification Course conducted at the Defence Police Training Centre located at Holsworthy NSW which will teach the knowledge and skills required, to conduct military investigations in accordance with military law and Defence procedures. This course is similar to a civil police detective's course found in most Australian Civilian Police services.

As crime has become sophisticated the military police have developed investigative techniques to match criminal trends. Military police must continually train and adapt to meet the pace of innovation and invention. The Cyber Crime Centre of the Royal military police has a digital forensic

Norwegian MPs investigating a serious crime in barracks, SIB members operate in peace and war investigating major crimes.

capability and acts as a centre of technical expertise for cyber-crime within the Service Police of the United Kingdom. As electronic devices increasingly embed themselves into modern culture, the opportunities for recovering digital evidence are ever present. Military police today must be able to exploit digital devices for evidence, using specialised hardware and software. Analysis of recovered data and produce detailed forensic reports to aid Service Police investigations. They must also be able to provide expert opinion at Courts Martials.

With advent of cameras and cell phones, military police have developed Multimedia & Evidential Imagery investigators who work with digital multimedia evidence. From enhancing CCTV footage retrieved at a crime scene, to digitally illustrating injuries on a 3D model, a role within this specialist area is challenging. Roles include the processing CCTV footage – including enhancement, and production of still images. Crime Scene Replication – using 360 photography, laser scanning and 3D modelling. Body Injury Mapping – to illustrate the result of complex medical testimony and show the impact of injuries on a victim. Video Reconstruction – of events and locations pertinent to an investigation.

SPECIALIST MILITARY POLICE ROLES

Previously the military police have had a long-established history with Mounted Units. Mounted Police in Britain had been established in Aldershot in 1853. This was the first occasion of the use of the term 'police' in a military context. On the 4th of July 1855, a total of twenty-one other ranks (Selected from 2nd Dragoons, 3rd Light Dragoons, 16th Lancers, 7th Hussars and 15th Hussars. Corps pay of 1s.6d daily for Sergeants and 1s.0d for privates, was authorised. JNCOs appear to have been overlooked.) were dispatched to form the 'Corps' and granted Corps pay, although they were retained as supernumeraries on the Muster Rolls of their parent regiments in order: *'To be employed as a Corps of Mounted Police for the preservation of Good Order in the camp at Aldershot, and for the protection of the inhabitants of the neighbourhood'.*

In 1865, the strength of the Corps increased to 32 mounted men. In 1872, a detachment of Mounted Police attended the Army's annual manoeuvres under an Assistant Provost Marshal appointed for the occasion, and two-years later the first set of printed orders were published for their guidance. These were signed by Major Thomas Trout, the first Provost Marshal to rise from the ranks of the Corps and whose appointment included the offices of Commandant, Quartermaster and

Officer-in-Charge of Records of the Military Mounted Police (MMP).[26]

The MMP was established as a distinct Corps for service at home and abroad on 1st August 1877 (The MMP was authorised on 31 July 1877, as a result of a Horse Guards letter (12709/200 C 10382) dated 12 May 1877. All serving personnel who came up the standards then set were transferred to the new Corps on 1 August 1877. Those not reaching the standards were returned to their parent regiments.), with an increased establishment of 75: 1 sergeant-Major; 7 sergeants; 13 corporals; 54 privates; and 71 horses. From this date the Corps maintained its own muster and pay rolls and all promotions were within the Corps. Military police were serving in Woolwich, Shorncliffe and Portsmouth in addition to Aldershot and on 1st April 1878, a second Quartermaster's Commission was granted when No. 1, Sergeant-Major William Silk (Trout's son-in-law) became the second officer in the Corps. Medals were earned and casualties suffered by Military Policemen in the Egyptian campaign of 1882–84, at Tel-el-Kebir and Suakin-el-Teb, and with the Nile Expeditionary Force – the MMP's first deployment overseas.

The 1st RAF Police Mounted Section was formed when the RAF were stationed at RAF Hinaidi near Baghdad in the Kingdom of Iraq. The terrain of the station was extremely difficult to patrol by mechanical means and the base was too large to patrol effectively on foot, therefore an alternative form of transport was required. After a short time in operation, horsepower quickly demonstrated their efficiency and proved to be an extremely cost-effective method of patrolling the sprawling airfield estate. Additionally, the very sight of RAF Police NCOs riding their large Arabian horses looked most imposing and gave a distinct air of authority. Due to its success further mounted sections were later established within North Africa, Germany, and RAF Akrotiri. Unfortunately, the RAF Police Mounted Section was disbanded in April 1972.

Horses were used throughout WWI and WWII the motorcycle slowly taking over the mounted MP role as technology improved. But it would not be the end of the mounted military police. Horses were used post WWII to patrol occupied countries, in fact the British MPs formed mounted units using former German Army mounts and equipment. Horse

---

26 https://www.britishmilitaryhistory.co.uk/docs-services-corps-military-police/

mounted patrols were seen as less aggressive to the occupied civilian population, than a loud armoured vehicle. They also made economic scene were petrol and other supplies during the Berlin Airlift were in short supply and could traverse bombed out areas and pathways vehicles could not.

The mounted troop of the military police of the U.S. army talks to a border guard from West Berlin during a ride out in Berlin on 25 March 1958. It was the last ride out of the mounted police. The horses were replaced with vehicles.

In more recent times the Royal Military Police employed equine mounted sections which were used to effectively patrol large areas of bases or open ground which were otherwise inaccessible. Not only were the horses a unique and effective form of transportation, but they also gave a visual deterrent to would be offenders. Her Majesty requested that she be attended and escorted on her silver Jubilee parade by the Royal Military Police Mounted Troop which took place on June 7th, 1977 (by this time the Mounted Troop consisted of around 20 NCO's). On 5th March 1995. The Mounted Troop of the Royal Military Police was officially disbanded after 140 years of service to the Crown and colours however there is a strong movement for its re-establishment.[27]

Horses have made their way back into the U.S. military, helping fight America's War on Terror in Third World countries. It's a war fought with laser guided bombs and jet fighters in the air, supported by ground forces on horseback. 21st century technology is now enlisting the cavalry skills of days long gone by. Today, 'hay burners' rather than 'gas-guzzlers' frequently are the vehicles of choice for elite Special Operations Forces in this battle waged in mountainous, treacherous terrain, inaccessible to tanks and other motor vehicles. Likewise, the US Air Force Police have

---

27 https://www.britishempire.co.uk/forces/armyunits/britishother/corpsofmilitary mountedpolice.htm

a long history of mounted patrols to cover large bases or patrol difficult terrain.

USAF Security Police grooming his horse prior to patrol.

Until very recent times horse patrols in Panama were common sight and the right tool for the job. The 23rd Security Forces at Howard Air Base in Panama had about 5 mounted horse patrols.

Other Air Force Security units that had horses are Clark Air Base in the Philippines and the US Air Force Academy. Vandenberg Air Force Base installation still employs military working horses, used for conducting patrols, search and rescue, crowd control and surveillance. The base's military working horse unit began in 1996 to employ a more environmentally friendly mode of transportation for the 30th Security Forces Squadron's game wardens. The military working horses are key for airmen patrolling the sprawling 99,400-acre base, where terrain ranges from remote sandy beaches to rugged hills choked with chaparral. The base is the Air Force's third largest installation.

Recognizing a member who is retiring from a career of long and honourable service is one of the oldest traditions of military service. The Air Force 30th Security Forces at Vandenberg Air Force Base recently bid farewell to two 1,200-pound, four-legged retirees sporting saddles and bridles who each served as the ultimate wingman, actually carrying colleagues on their backs through many critical missions. Willie and Judge, military working horses, retired following 'distinguished careers' as dozens of fellow members and equine counterparts watched. Judge, a 27-year-old quarter horse, recorded 20 years serving the Air Force, first at Howard AFB, Panama. Willie, an 18-year-old Arabian, logged 14 years of active-duty service after being acquired from a ranch in Northern California.

During their careers, Willie and Judge were involved in several key missions, such as helping locate lost hunters and patrolling areas around Titan or Delta 4-Heavy launch facilities prior to blast offs when activists tried to disrupt a launch. Some notable critics are:

- Judge, a 27-year-old quarter horse, served the Air Force for 20 years.
- Willie, 18-year-old Arabian, served 14 years on active duty.
- Judge patrolled 12,000 miles of jungle in Panama.
- Judge helped capture 100 trespassers in Panama.
- Judge and Willie patrolled VAFB beaches were they also contributed to the bust of an off-base marijuana grow that prevented $3 million of illegal drugs from reaching the streets.
- Both patrolled around launch sites to ensure the areas were clear.
- Both detected four Greenpeace activists who infiltrated VAFB to interrupt a missile-defence test in 2001.
- Both worked crowd control for 15 protests at VAFB.
- Both familiarized Navy Seals with horseback riding tactics in rugged terrain prior to their deployment to Afghanistan.

Retirement for the pair will take them to the 10-acre Jack Auchterlonie Memorial Equine Sanctuary, once at their retirement home, they will assist with events for disabled individuals and children as well as rehabilitation of other horses that are brought to the sanctuary. That's also where Vandenberg's other retired horses, Sarge, Alamo, and Duke landed. Each horse was presented a meritorious service medal, affixing the red-and-white ribbon with a brass circle depicting an eagle to their tack as the citation was read aloud spelling out their accomplishments. The pair of military working horses retire at the grade of sergeant.

After Judge's and Willie's retirements, the four-person Mounted Horse Patrol unit still has six young horses to fulfil the duties, although two remain in training. The team of four security forces members assigned to the 30th SFS mounted horse unit plan to expand the program to include 12–20 horses with as many riders. They are also putting efforts toward getting top-notched outside training for both the riders and the horses and one member is even being sent to farrier school.

The USAF mounted unit have also had a recent re-emergence in

Little Rock Air Force Base Arkansas, base security got a boost recently with the addition of three horses to form the 314th Security Forces Squadron mounted patrol. The horse patrol covers a designated area of Little Rock Air Force Base every day and focuses on remote areas of the perimeter, wooded areas behind housing and hunting areas that normally do not receive routine law enforcement coverage. Riders cover virtually every area of the base where the all-terrain vehicles get stuck and cover ground possibly not traversable by foot. It took about 90 days from concept approval to receiving three certified horses and riders at the Security Squadron. The horses are named Leadership, Teamwork and Growth. Finding three horses suitable for the work was just the start of an intensive project. Leadership made the journey from Colorado, while Growth and Teamwork were found in Fayetteville and El Paso, Ark. The Air Force were very selective in finding horses with the right temperament, size, and standardized colour and appearance. After that, saddles, tack and other riding and safety equipment had to be ordered. The mounted patrol will soon be wearing a new riding uniform with helmet, riding boots, navy-blue breeches, and a light-blue top, similar to a blue service uniform.

Another mounted patrol is at the first in Air Education and Training Command Colorado, a mounted unit from the Dallas Police Department volunteered to train the seven Air Force mounted patrol members. The mounted patrol learned basic care and maintenance of the horse and equipment, riding skills and proper police procedures from a mounted position, including handcuff and search tactics. The riders and horses also received advanced sensory training desensitizing the horse to loud noise and other events that could startle the horses. The sensory training was the most complex because the horse had to learn to ignore gunfire, sirens, and other stimuli and to focus on the rider while the rider had to learn to control the horse no matter what was going on. The student's main goal is to stay in the saddle at all times, so they really have to learn how to control the entire situation including themselves the horse and the suspect, all from the saddle. Similar to military working dog teams, the horse and rider must be properly trained and certified by the 314th Mission Support

Group commander prior to working patrol.

Operational mounted MP patrols provide a force multiplier and quick reaction force in isolated environments.

Horses possess several obvious advantages over foot mobile troops. They can cover distances quicker than troops on foot and well-cared for horses can last longer than troops on foot. Horses are not limited to roads and trails thus providing a degree of mobility not realized by wheeled or tracked vehicles.

Horses can be used to track bands of insurgents or trespassers on long range patrolling As shown by the Rhodesians and the South Africans in now Namibia indicates that healthy horses in good condition can sustain distances of 45–50 kilometres per day for extended periods of time. The horse's ability to provide surprise is a function of mobility and diminished sound. Mobility has already been discussed. Suffice it to say that there are places where horse-mounted troops can get to quicker. Diminished sound should speak for itself. The movement of horses is quieter than the movement of vehicles or aircraft.

Another aspect of security is the observation afforded to the rider by being mounted. Firstly, the perspective of the rider is enhanced by the height gained by being mounted, enabling the rider to see further. The rider can devote more attention toward observing his surroundings if he is not concerned, regardless how subliminally it may be, with where he is placing his feet.

With the ever-increased need for security in these times, great strides have taken place especially in electronic surveillance systems to detect intruders. The Military Police find physical security however is still the most effective form of security, putting a man on the ground in a given area means you own that area. Even if the most modern systems detect offenders a man still must respond to deal with the threat.

Most law enforcement departments worldwide, civilian police employ within their organisational structure, a Mounted unit. Time and again they have proved to be a valuable visual deterrent to offenders, a unique patrol platform increasing the operators' overall view. In post-war occupied West Germany, the US Army's constabulary units had several equine equipped Military Police units including the 287th and 759th MP Horse Platoons until 1957.

They have also had a recent re-emergence in Little Rock Air Force Base Arkansas recently where the USAF Security Police have established a horse mounted Squadron to patrol the perimeters of airfields, sighting them as *"providing the most effective combination of deterrence and manpower"*.

In Little Rock Air Force Base Arkansas, base security got a boost recently with the addition of three horses to form the 314th Security Forces Squadron mounted patrol. The horse patrol covers a designated area of Little Rock Air Force Base every day and focuses on remote areas of the perimeter, wooded areas behind housing and hunting areas that normally do not receive routine law enforcement coverage. Riders cover virtually every area of the base horses can go where vehicles can't, where even all-terrain vehicles get stuck and cover ground possibly not traversable by foot. Things that are normally obstacles to people and vehicles are not obstacles to these horses. The mounted patrol is the first in Air Education and Training Command and second in the Air Force. Security forces horse patrols was originally used at Clark Air Base in the Philippines and later at Howard Air Base in Panama. Those horses are currently in use at Vandenberg Air Force Base, California. Seeing these horses in action and the benefits of using them in remote areas of an air base prompted their introduction at Little Rock.

For the Military Police role, the horse can travel places that ATVs and motorized vehicles cannot. The roar of an ATV engine or headlights presents another advantage that horses have over motorized vehicles, stealth. Horses are quiet, and they can see at night, making it possible for a horse patrol to get close to camps or groups of illegals without being detected.

A Military Police horse also brings an air of authority to an explosive situation. Their size and speed can be intimidating, but they also have a calming effect on a large group ,detained by authorities. Search and rescue missions have made good use of horses because the animals can reach locations that are impenetrable except on foot. It's amazing what horses can do, climb steep hills, navigating difficult paths, and stay sure-footed even in the dark. The MP horse patrol has yet another advantage over all other high-tech methods of transport; horses are friendly to the environment such as when patrolling in remote areas designated as National parks which surround many Bases where much of the land is wilderness, undeveloped and rugged.

A modern Mounted Military Police force would not only contribute to the security of certain areas of a Countries Borders on UN type missions, but it would also create a cadre of experience that would prove useful should horse-mounted operations be needed in the future. In recent times British Mounted Military Police have been called upon to instructed Infantry Regiments to ride during tours of duty for the Falkland Islands Detachment. The mounted unit is a useful asset for patrols and counter-guerrilla operations. It is quite possible that a unit deployed on active service might find it prudent to have a platoon -sized mounted patrol element having an ability to move across country and use routes that are unlikely to be mined.

The U.S. Space Force, America's newest military branch entrusted with the absolute latest in military technology, also relies on horses. American Quarter Horses acquired from the Bureau of Land Management trained for Vandenberg Air Force Base's Conservation Working Horse Program. Military Working Horses (MWH) patrol the sprawling Vandenberg Air Force Base, the fifth largest air force base in America. Located in southern California, the 99,600-acre base incorporates such varied terrain as coastal hill country and beaches, and it is the only air force base in the country with such a program. The horses of the military working horse program do everything from enforcing fish and game laws to managing endangered species.

US Marine MP K9 team conducting search operations in Afghanistan. Photo supplied by handler.

Over the centuries dogs have had many roles with the military, but in modern times specific duties have been defined where dogs can give the best service. While in the past they have done everything from catch rats to draw fire to expose enemy positions, today dogs are given humane tasks, where their special skills can do the most good. Military Working Dog (MWD) teams can perform many combat support operations. These teams enable the tactical commander to free up soldiers and employ their resources in other areas. This force multiplier is especially valuable in area security and force protection and antiterrorism operations. The very area where Military Police operate. It is not surprising to find then that one of the largest users of dogs in modern times is the Military Police (MP).

There are many other units that use Military Working Dogs for example the Engineers are often associated with Explosive and Mine Detection dogs. Many Countries Infantry Regiments have a patrol dog capability and Special Forces use Military Working Dogs mainly duel trained to do both of these roles. Modern day Military Working Dogs provide a valuable asset to military police in peace time operations their senses of sight, smell, and hearing enhance their detection capabilities and provide commanders with a physical and psychological deterrent to criminal activity. Properly trained Military Working Dogs can prevent an intruder or suspect from escaping. When necessary, the Military Working Dog provides an added dimension of physical force as an alternative to the use of deadly force. Public knowledge of Military Working Dog team capabilities provides military police and various security forces with a formidable deterrent wherever the Military Working Dog team is employed. In peace time Military working dog teams support a variety of Military Police (MP) operations. They are used in peacetime environments to extend MP resources. And on the battlefield Military Working Dog teams can support MP tactical units involved in all MP missions. Military Working Dog teams can be used to help MP deter and detect the enemy and make a valuable contribution in the detection, investigation, or prevention of criminal activity. It has been the norm in many Countries that after the war or conflict has finished and the inevitable military reductions begin including the de-mobbing of animal resources, the one area were Military Working Dog have always found a home is with the MPs guarding facilities. In the past dogs have been used to guard nuclear weapons storage sites and Military Airfields. During the Viet Nam War the USAF Police employed dog teams as perimeter protection altering the presence of the enemy prior to Viet Cong attack. Likewise, today dogs are used to guard and patrol perimeters of Bases in Afghanistan.

Generally Military Police dogs are trained in man-work, tracking, article search, agility & obedience, whilst specialist dogs are trained in either Explosive or Narcotic roles. Some Forces train their General Duties dogs in a dual role, say Cannabis detection or as a Cadaver detection dog. As of course with such a big subject and worldwide operators there are many exceptions. Military Police Military Working Dogs used in the Explosive Detection Dog (EDD) role are perhaps at their most valuable trained to detect minuscule amounts of a wide range of explosives, make them an invaluable addition both to entry point security and patrolling within secure installations or with an Infantry unit in the streets of

Baghdad. These dogs are capable of achieving over a 98% success rate in bomb detection.

In the United Kingdom the Royal Air Force is the only Service Police force to operate military working dogs. The work undertaken by RAF Police dogs in theatre is invaluable, and they are considered a key asset for the Commander. Providing specialist arms explosive search capability and Force Protection, they act as a Force Multiplier, allowing the Commander greater flexibility with their personnel, whilst delivering maximum effect on the ground. In some situations, the Military Working Dog team can do the same amount of work as ten personnel.

Royal Air force K9 teams patrol bases in the UK and anywhere that RAF assets are deployed. What is more frightening the gun pointing at you or the 42 sharp teeth.

William the Conqueror used St. Hubert Hounds (Bloodhounds) to support his troops as well as to run down opponents. His St. Hubert Hounds guarded and defended his army's camps and followed remaining dissenters to the end of any trail. The Bayeux tapestry contains 55 dogs, it pictures the events before, during and after the Battle of Hastings in 1066 – it is believed some of the dogs are hunting but some are war dogs engaged in the battle itself. On the battle site has been discovered a dog collar, an open-work band of copper alloy backed by leather or velvet – attached to the metal through six small holes as proof.

In recent conflicts around the South Pacific Australian Military Police Dogs have been heavily evolved in conducting operations in East Timor and the Solomon's. MP dogs are multi-rolled to provide policing and physical security duties and immediate response tasks. Military Working Dog Handler (MWDH) also provide a man-trailing capability in support of ground defence operations, specifically scouting and clearing patrols. Australian Military Police Dog Handlers attached to the International Stabilization Force regularly undertake Patrols in and around the streets of suburban Dili. Military Police Dogs are a highly valued asset in peacekeeping operations. The dog teams were used as early warning detection devices tracking/man trailing, they also carry out building searchers, area searches, apprehension of the enemy, crowd control and as a force multiplier.

Photo courtesy of Capt. Bruce Page NZDF, supplied by RNZAF.

The Solomon Islands saw Australian MP dogs involved in security, crowd control and general police canine deterrent roles. The MP teams were used by International UN Police agencies in the execution of high-risk warrants and prisoner transport protection. In fact, when there was a dangerous offender involved, the MP dogs were called for support.

Today, the Royal Australian Air Force is the largest single corporate user of military working dogs in Australia. Its 195 Military Working Dog have an important role in the security of high-value RAAF assets at some 12 bases and establishments located across Australia. Operationally Military Working Dog Operation Cell, based at the Timor-Leste Aviation Group, provide security for Black Hawk helicopters and is on standby at all times for base security. They maintain a constant patrolling program from dusk to dawn.

Today MWD's are a vital asset, highly valued and as such receive similar protection as human soldiers including ear and eye protection, combat jackets and their handlers are trained in canine medicine, if need be.

Photo courtesy of Capt. Bruce Page NZDF.

A pair of Royal Military Police (RMP) Close Protection Operatives, carrying C8 CQB carbines, guard British Lt. Gen. John Cooper, the Deputy Commanding General for Multi-National Force-Iraq in As Samawah, Iraq. US DoD photo by Staff Sgt. Brendan Stephens.

Personal security is provided to high profile personnel or VIPs who are likely to be terrorist, criminal or military targets due to their position, assignment, symbolic value, vulnerabilities and/or location. Close Personal Protection (CPP) operatives are highly trained specialists in advanced weapons systems, close quarter fighting, driving, anti/counter surveillance, reconnaissance, as well as individual and team Close Personal Protection techniques.

Personal Protection is not a new role for Military Police formations, Bodyguards have been around since ancient times, however some early recorded Military Police personal protection formations were recorded in 1740, when Friedrich II established the *Feldjägerkorps zu Pferd*, from these troops were drawn men for duties as *Furierjäger* who task it was to accompany and protect members of the royal family and important officials.

One high profile Close Protection Unit is the Royal Military Police (CPU RMP) team. These special Royal Military Police teams provide close protection for military and civilian government VIPs, such as Generals and high-ranking Ministers abroad. Such a task was during the 1991 Gulf War when RMPs provided close protection to General Sir Peter de la Billiere the British Commander. These CPP operators often in plain clothes were frequently wrongly named by the media as Special Forces troops.

During the United Nations intervention in Bosnia RMP CPP teams were tasked to escort diplomats and VIPs from all Nations. Today they conduct the same role in the streets of Afghanistan. The British MPs have always been the world leaders in Close Protection. The history of RMP Close Protection from its origins during the Second World War, through to current operations around the globe. Although the forerunners of the RMP, as Military Mounted Police, Military Foot Police, Corps of Military Police and latterly the RMP, have always held responsibility for escorting senior commanders in operational theatres, and Her Majesty's Ambassadors and High Commissioners in high-risk appointments abroad, it was not until the 1980s that the RMP officially became the lead authority on Close Protection within the British Armed forces. Today, members of the RMP, Royal Marine Police Troop and Royal Air Force Police are deployed all around the world protecting VIPs from harm; be it the drug cartels in South America, Al Qaeda in Africa, or the Taliban in Afghanistan. Whether the threat against a VIP is posed by a terrorist or criminal, the level of protection provided by the military police remains one of professionalism, dedication, and unquestionable loyalty towards the principal.

The bodyguards within CPU RMP, known as Close Protection Operatives, carry a range of weapons, these include the 9mm pistol – typically a Sig Sauer or Glock. It can be carried concealed if required. The HK MP5K – a compact variant of the MP5, a 9mm sub machine gun. A C8 CQB – 5.56mm carbine with 10-inch barrel – a nice balance of firepower and compactness. Their training for RMP Close Protection

Operatives takes an extensive 8-week program that covers a range of disciplines, including: advanced shooting, advanced driving techniques, counter-surveillance, and hand-to-hand-combat. The training course is regarded as one of the hardest courses to pass in the British Army. Many more students undertake the course yet only a few make the final cut and even fewer are selected for operational teams. ••• culminates in an extended exercise in which the students must protect a 'VIP' over a period of several days. Royal Military Police Officers can apply for the Close Protection Unit after six months service with the RMP. Initially trained by the SAS, the RMP now runs its own close protection courses which train other units.

CPP members are often referred in the media as being Special Forces personnel. This has several underlying reasons, one being the training and skills required to conduct CPP operations is well above the average skills an ordinary soldier possesses. Secondly in peace time special forces have tried to take over this role in many countries to justify their status and budget, however in combat operations it is soon turned back over to the MPs as it is not seen as an SF core role in war.

In regard to the first point the MP is ideally suited as CPP operators as the role requires a person to be well disciplined, well educated, fast thinking and multi skilled.

The royal military police close protection unit carry out several courses each year and provide close protection operatives for both green (military protection) and black (high ranking diplomats and ambassadors). In regard to the latter this is done in plain clothes and often in low profile, unlike the US Secret Service which operate quit overtly. I found myself after a few months after completing my CPP course run by the New Zealand Military Police, on the other side of the World attached to guard that Countries Ambassador in Moscow, then still the USSR in 1988. Duties included Residential 24–7 occupation of the Embassy, Personal Bodyguard, Driver, and any other task no one else had in their portfolio.

Sometimes in uniform - often CP is conducted clandestinely.

CPP cannot be run by stringent doctrine, SOPs need to be constantly

updated and reviewed to ensure a team can provide the best level of CPP they can. Drops in performance levels or the development of an unwillingness to enhance the capability you provide, depletes the image of professionalism and the maintenance of your hard target posture. The image you display and the target you and your team display, have a direct effect on how others view the image and status of the principal you are protecting. Once you start looking as though you have vulnerabilities you are then seen as a soft target.

Iraq, especially Baghdad, is a constantly changing environment and, in terms of security, changes every few weeks. CPP Commanders need to be extremely flexible and adaptive with plans. What may be the 'norm' at the present time, will inevitably change within a matter of weeks. Commanders need to have the conviction to make decisions that provide best protection for the principal and his soldiers; more-so, individuals need to have the confidence and the maturity to make important decisions based purely off a commander's intent. Pre-deployment training, as a matter of priority, should focus on the development of these skills in the junior members of the team.

Private Liam Sharples (right), a SECDET XII rifleman, provides an armed escort for an Australian political advisor in Baghdad's International Zone. Photo by Captain Cameron Jamieson.

One example of a daily CPP operation is that of the Australian Military Police combined Security detachment in Iraq called SECDET and is recalled by a CPP operator who was there. "There was a recent handover the incoming team were keen and excited to take over and were chomping at the bit to get around and take part in as many jobs as possible. After a long and hard deployment, the team from SECDET XI were more than happy to handover as quickly as possible and take a much-needed rest. After the handover the new team kicked off with a flurry of business. The current Ambassador prefers to meet people in person rather than on the phone, so a usual day covers anywhere between 5 to 11 meetings with a dinner thrown in almost every second day just to maintain his profile. He, and the rest of his DFAT staff, definitely work very hard to maintain, develop and enhance the political culture of the region in order to ensure the reconstruction of Iraq progressed as planned".

SECDET (Security Detachment) XII is a Combat Team of about 110 personnel. The team is comprised of two infantry platoons, one cavalry troop, a military police detachment and a combat service support element. As part of Operation Catalyst SECDET provides security support to the Australian Embassy in Baghdad. SECDET uses Australian Light Armoured Vehicles (ASLAVs) and armoured Land cruisers to provide protected mobility for Australian Government personnel working at the Australian Embassy.

The Military Police Special Operation Battalion 'Cobra' is a Military Police unit of the Serbian Military, responsible for Counterterrorism, Close Protection. The unit was first established by the order of the Secretary of Defence in 1978. The unit was joined with the 282nd battalion of the Yugoslav People's Army in 1988. By the 1999 it became a separate anti-terrorist squad with a recognizable symbol of winged cobra. The wars in former Yugoslavia had cobras fighting with the British SAS, U.S. Marines in the fighting all cobras are coming out as winners which means that only one member lost in combat with the British SAS, as of 2007 this unit is directly subordinate to the military police. The unit consisted of 2 platoons and 60 members as of 2007. This unit is also responsible for Close Protection of military officials and the current president of Serbia, Mr Boris Tadic. Cobras are the best special forces unit of Serbia and cobras are one of the best trained special forces in Europe.

There are many sub-roles in Close Personal Protection and an MP operative is qualified in all of them. Each has its different challenges and demands but all require high degrees of fitness, discipline, constant awareness, and the ability to made instant decisions.

I am not deliberately going into operational details of how it's done or what drills or counter drills are used as this type of role require not just mystic but secrecy for ongoing operational considerations.

These different assignments however may include being a VIP Driver, who's task is to drive the principal from one location to another. Sounds simple enough but these persons are highly trained in all aspects of high-speed driving including evasive techniques, ambush drills and things you can do with a car both lightweight or heavily armoured that you only imagine in Hollywood. They are in effect a cross between a stunt driver-formula one race driver and gentle chaffer as required.

Residential Security teams provide protection at the VIP's home 24–7, this ensures the main protection team can rest once the principal is in residence.

Military Working Dogs can be used to patrol the grounds of the residence to give in-depth security. Specialist Explosive Detection Dog teams are used to search vehicles, baggage, persons, or any suspect items. The Residence is protected all the time so it can act as a known safe house if required.

The Bodyguard role (BG) is a specialist position within the team, these are exceptional people having to protect the principal at all times (24–7) without getting in his face or overtly being seen. A difficult job at the best of times. There are no real gender requirements, but a female BG might be used to guard a female VIP or vice-versa for obvious reasons due to having to go everywhere they go, yes this includes checking the loo before they use it. The Team itself typically deploys in small 3–4 person teams as an escort section. Additionally, security advance parties sometimes deploy ahead of the VIP's arrival at a given venue to search and secure it. An In-Situ Team Leader is in charge of the whole mission and team in the field.

Counterattack Teams (CAT) Operatives will act as a counter-attack force, ready to back-up the main CPP team. They usually trail a VIP convoy and are heavily armed. Depending on mission or Green or Black roles may have at their disposal heavy or light machine guns and anti-armour weapons. When the proverbial hits the fan this team springs to live to enable the ambushed VIP to get away.

The Headquarters Element maybe responsible for such things as investigation and intelligence gathering of not only the principal but potential threats. They might assign such tasks as Route Recon, Alternative routes, general planning, Liaison, Command and Control of the operation, usually from a central point.

MP TRANSPORT

Motorcycles used to be more common in an MPs arsenal than any other form of transport. Indeed, the United States and German Armies during WWII used road bikes extensively, with and without side cars. Due to their vulnerability to ambush they disappeared for a while. Today they are having a small resurgence in patrolling airfields or large facilities where the use of trail bikes and quad bikes are both economical as well as stealthy. They are an ideal platform when escorting convoys, enabling the MP to zig in and out of traffic getting ahead to the next intersection, and where he can control that point. They are also ideal for conducting route reconnaissance in combat areas. You will also see MPs riding them on Ceremonial occasions.

Patrol vehicles can be either soft skin or armoured depending on location, role, and risk factors. The normal daily garrison patrol vehicle is usually an off-shelf sedan similar to any civilian law enforcement agency. Specialist versions can carry K9s. For field operations in training and combat four-wheel drive military vehicles such as HUMVE are used. These vehicles require the mounting of support weaponry to act as protection for convoys.

The Military Police can find themselves doing numerous tasks, some within what is deemed a policing role, others outside the square. Many Commanders find due to their level of training, flexibility and I have to say it above average intelligence compared to many military formations, Military Police can turn their hand to accomplice most missions in peace and war.

Naval police the world over are often seen patrolling inshore facilities on the lookout for terrorist attacks.

Some examples are Army MPs can find themselves conducting water patrols in inflatable boats or purpose-built vessels when Naval resources are not available. Some Army Camps that boarder on rivers or the sea will usually have a water Military Police patrol boat. These duties are usually done ad-hoc or part time as required, nevertheless MPs have the skills to do such things.

Several US National Guard Military Police units have conducted such water patrols to assist in Homeland Security missions and the 1st Platoon, 153rd Military Police Company conducted River combat patrols in Baghdad, Iraq recently.

Naturally, this is a task most commonly conducted by Naval Military Police, protecting port facilities or hostile river areas. Such as in the case of the Bolivian Navy, where the Naval MP specialty is essentially similar to its counterpart in the Army, carrying out operations such as Important Persons Protection (IPP) Physical Security (SEF) or Patrol Facility (PAT). There, Naval detachments of MP cover all district headquarters and Naval Bases. Of course some Countries have full time water patrol MP branches in the Army such as in Finland. They use sleek fast riverine patrol boats.

Ideal for Military Police garrison patrol duties one of the fastest growing trends in law enforcement response today is utilization of mountain bicycles. Quiet, cost efficient, and amazingly effective, mountain bikes are able to bridge the gap between automobiles and foot patrol.

Bicycle officers are better able to use all of their senses, including smell and hearing, to detect and address crime. Bike patrol officers are often able to approach suspects virtually unnoticed, even in full uniform.

Mountain bikes have proven effective in a number of different environments. They are swift and agile in urban areas where traffic congestion and crowds delay motorized units. Bikes are also effective in less urban areas for park patrol, bushland, residential patrol, and military bases. They can be operated on streets, sidewalks, alleys, trails, and in any areas that are difficult to access with motor vehicles.

The USAF Security Police, US Army Military Police & Marine Military Police have established bike patrol units that patrol perimeters of airfields, Married quarters and Camp facilities sighting them as "*providing the most effective combination of deterrence and manpower*".

The Bicycle officer enjoys an observation platform of up to 1.5 meters a virtual mobile observation tower. Within the relatively flat Military Camp confides gives the capability of scanning a vast area which otherwise would require dozens of men to do. The Mountain bike will be able to respond to any incident day/night, faster than a running man in all weather conditions. The value of deterrence is difficult to calculate by virtue of its meaning however the sight of a bike mounted patrol has proven positive effects for other law enforcement agencies. The riders are capable of cycling 20 plus kilometres per shift around a Camp, they are of particular value patrolling married quarters, where a great deal of intelligence can be gathered by simply talking to people. Two patrolmen can thus be effective out of proportion to their number this is both operationally effective and economically advantageous.

In 2020 the New Zealand Defence Force is testing electric mopeds to patrol bases by Air force security police, quiet and environmentally friendly a compromise between the motorbike and cycle.

INTEROPERABILITY BETWEEN MILITARY POLICE SERVICES

German MPs frequently deploy with other NATO members as part of UN missions.

Throughout the world Military Police resources are being stretched due their increasing role in terrorist operations. Recent deployments by both the British and United States Forces in Iraq and Afghanistan have showed the need for better cooperation and joint training between Military Police Forces. This has been highlighted by several factors firstly one of manpower. Simply put there are not enough Military Police personnel within the US Army to cope with the Mission objectives. Therefore, the US Army Military Police are supplemented by their counterparts of the USAF Security Police Marines and Navy.

On August 4, 1998, Air Force General Michael Ryan and Acting Air Force Secretary F. Whitten Peters announced the Air Force would divide its forces into a number of nearly equally capable AEFs. Those AEFs would provide combat power on a rotating basis to combatant commanders worldwide, leveraging Air Force combat capabilities to better meet the national strategic requirements and joint operational objectives.

Working together is not a new concept WWI and WWII, Korea, Vietnam all saw MPs from different countries having to work together.

On September 11th, 2001, the AEF concept was put to the test during the Global War on Terrorism with simultaneous deployments in support of Operation Iraqi Freedom, Operation Enduring Freedom, and Operation Noble Eagle. By 2003, more than 107,000 Airmen were deployed, nearly twice as many as during Operation Desert Storm in 1991.

Since March 2004, the Air Force has provided airmen to serve combat support roles, despite the stress of working outside their usual duties. As a result, Air Force Chief of Staff Gen. T. Michael Moseley has sounded warnings about having airmen filling Army jobs they are not trained to do. Nevertheless, the Air Force steadily increased the number of Airmen serving in combat support roles for its sister services. The Air Force calls such missions 'in lieu of' taskings.

Fortunately for the United States the USAF Security Forces do undertake extensive ground combat training as their role also includes Airfield Defence. However, the needs of both Iraq and Afghanistan have shown an increase requirement for greater core combat skills within the Air Force Police role. They carry out functions including Route reconnaissance for military convoys, establishing Vehicle Control Check Points within various parts of the capital, the manning of Prisons such as Abbograde, and supplementing Army MPs manning levels wherever required. The main reason of course is to ensure inter-service operability.[28]

---

[28] As quoted by US Defence Forces article: *(www.Security Forces.com 2008).*

In November of 2007, it was announced by the U.S. Air Force:

That it was going to triple the number of Security Forces personnel in Iraq and Afghanistan to backfill Army and Marines Corps mission taskings. Many units are so over tasked with deployments that breaks between deployments can last only four to five months before deploying once again. Currently, many Security Forces Airman are now performing 'In Lieu of' operations with the Army and Marines in Iraq and other locations. These roles include combat patrols, assisting with the transportation of supply across Iraq's most dangerous routes, prison guard duty and EOD among many other functions the Air Force is being asked to assist with due to manning shortages within other services.

By 2011, twelve Air Force Security Forces members have died while supporting Operation Iraqi Freedom. These personnel total 22% of all Air Force casualties during OIF. Of those fatalities, seven were the result of hostile action such as small arms fire and Improvised Explosive Devices. The remaining five were the result of non-hostile action such as vehicle accidents and medical problems.

Likewise, in the British Forces Royal Air Force Police (RAFP) have had to fill major short falls within the Defence Military Police capability by deploying alongside their Army RMP counterparts. RAF Police are undertaking joint patrols of townships, convoy escorts of vital supplies from Airfields to major debarkation points, VIP Close Protection duties and as above conduct many Military Police roles that was once the sole realm of the Army. A UK defence commented said:

The RAFP also has a tactical deployable Squadron known as the Tactical Police Squadron, whose major role is forward policing and Line of Communication Policing (LoCP) in conflict zones. The TPS (formerly known as the Tactical Police Wing) was heavily involved in the recent Gulf conflict, and still have heavy involvement in the Iraq and Afghanistan theatres of operation, in addition to other less-publicized tasking around the world. RAFP members are also trained in Close Protection (CP) and carry out CP duties and operations wherever required to do so, ensuring the safety of VIPs and other dignitaries in hostile territories. The RAFP operates a large Police Dog Section, with detachments at many RAF stations. RAF Police dogs and their handlers currently support overseas operations in 'hot' theatres such as Iraq & Afghanistan in both patrol and specialist search roles.[29]

Military Police also provide training in such tasks as close protection for battlefield VIPs such as training individual regiments to look after their own Commanding Officers in combat.

In short, it's all about manpower and using the resources available to better fulfill the mission tasked to us. As the British and Americans have established by using existing Tri Service Police assets, it is a far better option than temporary recruitment increases in any one service to fill a mission requirement. The key is to ensure all Service Police can perform core skills that are inter-changeable with all three services, thus optimizing manpower.

Due to the advent of terrorism the future holds an ever-increasing role for Military Police functions. What was once known as secondary targets behind the lines is no longer applicable in fact these are the very perceived weak links terrorists are targeting.

It is these areas that many Military Police perform their security function. The demand for MPs on the battlefield and in garrison has been taxing for active-duty and reserve component Soldiers. Thousands of US Guard and Reserve members in artillery units have been reclassified as MPs and stationed at bases throughout the United States and Germany,

---

29 As quoted by RAF web article: *(www.world encyclpidea.com 2008).*

while active-duty MPs remain in Iraq. The Army has also enacted the Stop-Loss Program to keep active -and reserve – component MPs from dropping off the rolls. The US in particular rely on a large pool of National Guard trained MPs as many of these have a large number of civilian police officers in the unit.

They took a high-profile role in the war soon after the terrorist attack on Sept. 11, 2001, when the New York National Guard's 442nd MP Company contributed to rescue-and-recovery efforts at the World Trade Centre following the attack. The unit also provided security in New York City's mass transit systems. And in 2010, the 442nd's Soldiers returned from a year of duty in Iraq, where they trained Iraqi police.

One area of note where interoperability is taking place is with Military Police Working Dog teams. It is not unusual to find a US Marine Corps K9 dog team ahead of a patrol in the middle of Afghanistan in a platoon of soldiers from the 10th Mountain Division. Likewise, USAF explosive detection dogs checking vehicles at a Canadian check point near Camp Bastion in Iraq or a Naval Military search dog looking for narcotic at an Air Force base.

So common are tri-service police units working together in recent years, that to stop confusion whilst on international operations Air Force and Naval Service Police personnel have begun to wear the traditional Army MP insignia. The MP patch worn on the brassard or as an arm badge is instantly recognizable, particularly in its red and black traditional colour form. It is hoped that this will stop confusion in the field and make the identification of MPs instantly. Previously Military Police patches have included lettering such as SP, RAFP, AP, VZ and many others.

Royal Military Police, Spanish Military Police and an Italian Military Police work together at a traffic accident site. Interoperability is a key objective for NATOs Military Police. It enables a small force to expand quickly and work anywhere in the world.

Military Police units are working together from around the globe as part of United Nations or International force coalitions. Fortunately, most nations used their MPs in similar core skills such as Investigation, patrol, convoy security and traffic control. Thus joint co-operation is fairly straight forward.

When I was deployed to Mogadishu, Somalia as part of UNSOMII as an Air Force Policeman, I was attached to the United States Marine Corps 1st Military Police Company USMC 1st Division. Fortunately, due to universal MP training and similar doctrine I found myself leading convoy detachments and conducting MP night patrols in a squad Marines at night in downtown Mogadishu.

German Bundeswehr army military police and U.S. army soldiers with the 137th military police detachment patrol during a joint mission in Nawabad, north of Kunduz, northern Afghanistan December 11, 2010

In the future and at present multinational Military Police units are working together increasingly more as it is being shown that they have the right skill set for a Commander to deal with today's low to medium intensity conflicts.

The NATO Military Police Centre of Excellence enhances the capabilities of NATO MP, fosters interoperability, and provides subject matter expertise on MP activities, in accordance with the Alliance's strategic concept. It functions as a Military Police (MP) think tank and the motor for innovation and encourages co-operation and interoperability between NATO and its partners. The next conference is on 4–8 December 2020. The NATO Military Police Centre of Excellence is located in Bydgoszcz, Poland it runs courses to enhance joint operations and provides a framework to discuss doctrine, education, research and development and consultation in matters relating to military police operations.

IN ANY WEATHER IN ANY TERRAIN

Of course, most Nordic and European armies deploy in cold conditions within their homeland but have frequently seen themselves up to 2020 in the middle of deserts fighting terrorism.

We often imagine thanks to movies that MPs only patrol streets after hours in urban cities. Indeed, that's one role but the majority of operational roles are in the field. The one thing about the Military Police is they also have to be prepared to work and fight under all climatic and environmental conditions. They also have to work and fight in Jungles in open desert terrain or mountainous peaks. The 793rd MP Battalion seems to spend half its life in snow and the other half in the blazing sun. Take a quick look at these postings.

In May 2010, the 793rd Military Police Battalion was relocated to Fort Richardson, Alaska as part of the 3rd Manoeuvre Enhancement Brigade, US Army Alaska. Prior to this move, the Battalion had been part of the 18th Military Police Brigade, V Corps, in Germany. Its mission had

been to, on order, rapidly deploy and conduct combat, combat support and stability operations in support of the 18th Military Police Brigade and V Corps contingencies. The 793rd Military Police Battalion had been on continuous active duty since its activation at Camp Maxey, Texas, on 26 December 1942 a lovely warm state compared to Alaska. The colours of the unit's insignia, green and yellow, were also the colours of the Military Police Corps. The heraldic bend charged with the red *torteaux* symbolized the Battalion's route security and circulation control mission on the famous Red Ball Highway across France, Belgium and into Germany during World War II. The 2 *torteaux* represented campaign honours awarded for operations in World War II.

The unit was first on 10 December 1942 in the Army of the United States as the 793rd Military Police Battalion and activated on 26 December 1942 at Camp Maxey, Texas. The Battalion deployed to the snowy hills of Scotland in February 1944 for training prior to movement to France in August 1944, where it conducted route security operations on the famous Red Ball Highway until December 1944. From December 1944 to June 1945 the Battalion conducted port security operations in Antwerp, Belgium, and was cited in the Order of the Day by the Belgian Army.

In June 1945, the Battalion was assigned port security operations to sunny Marseilles, France until January 1946, when it entered Germany. The Battalion was subsequently assigned to the 1st Infantry Division and moved to Nurenberg where it conducted law and order operations as part of the occupation force, and security for the Nurenberg War Crimes Trial. The Battalion was awarded the Meritorious Unit Commendation for the European Theatre, and campaign streamers for Northern France 1944 and Rhineland 1944–1945, for military operations in Europe during World War II.

After the Second World War, the unit was reorganized and redesignated on 20 October 1947 as the 793rd Military Police Service Battalion. It was allotted to the Regular Army 22 June 1951. It was reorganized and redesignated on 20 September 1951 as the 793rd Military Police Battalion. During the Cold War era, the Battalion was assigned to VII Corps, United States Army, Europe. Companies A, B, and C were inactivated on 21 October 1977 in Germany. These organic companies were replaced by the 212th, 615th, and 630th Military Police Companies.

The Battalion deployed to the heat of Saudi Arabia in December 1990 in support of VII Corps during Operations Desert Shield and Desert Storm. The Battalion advanced into Iraq and Kuwait in February 1991 at the start of the ground offensive in support of the 1st Armoured Division, where it conducted extensive Enemy Prisoner of War operations. In April 1991, the Battalion supervised the evacuation of thousands of refugees from Iraq to Saudi Arabia. The Battalion was awarded the Meritorious Unit Commendation for Operation Desert Shield/Strom and campaign streamers for Defence of Saudi Arabia 1990–1991, Liberation and Defence of Kuwait 1991, and Southwest Asia Cease Fire, for military operations in Southwest Asia. The Battalion redeployed from Saudi Arabia to Germany in May 1991, and was subsequently reassigned to the 18th Military Police Brigade, V Corps.

The Battalion deployed to the sometimes-freezing conditions of Bosnia-Herzegovina in December 1995 in support of Task Force Eagle (led by the 1st Armoured Division) and Operation Joint Endeavour. For almost 11 months, soldiers of the Battalion performed a wide variety of missions including circulation control, area and route security operations, VIP security, and critical site security. During the Bosnian National Elections in September 1996, the Battalion provided around the clock support to nearly 200 election sites and counting houses in the Tuzla Valley. Upon the successful transfer of Military Police functions to the covering force of the 1st Infantry Division in November 1996, units of the Battalion redeployed to Germany, bringing an end to the second major deployment of the 'Spartans' outside of Germany since 1990. The Battalion was awarded the Army Superior Unit Award for military police support and operations in Bosnia.

The 793rd Military Police Battalion deployed to Kosovo between June 1999 to December 1999 in support of Task Force Falcon to implement the peace initiatives following the NATO led Air War with Yugoslavia and wouldn't you know it snows here too. They established the Bondsteel Detention Facility, the first facility of its kind in Kosovo, which further became the standard model for the Kosovo Force (KFOR). The 793rd Military Police Battalion returned to Kosovo in November 2000 to support Task Force Falcon, KFOR 2B, until May 2001. In October 2002, the 793rd Military Police Battalion again returned to Kosovo for a third tour as part of KFOR 4B and conducted operations in support of Multi-National Brigade East until August 2003.

The 793rd Military Police Battalion deployed to Iraq in December 2004 in support of Operation Iraqi Freedom 04–06. The Battalion secured the capitulated People's Mujahideen of Iran/Mujahedin-e Khalq forces at Camp Ashraf, Iraq. The Battalion also supported the 3rd Brigade Combat Team, 3rd Infantry Division in their area of operation. The Battalion redeployed to its home in Bamberg, Germany in November 2005 just in time for winter snow season. The 793rd Military Police Battalion was awarded the Meritorious Unit Commendation for Iraq and campaign streamer for Iraq, for military operations in support of Operation Iraqi Freedom.

Off to the sunny desert again from April 2008 to June 2009, the 793rd Military Police Battalion once again deployed to Iraq in support of Operation Iraqi Freedom 08–10 where they oversaw 12 subordinate units professionalizing the Iraqi Police across 7 provinces in central and southern Iraq, from Baghdad to Basra, serving under the Multi-National Division-Central, Multi-National Division-Southeast, and Multi-National Division South.

You guessed it, by 2011 they were back in the Alaskan snow.

Amphibious operations are far more complex than simply land base soldiers arriving to an operational area by sea. Many months of training and understanding limited logistics and limitations are needed. In 2019 MPs along with MP Dog teams were tasked to support Exercise SEA RAIDER as part of the Australian Defence Force's Australian Amphibious Task Group. The Task Group was designed to test the

Australian Defence Force's capacity to conduct amphibious warfare, stability and security operations, render humanitarian assistance and disaster relief and evacuate civilians from uncertain environments. MPs as seen during WWII and beyond, have provided quick access off beach heads, to ensure transport and logistics maintain movement to where they are needed and prevent choke points at the point of entry. What MPs can do to diminish time on target, increase speed of transition, provide specialist law enforcement advice, and generally work to add value to amphibious combat operations.

THE FUTURE

Croatian MPs form part of the joint Eastern MP Battalion.

The future for the military police looks extremely bright their numbers are in fact on the increase, many countries are converting whole regiments of soldiers from their current occupations to that of Military Police as recent operations have identified a need for this type of soldier in the field. Able to fight and think of alternative measures.

The Role of the Military Police soldier is varied on today's battlefield in places such as Iraq and Afghanistan other departments in the Army such as artillery, armour, and chemical Warfare soldiers have tried to work their way into military police roles because their own original missions are less critical. Soldiers from other branches have been trained to conduct several MP missions including limited law enforcement missions, route reconnaissance, traffic control, river crossings, route security, convoy security and internment/resettlement (I/R). One could argue that it is not the military police who are in danger of losing their mission. One could say that the military police mission, as demonstrated in Iraq and Afghanistan, is more critical than ever and is, in fact, understaffed.

However, the Military Police possess, due to their selection and training in law enforcement one task that cannot be explicitly found in an Army technical manual and that is 'How to Talk to People'. That is because it is not a task but a skill. Other branches can be taught military police tasks but cannot so easily learn military police skills. The military police soldier can set himself apart from his infantry counterpart with his ability to talk to the local man on the street and find out what is going on. It is in the nature of the infantryman to be up-front, forthright, and aggressive. However, such an attitude does not translate well to the common shop owner in Baghdad, or Kandahar. It takes a certain knack to approach a person calmly and coolly on a street in a country you have just invaded and, in a nonthreatening manner, find out what the word on the street is. It is in the military police soldier's nature to do this during routine law enforcement duties.[30]

The military police soldier has the potential to be the best intelligence gathering agent on the battlefield. Military police have been valuable in the under recognized role of intelligence collection. Military police soldiers in Iraq and Afghanistan have produced some of the most lucrative intelligence on the battlefield, discovering the location of high-value targets, large weapons caches, and criminal activity. Military police soldiers have done this by simply talking to local civilians during the course of other missions.

The nature of military operations changes daily in the contemporary operational environment and there is a demand to be flexible, adaptive thinkers and decision makers. Conventional warriors must also be diplomats to succeed in the myriad of stability operations. These new soldier-diplomats need a unique set of skills. The Military Police Corps are best suited to meet these new challenges. The military police soldier diplomat role was established in depth during operations in the Balkans, members had to learn to think not just as warriors but as politicians also.

Military police Soldiers also have received training that their combat arms counterparts have not. When executing law and order operations, military police Soldiers are trained in interpersonal skills and

---

30 https://researchcentre.army.gov.au/library/land-power-forum/military-police-contribution-evidence-based-operations

communication. They have developed the decision-making skills and the flexible responses needed in situations that require other than lethal force. Additionally, military police Soldiers have learned to use levels of force, evaluate situations, and apply procedures based on individualized events. The sensitive nature of many military police missions, such as detainee operations, has enabled military police leaders to think flexibly and use adaptive techniques instead of always relying on the textbook response.

Russia has realized the value of MPs; Military police units are filled with professional full-time soldiers not reservists.

The traditional concepts of the war fighter are changing every day. A mission conducted on the borders of Iraq, and another executed in the slums of Baghdad can occur simultaneously but may vary extensively in scope, methodology, purpose, and effects. Today's leaders must master a balance between conventional war fighting and a substantially more varied role that includes politics, diplomacy, and exceptional insight. Leaders within the Military Police Corps possess unique skills that will enable them to navigate this emerging battlefield successfully. Already trained to be adaptive and flexible thinkers, military police Soldiers have the ability to fulfill the need for war fighters as well as diplomats. As stability operations continue to advance throughout the globe, it is these diplomatic abilities that will mark the difference between success and failure.

An old and future role for Military Police is aid to civil power in times of national unrest or emergency. Military Police are frequently being used on the home front, in some cases they are used to support or supplement civilian law enforcement operations. In other cases, they are used as were several Commonwealth countries military police units in support of major events such as the Commonwealth games. In Australia MPs are used to aid civil power in state emergencies such as natural disasters. In the United Kingdom the RMP were seen assisting local law enforcement during the foot and mouth epidemic. During natural disasters the Military Police can have two faces, one to quell looting which comes with the full wrath of the force. The second a compassionate one helping victims clearing up after major flood or hurricanes incidents.

There are many stories to be told of Military Police units the world over helping on the home front like soldiers from the 92nd Military Police Battalion, Fort Leonard Wood, Missouri, who rose to the challenge of combating the effects of a December 2010 tornado that left 4 people on the installation with minor injuries and more than 150 military homes uninhabitable.

The MP patrols on duty that day were instructed to follow the storm's path to conduct damage assessments and check for any injured people. US Military police Soldiers are trained in the area of first response during Advanced Individual Training, and they receive follow up training at the unit level.

Military police provided augmentation and assistance in cordoning off areas that were considered to be unsafe for public transportation. Within the first week of the disaster, more than 7,000 hours were dedicated to tornado law enforcement and emergency responder augmentation.

Weeks later, military police continue to provide security for the homes and personal property affected by the tornado. Military police have been called upon during several natural disasters, from Haiti to Gulf Coast hurricanes, they play a vital role in emergency response not just overseas, but at home too.

MPs are also taking the lead in homeland security. MPs are frequently the only military personnel on a base in the dark hours awake patrolling ensuring facility security when everyone else is asleep. It is a 24-hour, seven day a week job and many other service personnel on their weekend off, tend to forget that. They are truly the thin red line of defence.

Who escorts the high-ranking officers or dignitaries around the battlefield? – The MPs.

Who conducts security materials from wages to Nuclear material? – The MPs.

Who is responsible for ensuring vital supplies or documentation are escorted under protection? – The MPs.

Who responds to a prowler in the defence housing area when serviceman dependents are alone? – The MPs.

Who is securing the base when others are asleep? – The MPs

A sample of the abilities that a single MP company poses is best explained by the actions of the 4th MP Company of the 4th Infantry Division deployed as Task Force Ironhorse in support of Operation Iraqi Freedom. During the deployment, the military police contribution was wide-ranging, covering long distances and in a battle space that expanded far beyond its doctrinal capability.

Within 12 hours of receiving notification of deployment, the 4th Military Police Company had combat-loaded its equipment and had its vehicles staged and ready for movement to the deployment ready-reaction field. At the 96-hour point, the company had all cargo loaded on ships. The unit moved into its first combat encounter in almost a quarter of a century.

The 4th Military Police Company under division control had only 41 high-mobility, multipurpose wheeled vehicle assigned to the company, it faced a monumental task. Another factor making the operation even more challenging was the lack of sufficient maps of Kuwait and southern Iraq since initial deployment plans had been based on entrance through Turkey. Fortunately, the company had soldiers and non-commissioned officers (NCOs) who had recently redeployed from Kuwait as part of Operation Desert Spring. That knowledge, coupled with the discipline and technical and tactical proficiency of the unit's soldiers and junior NCOs, set the stage for the 4th Military Police Company's first combat support mission since Vietnam.

The company based its 1st and 2nd Platoons at the aerial port of debarkation in Kuwait, where they were responsible for moving personnel and equipment from there to their base camps and back. The 5th Platoon operated out of the Kuwaiti Naval Base and escorted convoys carrying the division's authorized basic load to Camp Udari, covering an average of 200 miles during the 16-hour round trip. Squad and team leaders assumed a great deal of responsibility in not only securing the convoys but in navigating and communicating with local national support personnel. The military police became a great asset to convoy commanders since they were able to provide valuable information on the status of routes and the local population. In many cases, the convoy commanders handed the reins of the convoy to junior non-commissioned military police.

The company headquarters and the 3rd and 4th Platoons moved to Camp New Jersey to conduct integration tasks and begin preparations for the division's movement into Iraq.

Conditions for this movement improved greatly as electronic map sheets of Kuwait and Iraq became available. This gave squad and team leaders the ability to create route overlays and e-mail them to other vehicles in the convoy including the convoy commander's vehicle. It also allowed teams to maintain situational awareness and conduct text messaging when escorting large convoys that were out of radio range.

The first element of the 4th Military Police Company to cross the line of departure was 3rd Platoon. Its mission was to provide in-transit security for the Task Force Ironhorse advance party as it moved to Tactical Assembly Area Ironhorse, just south of Baghdad. There, 3rd Platoon provided area security as units downloaded combat platforms from heavy-equipment transporters and then secured their convoys up to the 3rd Infantry Division battle handoff line. In addition, 3rd Platoon escorted convoys that were moving elements north to Taji, Samara, Baquba, Tikrit, Bayji, and Kirkuk.

The 4th Platoon secured the movement of the Task Force Ironhorse tactical command post and continued to provide area security when it established operations at Baghdad International Airport and later at the Tikrit Palace complex. The remainder of the company provided convoy escorts for the rest of Task Force Ironhorse, from the base camps to Tactical Assembly Area Ironhorse. Squad and team leaders were continually put to the test as they escorted convoys ranging in size from 100 to 250 vehicles on a 550-mile round trip that took 48 to 60 hours to complete. By the end of the movement, the 4th Military Police Company had escorted more than 30,000 soldiers and 14,000 pieces of equipment more than 600 miles without a single accident. Each platoon averaged 13,000 miles during the three-week period.

Five days into the movement, the 978th Military Police Company was attached to Task Force Ironhorse and took over the remaining escorts and security operations for the division support element. This allowed the 4th to move the rest of the unit to the Tikrit Palace complex and begin security operations.

In Iraq, the 4th Military Police Company began conducting operations to secure the main command posts of Task Force Ironhorse and its senior leaders. The company developed a force protection plan for the Tikrit Palace complex, which incorporated mounted military police patrols, static access control points, a mechanized quick-reaction force, air defence artillery sections, engineer boat patrols, and tower guard forces. The company command post served as the command and control for the force and coordinated the force protection effort. During the mission, the integrity of the command posts was never compromised.

The company also developed a comprehensive counter-reconnaissance zone plan for the city of Tikrit by establishing a strong military presence. The plan consisted of mobile military police patrols used to enforce curfews and establish order and discipline. The patrols were also successful in confiscating many weapons and other contraband. A coordinated raid with the 1st Brigade Combat Team quick-reaction force led to the capture of a 60-millimeter mortar round, several AK-47 assault rifles, and ammunition. Counter-reconnaissance zone patrols enabled the task force to saturate the city of Tikrit with a military police presence, never allowing the enemy freedom of movement to coordinate attacks.

The 4th Military Police Company also provided a protective services detail (PSD) for the 4ID Commander, the Assistant Division Commander for Support, and the Assistant Division Commander for Manoeuvre. These PSDs provided senior leaders around-the-clock protection during ground and air movements. The company also provided a PSD for the Army Chief of Staff, General Eric K. Shinseki, during his visit to Task Force Ironhorse.

In addition to providing site security of command-and-control nodes, and personnel, the company also received a no-notice mission to secure two downed CH-47 Chinook helicopters from the 101st Airborne Division. Within an hour of the aircraft touching down, the company had a platoon on-site to provide 360-degree security. The military police flawlessly executed the 3-day security mission, in an area sympathetic to the Ba'ath Party, without incident. After the security of the task force was well established, the commander was able to release direct-support military police platoons to their respective brigade combat teams. Direct-support military police platoons continued to provide the brigade combat team assets for area security, as well as critical convoy escorts, flash checkpoints, and raids. Once in place, the soldiers of the 4th provided support in every major area of Task Force Ironhorse operations an area of more than 40,000 square kilometres.

In addition to providing the task force freedom of movement and area security, the 4th Military Police Company also established and operated the central collection point to manage the large number of captured enemy prisoners of war (POWs) and civilian internees (CIs). The unit developed a 'team POW' concept. This consisted of a military police platoon (the 5th Platoon) designated to run the central collection point and provide POW escorts; transportation assets from B Company, 704th Division Support Battalion; and CI interrogators from the 104th Military Intelligence Battalion. More than 800 POWs/CIs were processed, interrogated, and evacuated during the first 45 days of the operation, including several Ba'ath Party members and Saddam loyalists. Despite a challenging mission, team POW had no incidents, uprisings, or escapes.

As the company transitions from combat to stability operations and support operations the greatest lesson, they have learned is that they did it right. Too often soldiers, NCOs, officers, and leaders relate their 'significance' in an operation by the number of enemy killed. Significance is more accurately measured through mission accomplishment. Although the company had several armed engagements with paramilitary forces and inflicted casualties upon them, the most junior to the most senior soldier in the unit understands how military police best support the division.

The 4th Infantry Division has more than 40 manoeuvre companies, whose primary mission is to close in and destroy the enemy. It has only one military police company and that company was ready when it was needed. More than 30,000 soldiers and 14,000 pieces of equipment were moved; three main command posts and their leaders were secured; and more than 800 POWs were processed, interned, and evacuated. Without a doubt, the 4th Military Police Company distinguished itself as a combat multiplier and confirmed the key role military police will play in future operations.

As we have noted several Nations have either used Naval or Air force personnel to fill gaps in Military Police operations or substitute MPs with members from Regiments such as Artillery that due to the type of conflict are not needed, at least in large numbers, therefore they are in effect spare. Both have their advantages and disadvantages; it is however important that Armies must train for war not peace keeping operations. If we fall into this trap, then when we need to go to war, we will have not resources or skill sets. However, given anything other than a world war the trend at least since the last world war has been, fairly highly intensive war operations followed by protracted stabilization /occupation operations.

The latter role fits the modern Military Police modus operandi to a tee. Therefore, I wonder if more Military Police formations need to be established. This could be done by converting existing Regiments with a mission that is limited (but still needed in war) to Military Police Regiments and reverting the other Regiment to a Reserve or National Guard status. Naturally the existing manpower is retained and retrained so no one losses employment.

By using larger self-contained Military Police formations with generic helicopter support, water patrol assets, Canine units, General Patrol, Forensic and Investigative branches a commander can conduct operations like a large city police force ensuring immediately after the conflict has ended, law enforcement is in place. As happened post Iraqi and several Balkan States the time delay between the war fighting ending and the rule of law establishing a safe community is vital. The above countries suffered in a delay in infrastructure especially law enforcement causing lawlessness, riots and violence to erupt between rival groups.

This is why after all you can never do without a civil Police Force in any Country as anarchy will rule. It is the Military Police role to be that Civilian Police Force until the local population can establish its own.

The future use of technology will assist military police preform their roles even more effectively. In 2020 MPs from the 287th Military Police Company, 97th Military Police Battalion, 89th Military Police Brigade based at Fort Riley, Kansas, utilised the Raven during the Allied Spirit VIII exercise in Germany. The Raven system is designed for rapid deployment and high mobility. At just over four pounds, its lightweight frame makes transport easy for ground troops. The UAV has a range up to 10 kilometres from its launch point. The MPs role is to ensure traffic flow and to mark any route a military convoy is likely to take. By using small UAVs the MPs can monitor traffic from above, identify likely problem areas and identify possible hazards or threats in the area instantly.[31]

Army Spc. William Ritter, a military policeman with 287th Military Police Company. Army photo by Spc. Dustin D. Biven.

Since 2018 a new counter-poaching task force has trained more than 120 rangers to protect endangered wildlife in Malawi. Malawi and South African. Photo: Forces TV.

---

31 https://www.defense.gov/Explore/News/Article/Article/1427660/military-police-use-raven-uavs-at-allied-spirit-exercise/

The Armed Forces make a huge contribution to everyday life; serving personnel are mobilized during natural disasters, terrorist attacks, humanitarian and environmental crises and as a peacekeeping force around the world.

Conservation is becoming more militarised, and it is cause for serious concern. Rising rates of elephant and rhino poaching in Africa, and fears of a link between poachers and terrorists, have led to foreign national armies, private military companies and even UN peacekeeping forces all moving into wildlife protection. In 2018 a new British military counter-poaching task force was developed after £900,000 of funding was announced by the UK Government. The funding will be used to train African park rangers in more effective counter-poaching techniques.[32]

Military Police are called upon to mobilize during natural disasters, terrorist attacks, humanitarian, and environmental crises such as the current Covid-Virus pandemic and as peacekeeping forces around the world. Currently several infantry-based units have been embedded with African park rangers and would go out on long-range patrols working alongside them to enhance their capability. Rangers are natural trackers, but the military are able to enhance their technological advances such as night vision equipment and even aerial drones.

Although one of the smallest Corps in a Military Force in most Countries, the MPs I have met and worked with have several things in common. They fight well above their weight. Their abilities and tasks they perform far outweigh their physical numbers and they can always be counted on to be professional.

Since the creation of time there has always existed some form of Law Enforcement. In any ancient army there has been someone to take the job of the Provost Marshal. The facts are someone did the job because it was vital to the effectiveness of the Army. Francis Markham's *Five Decades of Epistles of Warre,* published in 1622, states that the Provost Marshal would be a soldier of great judgment and experience in all martial discipline, well seen in the laws and ordinances of the Post or Camp.

Finally, many claim to be the first in or the last out of the battlefield

---

32 https://www.forces.net/news/uk-military-develop-anti-poaching-force-ps900k-new-funding

and quite often this is true to Special Forces units. However it is the Military Police that consistently play this role during peace and war time operations. They will continue to be in the forefront of military operations well into the future.

As General Pattern stated in WWII,

> "*When all else fails around me at least I still have the MPs, my Pretorian Guard*".

"At dusty cross roads you see him stand,
Directing traffic with white gloved hand,
often the recipient of ribald yells.

The target of snipers and falling shells, the
armband he wears denotes his rank, the
jeep is his transport, he'd scorn a tank.

When out of the line and in the rear,
the standard of excellence is very clear,
like a London Bobby patrolling his beat,
there are standards he feels, that he must keep,
his boots are the brightest, his belt snowy white,
the cap badge is burnished, the set is just right,
his symbol of authority is plain to see,
his armband's emblazoned with two letters – MP."

– by Les Payne

PART TWO

MPS OF THE WORLD

The next several chapters of the book deals with a selection of Military Police units from around the world, a little about their history but mainly their functions today. I have not included all MP Corps just the predominant ones that either I have worked with, attached to, or who are simple involved in predominate operations today in the fight against terrorism.

Several Eastern Countries have formed a joint Multinational Military Police Battalion, they conduct mutual training and deployments. Some of the units are discussed in this chapter, frequently join forces to form a Battalion, usually each country provides manpower at Company strength. The advantages are smaller forces can become part of a larger operation giving commitment to NATO or United Nations operations. Another advantage is uniformity of their training and in most cases similar weapons systems and doctrine are used.

We have seen how effective military police are in the counter-insurgency role overseas, it was only logical that the same skills set be used on the home front to counter terrorism. In countries like Australia MPs were used in both G20 summit meetings and the 2018 Commonwealth Games to supplement civilian police assets.

During the present Covid-epidemic Military Police have been the obvious first choice to aid civil power. Many Military Police units are used across the globe to back up civilian police who are stretched to their limits.

NORTH AMERICA

The US Military Police Corps

Female MP of the 101 Airborne

The Military Police Corps achieved permanent status in the U.S. Army on 26 September 1941, yet its traditions of duty, service, and security date back to the Revolutionary War. Over the last two centuries the military police – or provost marshals as they were called during much of their history – evolved from a group of miscellaneous units and men organized on a temporary basis in time of national emergency to perform a limited range of law-and-order responsibilities into today's highly organized and trained combat support force. During the 1980s military police units carried out many of the wide-ranging duties they have assumed in the Army, such as fighting in Grenada; guarding the summer Olympics in Seoul, Korea; helping to quell civil disturbances in the Virgin Islands in the aftermath

of Hurricane Hugo; and playing an essential role in JUST CAUSE, the Army's operation in Panama in 1989–1990. Based on a tradition of service that stretches back more than two hundred years, military police have come to be recognized as an important element of the Army in both peace and war.

The Military Police Corps traces its beginnings to the formation of a provost unit, the *Maréchaussée* Corps, in the Continental Army. Authorized by Congress on 27 May 1778 with a name borrowed from the French term for provost troops, the special unit was assigned by General George Washington to perform those necessary police functions required in camp and in the field. The first American military police unit was organized along the lines of a regular Continental Army company with 1 captain, 4 lieutenants, 1 clerk, 1 quartermaster sergeant, 2 trumpeters, 2 sergeants, 5 corporals, 43 provosts, and 4 executioners. Reflecting the unit's special requirements for speed and equipment, the corps was mounted and accoutred as light dragoons.

Washington appointed Bartholomew Von Heer a professional Prussian soldier provost marshal of the Continental Army and commander of the Marechaussee Corps with the rank of captain. Von Heer and his men were expected to patrol the camp and its vicinity in order to detain fugitives and arrest rioters and thieves. During combat the unit was to patrol the flanks and rear, watching for spies and stragglers and safeguarding the baggage and supplies. The Marechaussee Corps also supervised relations with the sutlers, the merchants who supplied the Army, and assumed general responsibility for the collection, security, and movement of prisoners of war. In November 1780 Washington directed the Corps to join Colonel Stephen Moylan and proceed to the Hackensack. They were to secure all its crossings to prevent persons from carrying intelligence to the enemy. In 1779 they were instructed to organize patrols to obtain intelligence of the enemy's movement such as on the south side of the Raritan toward Amboy, New Jersey. During the Battle of the Springfield, a shortage of cavalry led Washington to employ the Marechaussee Corps in a combat role fighting with General Nathaniel Greene's army in the victorious Battle of Springfield, New Jersey, in June 1780. At the Battle of Yorktown in 1781, the Marechaussee Corps provided security for Washington's headquarters which was near Dobbs Ferry, Virginia. In September 1782 the Provost Corps was temporarily attached to General Washington's Lifeguard. The Corps was disbanded on 4 November 1783 at Rock Hill, New Jersey. A small detachment was retained as part of Washington's Lifeguard to provide security at Army headquarters. It escorted the Commander back to his home at Mount Vernon. The Marechaussee Corps was the first MP-like organization in the United States and performed many duties much like the Army Military Police Corps of today. They are also connected to the crossed flintlock pistols, the symbol of today's Military Police Corps. They normally carried a pair of flintlock pistols in holsters on their saddles and used them when necessary.[33]

In 2017 a beautiful full-scale bronze statue of a member of the Marechaussee was unveiled at the Memorial Park, Fort Leonard Wood, Missouri, 19th September 2016 - "Marechaussee on Horseback" by sculptor James Hall III. Photo courtesy of United States Army Military Police Corps Regimental Museum.

33 https://allthingsliberty.com/2014/10/bartholomew-von-heer-and-marechaussee-corps/

A second, larger military police force, this one organized in 1779 by the Commonwealth of Virginia, administered the prisoner-of-war compound established at Charlottesville to secure the British and German soldiers captured at Saratoga. Although the existence of both units was short-lived-the prisoner guards were disbanded in 1781.

No other military police units were formally organized in the U.S. Army until the outbreak of the Civil War, although commanders during that extended period often detailed certain officers and men to perform similar functions. During the War of 1812, and the Mexican War, 1845 – 1848, the lack of an organized Military Police Corps reflected the general ill-preparedness of the total Armed Forces of the Unites States to conduct military operations. Many politicians in Congress were wary of a strong military and did little to provide for an adequate peacetime Army or Navy. In was, commanders had to marshal citizen militia to maintain a sufficient force. Once a battle ended and the Army relocated, few of the military troops remained with it. Facing serious shortages of troops and equipment, commanders focused their resources on infantry and artillery tactics instead of police matters. Article 58 of the Army's General Regulations issued in 1820 did outline the duties of military police and recommended that commanding officers select personnel of superior physical ability and intelligence to fulfil them. However, the article did not require that the men assigned to be military police receive any specific training, and in practise those commanders who established such a force normally assigned the duty on a temporary basis.[34]

Nevertheless, in the Mexican War, the duties performed by modern military police were not totally ignored. When General Winfield Scott took his army into Central Mexico, he proclaimed a code of martial law in the occupied areas and appointed military governors to enforce it. In Mexico City he also organized four hundred picket soldiers as a police force to supplement the native establishment. Throughout the Mexican War, units were detailed to perform provost-type duties. For example, after American forces captured Santa Fe, New Mexico, the Second Missouri

---

34 To Captain Bartholomew from George Washington, 27 July 1778,"in *The Papers of George Washington,* Revolutionary War Series, *1 July – 14 September 1778*, ed., David R. Hoth (Charlottesville: University of Virginia Press, 2006), 185.

Mounted was detailed to keep the peace in that city. Likewise, in April 1846, General Zachary Taylor assigned the Second Dragoons to provide small patrols in the around Fort Brown, Texas, to present the infiltration of Mexican soldiers in the area. After Mexico City was captured, the central valley of Mexico was in complete discord. Dragoons were used to patrol the area, break up fighting, and impose military law. The Army also utilized a small section of its various units to collect stragglers on long marches, to patrol camps and towns, to enforce regulations, and to ensure that orders for discipline were enforced. This method, deemed unsatisfactory in many respects, nevertheless helped maintain order and discipline during the War and frequent clashes with Indian tribes along the frontier.

Increasingly during this period, the Army came to assume new responsibilities that called for units capable of extending national security authority along the new nation's frontiers. Serving essentially as military police, federal troops played a vital role throughout the settlement of the trans-Appalachian West. Because of the proximity of Army outposts and the general scarcity of civil law enforcement authority, settlers looked to the military as the primary source of law and order.

Not only were federal units used to police many of the towns and lines of communications along the new American frontier, but they also assumed responsibility for quelling some of the civil disturbances which occurred during the period. An important example of federal troops being used in this manner occurred in the summer of 1794 during the so-called Whiskey Rebellion.

Faced with a large-scale threat to law and order by farmers in western Pennsylvania who were up in arms against the newly imposed excise tax on whiskey, President Washington ordered the federalization of militia units, which marched in force to the scene of the troubles. While not military police in the strict sense of the term, these troops assumed police duties, made numerous arrests, and occupied several counties, performing provost marshal functions that would become standard in the future.

A commander's military police responsibilities received greater recognition in 1821 when the War Department tried, through a series of general regulations, to establish a uniformity of organizations within the

Army. Article 58 of these regulations, entitled 'General Police,' outlined the duties of military police and recommended that commanders select personnel of superior intelligence and physical ability to perform these duties. Significantly, throughout the Army's history these qualities have always been identified as prerequisites for the soldiers selected to perform military police duties. But the regulation made no provision for special training for these provost troops, nor did it order the organization of military police units, maintaining that military police forces would, in usual circumstances, be assigned temporary status within larger military organizations.

The Civil War created an urgent need for provost marshals and military police units within the federal Army. As early as 18 July 1861, Brig. Gen. Irvin McDowell, the Union Army's first field commander, authorized the commander of each regiment in the Department of Northeastern Virginia to select a commissioned officer as regimental provost marshal along with a permanent guard of ten enlisted men.[35] McDowell was responding to reports of widespread marauding in the ranks as his units marched across northern Virginia on the way to Bull Run. He wanted these units assigned the "special and sole duty" of preserving property from depredation and of arresting "all wrong-doers, of whatever regiment or corps they may be." Wrongdoers, he went on to order, "will be reported to headquarters, and the least that will be done to them will be to send them to the Alexandria jail." In those early days of the war, commanders were particularly sensitive to the political implications of interfering with local law enforcement, and McDowell also made it clear that his provosts were not to arrest civilians. His troops were to fight the enemy, "not to judge and punish the unarmed and helpless, however guilty they may be."

In the wake of the Union's defeat at Bull Run, the newly appointed commander of the Army of the Potomac, Maj. Gen. George B. McClellan,

35 https://www.battlefields.org/learn/biographies/irvin-mcdowell

reported "with much regret" that large numbers of soldiers stationed in the vicinity of the capital were in the habit of frequenting the streets and hotels of the city. Calling the practice "eminently prejudicial to good order and military discipline," he appointed Col. Andrew Porter provost marshal of Washington and assigned him the duty of keeping the officers and men in camp unless under special pass. He gave Porter some 1,000 officers and men-all the Regulars in the city, including infantry, cavalry, and artillery units-to suppress gambling, marauding, and looting in the capital area and to intercept stragglers and fugitives from nearby Army units. To carry out its mission, the provost guard was allowed to impose curfews on soldiers, all of whom were obliged to carry passes. Eventually, Porter was also empowered to search citizens, seize weapons and contraband, and make arrests. Thus began the gradual extension of the jurisdiction of provost marshals during the Civil War from responsibility for maintaining law and order within the military to include the protection and, to some extent, the control of the civilian population.

Although organized military police units were relatively rare in the Union Army, General McClellan established the Office of Provost Marshal General of the Army of the Potomac and appointed Colonel Porter, lately returned from his duties in Washington, to command the unit.[36] McClellan gave Porter a sizable force to carry out military police functions in his army, including battalions from the 8th and 17th Infantry and the entire 2nd Cavalry, as well as several units of Regular artillery. McClellan later enumerated the duties of his provost marshal, which, in addition to those already made familiar by Porter's troops in Washington, included regulation of places of public accommodation and amusement, distribution of passes to civilians for purposes of trade within the lines, and "searches, seizures, and arrests" within the army area.

Porter coordinated, but did not supervise, the activities of the provost units McClellan was also organizing in the separate divisions of the Army

---

[36] The provost marshals were the Union's military police. They hunted and arrested deserters, spies, and civilians suspected of disloyalty; confined prisoners; maintained records of paroles and oaths of allegiance; controlled the passage of civilians in military zones and those using Government transportation; and investigated the theft of Government property. In some instances, provost courts were set up to try cases that fell under the provost marshal's jurisdiction and those cases where military personnel were accused of civil crimes.

of the Potomac. Following Porter's appointment, McClellan ordered each of his division commanders to organize a provost guard within his command. Serving under a divisional provost marshal, again with an enlisted strength of ten men, these units were primarily responsible for protecting civilian property from the sometimes-sticky hands of soldiers on the march as well as all other duties associated with the discipline and orderly activities of the army. They also carried on the many collateral duties already made familiar in the Continental Army. They supervised and otherwise inspected the trade between local private merchants and Army units and individual soldiers, and they also assumed certain intelligence responsibilities, collecting and disseminating information on enemy forces.

Rivalling the work of military police in the field, provost marshals also assumed the enormous task of enforcing the nation's first conscription law. When demands for manpower led the Union to abandon its dependence on volunteer enlistments and turn to conscription, Congress created the Office of the Provost Marshal General of the Army on 3 March 1863 and appointed James B. Fry to the position in the rank of colonel of cavalry The new draft law charged the provost marshal general with overseeing the administration and enforcement of military recruitment and conscription along with a number of other quasi-military police duties associated with the war effort. It also empowered Fry to arrest summarily anyone engaged in impeding or avoiding conscription.

The energetic Fry quickly organized a small army of civilian bureaucrats to supervise the draft calls. To assist him in this and an ever-increasing number of other duties largely unrelated to the draft, the War Department authorized the creation on 28 April 1863 of a new organization, the Invalid Corps (later renamed the Veteran Reserve Corps). Manned by soldiers wounded on the battlefield or weakened by illness and judged unfit for further frontline service, this special force reached a strength of more than 30,000 officers and men by the end of the war. Its units served as provost guards in large cities and towns, escorts for prisoners of war, security guards for railroads, and during the raid on Washington in 1864, they were committed to battle when the enemy penetrated into rear areas.

One of their most important functions remained to guard the many district draft offices established by the provost marshal general to supervise the selection of men under the provisions of the draft act. That legislation proved extremely unpopular and placed the Invalid Corps in a perilous position when massive resistance to conscription spread across the North. Their most notable service came in the valiant but futile effort to preserve order at the outbreak of the riots that shook New York City in July 1863. Few in number, the provost troops were quickly overwhelmed. The riots continued unimpeded until Washington brought in more than 100,000 combat troops, ending what would become the nation's deadliest civil disturbance.

Following the pattern set at the end of the Revolutionary War, the Office of Provost Marshal General was discontinued in 1866. With the expansion of the Army due to the Spanish American War in 1898, the military police command function became greater than at any time during the preceding thirty years. A major development was the appointment of Brigadier General Arthur MacArthur as Military Governor and Provost Marshal General of the walled city of Manila in the Philippines. He was ordered to relieve the civil governor and "to take possession of the office, clerks, and machinery of that office." Subsequently, a Provost Guard Brigade composed of troops drawn from the Cavalry. Infantry, and Artillery units was established to maintain martial law in the city of Manila. Brigadier General Harry H. Bandholtz became chief of this Police Brigade. The reports of General MacArthur from Manila to the War Department referred to the men performing police and patrol duties as military police. At the same time, the report from the Chief of Police enumerated the number of arrests made for various offenses by "military and native police." For the first time, men performing police duties in the military were referred to specifically as military police.[37]

World War I marked a significant step in the military police's journey toward permanent branch status within the Army. Once again, the Army organized units both at the War Department level and in the field to carry out military police duties. Following America's entry into the war in 1917,

---

37 Kathy West, Historian Assistant, U.S. Army Military Police Corps Bulletin, 11 August 2010.

the War Department appointed Maj. Enoch H. Crowder provost marshal general of the Army. Again, the paramount mission of this official and the units placed under his command was to administer a selective service law. In July 1917 General John J. Pershing appointed Lt. Col. Hanson E. Ely as provost marshal general of the American Expeditionary Forces (AEF) to advise him "on military police and provost marshal matters.

Anticipating the need for military police in the AEF, the War Department approved a divisional table of organization in May 1917 that included authorization of a headquarters and two military police companies, a total of 316 officers and men in each division. Based on this guidance, the AEF organized two military police companies in the 1st Division in July, marking the first use of an organization officially called military police. General Pershing's plan called for placing these companies in the divisional train. Divisional returns of 4 September 1917 listed 95 men in the 1st Division's train headquarters and two military police companies with a strength of 150 and 152 officers and men respectively. To supplement the direct support units, a general support military police regiment, the First Army Headquarters Regiment, was formed by converting a French-speaking New Hampshire National Guard infantry organization and filling it out with men with civilian experience as detectives.

During the war the AEF organized military police units in sixty-one separate divisions, but in July 1918 Pershing also received permission to organize military police units in each corps and army with additional separate companies posted to the various sections of the Service of Supply, the Training Depot, and "to tactical units as may be necessary." Ironically, the increase in the number of military police companies resulted in a weakening in the strength of all military police companies in the AEF, because Pershing was forced to cut down on the size and number of divisional military police units in order to provide trained manpower for the new units. In the months following the end of hostilities, the AEF could count military police battalions in each of its three armies with a fourth battalion attached to the AEF's general headquarters at Chaumont, France.

The AEF's military police performed all those activities made familiar in earlier wars but with some significant additions. A constant concern of senior commanders in this era of massive military units fighting on wide fronts was the control of traffic in the rear areas and prevention of unauthorized individuals from entering the zones of operations. Borrowing a method devised by the French, Brig. Gen. Harry H. Bandholtz, a successor to Ely as the AEF provost marshal general, organized military police units to check all individuals travelling in leave areas, major cities, and examining points in rear Army areas.

World War I also altered the Army's traditional way of administering and caring for prisoners of war. In distinction to most earlier conflicts, where prisoners of war were usually held for short periods of time until exchanges could be affected, World War I created massive numbers of prisoners that had to be confined for long periods. During the ten-month period in which the United States processed foreign troops through its temporary prisoner-of-war camps, escort guard companies of military police handled some 48,000 prisoners. These guard companies were responsible for transporting all prisoners from division cages to a central prisoner-of-war enclosure. Reminiscent of the Civil War, soldiers judged unfit for full combat duty manned these companies.

Although the need for military police was universally recognized and thousands of men were performing military police functions throughout the Army, the pressing need for their services left selection of personnel haphazard and specialized professional training limited. General Bandholtz had established a service school at Autun, France, during the last months of the war that trained and graduated over 4,000 officers and men during its brief existence. Nevertheless, familiar patterns continued to persist. Men, usually with no experience in such duties, were drafted out of military units and thrust into military police organizations where they were expected to learn on the job.

The existence of a formal branch, especially if perpetuated in the peacetime Army, would allow for the systematic selection of personnel based on aptitude and fitness for these duties. It would also lead to a permanent training establishment where men could receive specialized instruction before assignment to regularly organized military police units throughout the Army. Then military police could be expected to have special supervision during a systemized training program before assignment to units. The promises implicit in the formation of such a corps were not to be fulfilled. Although under wartime legislation, Congress finally authorized establishment of a Military Police Corps, it was not until the closing weeks of the war, on 15 October 1918.

The new corps was to consist of the Provost Marshal General Department, AEF, all military police units in the AEF, and 'additional personnel.' The basic organizational unit remained the military police company, which as of October 1918 consisted of 205 officers and men.

Equipment for the AEF military police company was listed in the new legislation. Including 50 horses, 6 mules, 1 wagon, 18 motorcycles, and 105 bicycles, it was one of the most mobile organizations in the Army.

With the cessation of hostilities, the military police in the AEF were made extra busy by the hordes of American GIs who took unauthorized leave to see 'Paree' and the other fabled sights of a Europe now at peace. At the time of the Armistice agreement, the strength of the new corps stood at 463 officers and 15,912 men, who were stationed throughout France and with those troops of the Third Army who would participate in the occupation of the Rhineland.

In an effort to preserve the new branch as the Army entered its usual post-war drawdown in strength and also to preserve and document the role played by military police during the war, General Bandholtz requested all division commanders to submit reports concerning military police activities in their areas. Most of these reports strongly endorsed the work of the corps, and subsequently Bandholtz proposed to the War Department that a permanent military police corps be retained in the Regular Army. Citing the inadequacies in assigning non-specialists to such technically demanding duties, he stressed the obvious point that a permanent corps would ensure the existence of stable and efficient military police units in future emergencies.

Although Congress rejected the idea of a permanent corps, it did ratify the permanent organization of military police units in the Army in the National Defence Act of 1920. To save spaces in the Regular divisions, Congress combined the headquarters company and military police company. It also organized a Military Police Branch in the Officers' Reserve Corps. In the 1920s military police duties were once again performed by troops drawn from posts, camps, and stations and tactical units, usually on the basis of rosters drawn up by local commanders. Provost marshals existed in the reserve commands but never above the corps area level. Despite its organizational preservation in the severely reduced post-war Army, the military police function was again allowed to drift.

Between 1921 and 1940, forty-five military police battalions were constituted and added to the rolls of the Army. Of these, four were in the Regular Army, eleven were in the National Guard, and the remainder were in the Organized Reserve. None of the four Regular Army battalions served on active duty, but all were organized as RAI units. Only one National Guard unit, the 101st Military Police Battalion, was organized. Most of the Reserve battalions were organized at various times in the 1920s and 1930s.

There were two types of MP battalions; one assigned to the field army and the other assigned to the corps. The primary difference between the two was that the army battalion was authorized one additional MP company for a total of five.

With the outbreak of war in Europe in 1939 the creation of a military police corps became almost a necessity. In conjunction with a rising national concern over possible subversion and the perceived need to control hostile aliens, the Secretary of War Henry L. Stimson appointed Maj. Gen. Allen W. Guillon, the adjutant general of the Army, as acting provost marshal on 31 July 1941. To meet the demands associated with an army mobilizing for war, the War Department also recognized that a centralized authority above the corps level was necessary. On 26 September 1941, the official birthday of the corps, the secretary of war established the Military Police Corps as a permanent branch of the Army.

The duties of the new branch were published the day the United States declared war. The military police became responsible for investigating all crimes and offenses committed by persons "subject to military law within the area under the control of the organization to which they are assigned or attached." The branch was also charged with fighting crime, enforcing all police regulations pertaining to their area, reporting violations of orders "given by them in the proper execution of their duties regardless of the grade or status of the offender," and preventing the commission of acts "which are subversive of discipline or that cast discredit in any way on the United States Army." The branch was expected to perform those duties traditionally associated with their specialty controlling the movement of traffic both in the battlefield area as well as in camps, posts, and stations; safeguarding soldiers from violence or accidents; recovering lost, stolen, and abandoned property within the Army; and relieving combat organizations of the custody of prisoners of war and operating the prisoner-of-war system-along with some new military duties, including assisting in destroying hostile airborne troops when combat troops were unavailable or inadequate to the task.

The enforcement of military laws and regulations, the maintenance of order, and the control of traffic remained the most important wartime duties of the military police. But as usual in wartime, the corps was also expected to assume some duties more usually associated with civilian law enforcement. These included protecting designated buildings, public works, and localities of special importance from pillage, sabotage, and damage; supervising and controlling the evacuation and repatriation of civilian populations; assisting in the enforcement of gas defence, passive antiaircraft measures, and blackouts; and performing security investigations and other general measures for security and secrecy.

To perform military police responsibilities in the field, the War Department authorized larger military police units, with the battalion (later in the war it changed to group) prescribed as the largest unit in higher headquarters. It created the position of provost marshal general to serve on the staff of these headquarters to assist the commanders "in the supervision and operation of police matters." Describing it as a wartime measure, the War Department also authorized the appointment of a provost marshal general at each general headquarters or theatre of operations and on the staff of all divisions and higher units. In distinction to those serving in the tactical units, these general headquarters officers, with certain exceptions, were assigned to the special staff and exercised no command function over the military police units in the command.

The War Department initially organized three new battalions and four separate companies of military police from already existing assets. It also transferred all officers and enlisted men performing military police duties as well as all units performing such functions to the new corps. As a consequence, by mid-1942 the number of military police units had increased to seventeen battalions organized under the tables of organization. By that time, as the Army was rapidly expanding toward its full wartime strength, military police companies had become increasingly specialized as planning became more sophisticated. Some served exclusively as zone of interior guards, escort guards, and post, camp, and station garrisons. Others focused on duties relating to prisoners of war or in security processing while still another large number of companies became exclusively involved in criminal investigations. The corps, which started with a paltry 2,000 men in 1941, grew to a strength of more than 200,000 during the course of the war.

As a result of the rapid expansion of the military police and the ever-increasing need for trained personnel, the corps created the Military Police Service School at the Arlington Cantonment, Fort Myer, Virginia, on 19 December 1941. The school was similar to the one established in France in 1918 for training military police in the AEF. Its curriculum emphasized internal security and intelligence functions. The Provost Marshal General's School, as it was renamed on 15 January 1942, had four basic departments: Military Law, Traffic Control, Police Methods, and Criminal Investigation. The corps also established a replacement training centre and a unit training centre. By V-J Day some 40,000 men had processed through the replacement training centre.

Based on its experiences during the war and faced with the challenge of a new conflict in Korea, the Department of the Army issued new guidance concerning the responsibilities and organization of the military police in September 1950. It redefined the responsibilities of the provost marshals who henceforth would not only advise the commander on policy matters, but directly supervise the operations of the military police of the command.

The Korean War also introduced a new duty for military police. The war witnessed a dramatic increase in black-market activities associated with an army fighting in a third world nation. In previous decades control of the black market fell to civil affairs units, but the massiveness of the problem that began to appear in 1951 quickly involved the resources of the military police and, eventually, the corps added control and eradication of black-market activities to its list of responsibilities. Noting that the destruction caused by military operations and the usual local shortages of supplies in occupied territories created an extensive demand for items such as cigarettes, gasoline, food, weapons, and vehicles, the Department of the Army called on the military police, subject to the Uniform Code of Military justice, to detect and apprehend military personnel and civilians participating in black-marketing.

In ensuing decades America's involvement in Southeast Asia brought about yet another significant expansion in military police responsibilities, underscoring new and varied uses for military police in a war without defined rear areas. In addition to their usual wartime functions, military police units served in a direct combat support role. They provided convoy security, often escorting supplies and equipment through districts subject to direct enemy attack. They controlled traffic throughout the four combat zones where front lines had ceased to exist in the usual sense of the word. They secured highways and bridges against both local subversives and North Vietnamese regulars. They joined combat troops in the hazardous task of locating and destroying enemy tunnels. They supervised the movement of refugees and the control of political detainees in a war where determining friends and enemies could be a deadly decision. Military police also became frontline fighters during the successful effort to repel the North Vietnamese during the Tet offensive in 1968. At one point in the war military police were given exclusive responsibility for a specific tactical area, including responsibility for civic action functions in that area.

This increase in responsibility was recognized organizationally by the expansion in the number of military police units in Vietnam and by their organization for command-and-control purposes under a military police brigade. The seven military police battalions that served in Vietnam were organized into three military police groups: the 8th performed all criminal investigative work in the theatre; the 16th provided command

and control of all military police units assigned to the I and II tactical zones; the 89th controlled those units in zones III and IV. These units in turn were organized under the 18th Military Police Brigade, the first military police unit of its level to be employed in the Army. The brigade commander also served as provost marshal of the Military Assistance Command, Vietnam.

During 1968 the Army Chief of Staff, acknowledging the Military Police Corps' active involvement in support of military operations in Vietnam, approved changing the branch's identification from combat service support to combat support. This change was clearly justified by the responsibilities assumed by the corps in Vietnam where military police units were organized, trained, and equipped to perform operations in a combat support role. As a combat support branch, the Military Police Corps was placed under the U.S. Army Regimental System in September 1986.

The experience of Vietnam and the implementation of Air Land Battle doctrine for the battlefield of the future placed further responsibilities upon the military police in recent years. In 1988 the Army redefined and enlarged the branch's battlefield mission as first outlined in the publication of Air Land doctrine in 1986. Army doctrine posited that where in previous wars military police usually performed a rear security role, the battlefield of the future would find the need for protection against rear area threats vastly increased. The military police in the rear area must be ready and able for short periods of time to assume a direct combat role. The battle of the future, the new doctrine presupposed, would be fast paced and short in duration. Therefore, the military police unit, with its special ability to move and communicate with great speed and with its possession of unusually heavy firepower for such a highly mobile unit, could significantly enhance a commander's combat options. In addition, its versatility in controlling traffic and troop movement would allow commanders to mobilize much more quickly than in the past. In a future when a small force structure would be used in low intensity conflicts worldwide, military police could be expected to play an increasingly important operational role.

Grenada

On October 25, 1983, the 82nd Airborne Division, America's Guard of Honour, was called into combat to free American students and liberate the oppressed people of the tiny Caribbean island of Grenada. One of the key elements contributing to the overall success of that operation was the performance of the men of the 82nd MP Company. In Operation 'Urgent Fury' the 82nd's MPs were tasked with a multitude of missions, ranging from combat action to garrison duty, under tough conditions. Upon notification of the operation, the Division's Provost Marshal Office and the MP company supported the division's deployment. MPs provided numerous escorts, as well as traffic control points, to ensure the expeditious movement of personnel and equipment to staging areas. Due to the nature of the operation, the general support platoon significantly increased security at division headquarters. As the deployment schedule for the MP company became clear, provision was made with the XVIII Airborne Corps Provost Marshal Office for the latter to assume the division's MP garrison law enforcement mission, as well as Grenada to provide required deployment support. Coordination and implementation of the move went smoothly and were affected on 29 October.

On October 25, three squads of the 2nd MP Platoon deployed with the 2nd Battalion (Abn), 325th Infantry. Upon arrival in Grenada, the 2nd Squad of the platoon was immediately assigned the duty of enemy prisoner of war collection, as well as holding and processing them for the task force. The 1st and 3rd MP Squads handled detainee and refugee control at the Point Salines airfield along with clearing manmade structures from it. The 4th MP Squad arrived later that day and took over security for the battalion tactical operations centre. On October 26, the 1st and 3rd MP Squads were moved to the True Blue Medical College, which served as a refugee centre.

Given the mission of providing security for and evacuation of US and foreign civilians, these squads remained there until October 28, when they were relieved by the 118th Military Police Company. The 2nd MP Squad was assigned duties assisting the Caribbean Peacekeeping Force at the enemy prisoner of war camp and remained there until relieved by the 118th Military Police Company (Abn) on October 28. After being attached to the Combat Support Company, 3rd Battalion (Abn), 325th Infantry, the 4th MP Squad performed area reconnaissance and cleared buildings until assuming responsibility for security at the brigade tactical operations centre. On October 29, three squads of the 2nd MP Platoon were pulled by division and assigned law enforcement duties working with the Caribbean Peacekeeping Force in St. George's. They were joined there by the remaining squad after its release from Division Tactical Operations Centre security duties by the GS Platoon on October 30. Responsibilities of the 2nd MP Platoon in St. George's included joint patrols with the Caribbean Peacekeeping Force, checking out suspected Cuban hideouts and weapon caches, prison security, and VIP security. These missions continued until the 2nd MP Platoon was relieved by a platoon of the 21st Military Police Company, 503rd Military Police Battalion.

Late in the evening of the 26th, the 82nd Division's 3rd Brigade began to deploy across the island. The 3rd Military Police Platoon moved out by squad with their parent battalions and remained under the operational control of those battalions throughout the operation. Missions performed included enemy prisoner of war escort from battalion/brigade to the prison camp; clearing operations; investigating with the S-2 reported Cuban hideouts and weapons caches; providing tactical operations centre security; and escorting dignitaries. The 3rd MP Platoon remained with the 3rd Brigade Task Force after all other units returned to Fort Bragg, North Carolina. The majority of their time was spent performing brigade and battalion tactical operations centre security, conducting hasty route reconnaissance, manning civilian control points, performing reaction force duties, responding to snipers, and guarding the Cuban Embassy. Just prior to redeployment, three squads were detached to the 503rd Military Police Battalion to assist the 21st Military Police Company in manning checkpoints in and around St. George's. On December 12, the 3rd MP Platoon returned home with the last elements of the 82nd Airborne Division.

A three-person advance Provost Marshal cell, headed by the PM operations officer, was deployed October 26. The cell's primary missions were to coordinate MP activities, identify requirements, and keep the task force commander and staff informed of MP activities. Primary problem areas were eliminating equipment and supply shortages, rectifying overcrowding at the enemy prisoner of war camp, managing the evacuation of US and foreign nationals. and handling refugee problems at the True-Blue Refugee Centre.

Because of the magnitude of the enemy prisoner of war operations, as well as the MP requirements for evacuating US and foreign nationals, the 118th MP Company was attached to the 82nd Airborne Division and placed under operational control of the Provost Marshal. They assumed duties at the enemy prisoner of war camp and True-Blue evacuation site from the 2nd MP Platoon on October 28. Shortly after the 118th's arrival at the enemy prisoner of war camp, all the Caribbean Peacekeeping Forces personnel withdrew, leaving responsibility for the operation of the camp in MP hands. With the arrival of the Provost Marshal on 30 October, a thorough analysis of the prisoner situation was completed. Arrangements were made with G5 and the State Department to evacuate neutral personnel. Due to the overcrowded conditions on the initial site, construction of a new 1,000-man compound closer to the ocean was begun on November 1. The 118th Military Police Company selected seven non-commissioned officers, who spoke Spanish fluently, to direct the construction of the camp. Construction was achieved by utilizing captured Cuban labour and captured supplies obtained from the Infantry and Engineers. Stipulations of the Geneva Convention relating to the sheltering of prisoners were met by distributing confiscated Cuban foam mattresses and Cuban G. P. medium tents. Showers and latrines were built by Cuban plumbers while others laid the concertina wire needed for security. Approximately 115 Cubans, under the direction of the non-commissioned officers, were utilized in building the camp. Food supplies were trucked in by confiscated Cuban vehicles while the water supply was provided by a fire truck.

Provisions for the removal of solid waste and entomology services were coordinated with the Army contractor and local Grenadians. Under the guidance of the 307th Engineers and the 118th Military Police Company, the facility was completed. Thirty hours after construction began, over seven hundred captured Cubans had been moved to the new camp.

Prisoner of war evacuation began November 3, with approximately one hundred Cubans being flown out. Fifty more left on November 4, and this procedure continued until all prisoners had been repatriated.

Operation 'Urgent Fury' demonstrated that the military police have a vital role to play in division combat operations and that the troopers of the 82nd Military Police Company could be counted on to perform that role with distinction. The results speak for themselves: 14 Cubans and 47 members of the People's Revolutionary Army captured and 109 rifles, 18 pistols, 2 machine guns, and more than 3,000 rounds of ammunition recovered. Some 700 prisoners of war were processed, and more than 1,500 refugees assisted. Operating primarily at the squad level, MPs were confronted with a myriad of missions which they met with decisiveness, ingenuity, and resourcefulness. They also demonstrated that they were equally capable of performing purely combat-type missions, such as ambushes. Missions performed by MPs ranged from assisting the infantry in carrying out clearing operations to peacetime missions such as working with the Caribbean Peacekeeping Forces in restoring law and order to St. George's. More importantly, these MPs adeptly made the rapid transition from combat support to peacetime missions.

The 82nd Military Police Company also was assigned responsibility for performing customs inspections on all departing personnel. This short-fused mission required the dedication of forty percent of available military police assets to fulfil it and was performed concurrently with supporting combat missions. Such a task is normally assigned to a Corps' military police unit.

Maximum flexibility was demonstrated by customs inspectors who successfully responded to battalion commanders' requests to inspect their massed battalions at locations away from established customs stations. This was accomplished while continuing to maintain normal customs operations for other departing personnel. The operation validated the concept of attaching a Corps' military police company to the division Provost Marshal for use in performing enemy prisoner of war and refugee control operations. While most operational plans call for this to occur, there had been some scepticism as to its implementation. The plan indeed worked well. Operation 'Urgent Fury' for the 82nd Military Police

Company and the 82nd Airborne Division was an outstanding success.

The need for military police has been evident to American military commanders since the struggle for our national independence. Whenever the United States engaged in warfare, some form of police element emerged to assist its leaders in maintaining various aspects of discipline. Surfacing when necessity dictated, the Military Police Corps evolved through several phases, each meeting the needs of a particular period in American history. Assuming increased responsibilities, military police established their place as combat soldiers who have the professional knowledge and flexibility needed to perform a variety of missions in war and peace.

The assets that make the Military Police Corps so valuable in contemporary battlefield doctrine are actually quite similar to those possessed by the Marechaussee Corps in the Revolutionary War. While travelling a difficult road to organizational permanence and recognition as an organic element of the Army's fighting team, military police have along the way carefully adapted their mobility and communications capability to a myriad of new duties and responsibilities, leaving the corps ready to assume greater responsibilities and duties in the Army of the future.

There are numerous Military Police Battalions in today's US Army, here is a look at just one unit.

The 504th Military Police Battalion is a combat Military Police Battalion with a Headquarters Detachment and three line companies A, B, and C, and is the most decorated Military Police Battalion on active duty today. The Battalion was Constituted 29 July 1921, in the Organized Reserves as the 304th MP Battalion. Organized in April 1922 in Tennessee.

Inactivated, January 1938 in Tennessee; concurrently, withdrawn from the Organized reserves and allotted to the Regular Army. Redesignated 1 June 1940 as the 504th Military Police Battalion. Activated 15 May 1941 at Fort Sam Houston, TX. The battalion now celebrates this day as its birthday. The 504th had no sooner formed than it began training for its first major challenge. For two years, the battalion prepared for its baptism of fire. Company D, 504th Military Police Battalion was inactivated 20 June 1942 at Fort Sam Houston, TX. In February 1943, the 504th was alerted for deployment to Europe, and on 18 March 1943, landed on the beaches of North Africa as part of the first Allied force of World War II to fight against Rommel's Africa Korps. As the battle widened the battalion spread over some 400,000 square miles of desert. As the Africa Korps gradually fell against the combined American-British advance, the 504th assumed control of huge numbers of German prisoners. But the battalion's attention was quickly turned to the north as the Allied force prepared for their first landing on the European continent to strike against the 'soft underbelly' of the Third Reich. On 10 July 1943, elements of the 504th joined 800,000 Allied soldiers as part of Operation " AVALANCHE", the Allied landing at Salerno. Soldiers of the battalion had now been combat tested in nearly every type of operation for which the military police were then trained. Later actions of the 504th during World War II included the August 1944 landing in Southern France to support the earlier D-Day invasion of Normandy and its movement across 500 miles in Europe in one month as part of the Seventh Army. Following the Allied victory over the European Axis powers, the battalion was assigned to the Third Army Headquarters in Munich. In 26 months of fighting, the 504th had emerged from World War II as the most decorated MP battalion of the conflict by earning nine battle stars and four bronze arrowheads for amphibious landings. The battalion was Inactivated 20 January 1947, at Heidelberg, Germany. Its colours would not fly again until 1950, with the start of the Korean Conflict. The battalion restationed to Ft. Lewis in June 1984. The present-day configuration of the 504th Military Police Battalion is a combat Military Police Battalion with a Headquarters Detachment and three line companies; the 66th MP Company, the 170th MP Company and the 571st MP Company. The 504th also fulfills the Law-and-Order mission for Fort Lewis and Yakima Training centre. 'DUTY, JUSTICE, AND HONOR'

Established in May 1918, the War Department created yet another military police organization on the Army staff, the Criminal Investigation Division (CID). Charged with investigating criminal wrongdoing within the service, the CID was organized along the lines of a detective squad similar to those found in any large city police department of the era. Initially the CID consisted of eight companies, each with 5 officers and 100 enlisted men. Its members were selected by the provost marshals in the various army areas from among those soldiers with civilian experience as police detectives, lawyers, and journalists. Its full organizational structure was not established until the last weeks of the war. During 1918 the CID was involved in some 4,500 cases pertaining to the investigation of black-market activities, fraudulent passes sold in troop areas, worthless check-cashing operations, mail theft, and theft and illegal sale of government supplies.

Today as the Army's primary criminal investigative organization and Department of Defence's premier investigative organization, CID is responsible for conducting criminal investigations in which the Army is, or may be, a party of interest. Headquartered at Quantico, Virginia and operating throughout the world, CID Special Agents conduct criminal investigations that range from death to fraud, on and off military reservations and when appropriate, with local, state, and other federal investigative agencies. CID supports the Army through the deployment, in peace and war, of highly trained Special Agents and support personnel, the operation of a certified forensic laboratory, a protective services unit, computer crimes specialists, polygraph services, criminal intelligence collection and analysis and a variety of other services normally associated with law enforcement activities.

CID's mission is the same in both the installation and battlefield environments; however, CID's traditional roles are expanded once deployed to the battlefield or to a contingency operation.

CID's advanced theatre operations often include mentoring local national investigators and police in developing the rule of law, conducting site exploitation and recovery of forensic and biometric evidence, and developing criminal intelligence. CID also provides logistics security and conducts protective service and force protection operations. During battlefield operations, CID's criminal investigations can include war crimes, anti-terrorism and crimes against coalition forces and host nation personnel. Investigating these complex criminal scenarios allows combatant commanders to take the fight to the enemy and most importantly, save lives.

Primary Mission Requirements:

- Investigate serious crime
- Conduct sensitive/serious investigations
- Collect, analyse, and disseminate criminal intelligence
- Conduct protective service operations
- Provide forensic laboratory support
- Maintain Army criminal records

US Naval MPs patrol dockside.

The US Navy has formed a 'Military Police' force. This was something the navy never had previously. For a long time, marines were used for many security tasks. But the marines have been withdrawn from those duties over the last two decades. So now the navy needs more security and is doing it itself. In response to the suicide boat attack on the USS Cole in 2000, and the war on terror after September 11, 2001, the U.S. Navy decided it needed better port security, and decided to greatly expand its 'Masters at Arms' (MAAs) force.

The master-at-arms rating started out in the post-American Revolutionary War on board the ships of the United States' early Navy. Taking on many customs and traditions of the Royal Navy, the existence of the rating did not take effect until the Naval Act of 1 July 1797 (a previous Act of 27 March 1794 authorized the same, but was allowed to expire) or known as the Congressional Act to provide for a naval armament, which authorized the President of the United States to provide four ships of 44 guns and two ships of 36 guns each, to be employed on each ship various officers, marines, and petty officers under the command of a commissioned officer as the captain.

"And be it further enacted, that there shall be employed, in each of the said ships, the following warrant officers, who shall be appointed by the President of the United States, to wit: One sailing-master, one purser, one boatswain, one gunner, one sail-maker, one carpenter, and eight midshipmen; and the following petty officers, who shall be appointed by the captains of the ships, respectively, in which they are to be employed, viz: two master's mates, one captain's clerk, two boatswain's mates, one cockswain, one sail-maker's mate, two gunner's mates, one yeoman of the gun room, nine quarter-gunners, (and for the four larger ships two additional quarter-gunners,) two carpenter's mates, one armourer, one steward, one cooper, one master-at-arms, and one cook."

The call for a naval armament, and the change of the United States' isolationism was in direct response to the hostile acts of the Barbary States' pirates. Because of this Congressional Act, the MA rating is recognized as one of the 'oldest' ratings still existing in today's modern U.S. Navy. According to the Naval History and Heritage Command, the MA rating was officially established in 1797, disestablished in 1921, only to be re-established by the Chief of Naval Personnel on 1 August 1973, thereby making that date 'August 1st' as the official birthday of the modern U.S. Navy Master-at-Arms.

MA is the rating primarily concerned with law enforcement, and good order and discipline. They serve as a military police force onboard naval ships and installations, both Continental United States and outside Continental United States. MAs traditionally report to the commanding officer of the command, through the executive officer or operations officer, in maintaining good order and discipline, enforcing rules and regulations, and protecting life and property. MA rating can expect to see duties on board a variety of warships such aircraft carriers, cruisers, and destroyers, aboard naval shore and aviation installations, overseas in remote locations such as Bahrain and Diego Garcia, forward deployed to Iraq, Afghanistan, or Africa, or assigned to expeditionary or naval special warfare units. MAs are expected to perform their duties independently and advise their commander on matters pertaining to law enforcement or anti-terrorism force protection.[38]

In support of the Global war on terrorism, today's MA force is being forward deployed to many places around the world including Cuba,

---

38 Connell, Royal H. and Mack, William P. (2004), *Naval Ceremonies, Customs, and Traditions*, Naval Institute Press, ISBN 1-55750-330-3 (p. 314)

Iraq, Afghanistan, and Djibouti, among other locations. These missions typically include protective services and embarked security teams aboard ships with minimal self-defence capability responsible for fortifying landside locations and securing foreign ports for use by U.S. warships. The current active-duty number of MAs is approximately 11,000. It is a direct reflection of the requirement due to global terrorism as this is a significant increase from the previous manning level in the year 2000 which consisted of approximately 3,500 personnel.

No, it's not Special Agent Gibbs saving the world with his three sidekicks as the TV series would have us believe. The real NCIS is quite a large organization with many people combining to solve crime. As the name of NCIS has changed, so has its mission. The history of NCIS can be traced to the establishment of the Office of Naval Intelligence (ONI).

Subsequently, the name changed to the Naval Intelligence Investigative Service (NIIS), the Naval Secret Service (NSS), back to ONI, then the Naval Investigative Service (NIS), the Naval Security and Investigative Command (NSIC), the Naval Investigative Service Command (NISCOM), and finally, in 1992 what it is today, the Naval Criminal Investigative Service (NCIS).

The Mission today of the Naval Criminal Investigative Service (NCIS) is to investigate and defeat criminal, terrorist, and foreign intelligence threats to the United States Navy and Marine Corps, wherever they operate, ashore or afloat.

The Office of Naval Intelligence (ONI) was established when Secretary of the Navy William H. Hunt signed Navy Department General Order 292 in 1882. ONI was initially tasked with collecting information on the characteristics and weaponry of foreign vessels, charting foreign passages, rivers, or other bodies of water, and touring overseas fortifications, industrial plants, and shipyards. By 1915 in anticipation of the United States' entry into World War I, ONI's responsibilities expanded to include espionage, sabotage, and all manner of information on the Navy's potential adversaries. This mission expansion is credited to Marine Major John Henry Russell, who went on to become the 16th Commandant of the Marine Corps. He is credited with making investigations part of the NCIS mission.

In fall of 1916 the first Branch Office (a small undercover unit) was established in New York City under the supervision of ONI. Heavy reliance was placed on both reservists on active duty and civilian operatives, many of the latter serving voluntarily and without pay. The office served as a model for others developed during World War I and accounted for some impressive successes in the field of counterespionage. Following WWI, responsibilities for criminal investigations were placed under naval aides for information, who were assigned to the staffs of each of the 15 naval district commandants, and later placed under the district aide. The counterintelligence units under the aides were collectively designated as the Naval Secret Service with the first investigators known as secret service agents. Eventually, all operatives were known as Special Agents of the Office of Naval Intelligence.

NCIS has several roles protecting the naval forces from violent extremist organizations and individuals is one of NCIS' highest priorities. As the primary law enforcement and counterintelligence component for the naval services, NCIS is focused on countering threats to the physical security of Sailors, Marines, and Department of the Navy (DON) civilian personnel and on preventing terrorist attacks against installations and ships.

NCIS is responsible for detecting, deterring, and disrupting terrorism worldwide through a wide array of offensive and defensive capabilities. Offensive operations aim at identifying and interdicting terrorist activities. In defensive operations, NCIS supports key DON leaders with protective services and performs physical security assessments of military installations and related facilities – including ports, airfields, and exercise areas to which naval expeditionary forces deploy.

counterintelligence, Within the Department of the Navy, NCIS has exclusive investigative jurisdiction into actual, potential or suspected acts of espionage, sabotage, assassination, and defection.

The safeguarding of classified information, vetting personnel for trustworthiness and protecting classified information within industry.

The NCIS Cyber Department utilizes advanced cyber technologies and methodologies to identify and process electronic data of intelligence or evidentiary value.

NCIS works to neutralize foreign intelligence services and foreign commercial activities seeking information about critical naval programs and research, development, test and evaluation facilities. To prevent the compromise of military technology, NCIS pursues a robust Research and Technology Protection program, which works to safeguard the nation's vital defence technology.

NCIS has computer investigations and operations agents assigned throughout the world focusing on hackers, criminal groups, foreign intelligence services, terrorists, and insiders.

As the felony investigative arm of the Department of the Navy (DON), NCIS civilian Special Agents have investigative responsibility within the DON for all crimes punishable under the Uniform Code of Military Justice by confinement of more than one year. The agency also frequently conducts felony investigations under the criminal laws of the United States when DON equities are involved.

Criminal investigations are at the core of everything that NCIS does. Agents are trained at the NCIS Special Agent Basic Training Program (SABTP) and Criminal Investigators Training Program (CITP) at the Federal Law Enforcement Training centre (FLETC), Glynco, GA. After gaining field experience with NCIS in basic criminal investigations, agents can move into specialty areas and are eligible for additional training.

Types of crimes investigated by NCIS include rape, child physical and sexual abuse, burglary and robbery, theft of government and personal property, and homicide. NCIS also has responsibility for investigating any non-combat death involving a naval service member where the cause of death cannot be medically attributable to disease or natural causes.

A US Naval Master at Arms, on patrol with a US Army unit.

US Marine Military Police perform assigned military law enforcement duties to uphold the criminal justice system, maintain good order and discipline, and support the commander's law enforcement and security requirements in peacetime and combat operations. It is very demanding in that the Military Police are confronted with every form of violation and criminal liability, misdemeanour through felony.

The United States Marine Corps traces its institutional roots to the Continental Marines of the Revolutionary War, formed in November 1775. Disbanded in April 1783 and resurrected again in July 1798 for service in the new-build Frigates. Marines had a role and reputation as expert marksmen in ship-to-ship actions. However Marine Military Police were no strangers to some of the roles performed by MP today, many Marines in the early years of their formation acted as the captains' bodyguard, reaction force and disciplinarians onboard Naval ships. Even though today most Navies have a Master-At-Arms or Naval Police of their own the British and US Marines can be still used in their original role.

Military police have become an essential part of logistical battlefield support in modern warfare. Today each of the Armed Services has its own Military Police Force, and the Marine Corps have some of the best-trained Military Police officers in the world. With the current state of military operations Marine Corps Military policemen are some of the most active police officers in the world. The Marine Corps MP specialty are useful both during direct combat operations and also during peacetime. There are many different duties, but five main functions that the Marine Corps Military Police perform: They maintain order and law, they perform Police intelligence operations, they maintain area security posts and security operations, they act as resettlement and interment officers in various interment operations, and they act as support for mobility operations. These are the five main processes that the Marine Corps and other services Military police provide to area commanders.

As modern warfare has developed, there has been an increasing need for soldiers to be tasked with securing outposts, checkpoints, prisoners of war and investigating the criminal acts of their own soldiers. Marine Corps military police forces were first established in 1945 to handle order and discipline during peace and prisoner of war internment during wartime. But the role of Marine military police expanded during the Vietnam War. From that point, Marine Corps MPs provided dog scout teams, investigated black-market activity, vehicle accidents and war crimes, while also taking control of overall rear echelon security.

As military police operations became more complex, a need developed for soldiers to direct forces through rear areas and protect logistical support units in case of a counterattack. This gave Marine Corps military police, a support branch that doesn't have official combat responsibilities, the job of backup defence force in case of an attack in the rear. This is significant because females are not allowed into combat branches, but they are allowed into the military police branch. That branch now performs regular combat operations in which female soldiers participate.

Marine Corps military police are responsible for the order and discipline of all Marines through the Uniform Code of Military Justice. They investigate crimes, patrol, make arrests and incarcerate criminals just like a civilian police force. During combat operations, Marine Corps military police continue to conduct police force operations, but they also handle prisoners of war, conduct police intelligence operations and maintain battlefield circulation control throughout the rear areas.

There is one level of Marine Corps military police training for enlisted personnel and another level of training for officers entering the military police branch. Enlisted military police are trained to use breathalyser and radar equipment, conduct traffic accident investigations, handle working dogs and work on special reaction teams. Officers in the military police are trained to command divisional military police companies that are responsible for all criminal justice within that division. These officers are required to take much more classroom time on the Uniform Code of Military Justice than enlisted military police.

Marine Corps military police are trained at the U.S. Army Military

Police School in Fort Leonard Wood, where they receive the benefit of training from the Army's military police branch. Marine Corps instructors at the USMC Military Police (MP) Schoolhouse at Fort Leonard Wood (FLW), Missouri are responsible for preparing Marine MP Forces for deployment throughout the world. The curriculum for its eleven-week course constitutes the same standard of training as for all services.

Traffic enforcement is just one role the USMC MPs conduct. The USMC has begun a program to improve safety on the roads by its members and the Military Police ensure traffic regulations are obeyed on Base roads and operational routes on the Battlefield. The reason is more Marines have died on the nation's highways in fiscal 2008 than on foreign battlefields.

US Marine Corps (USMC) Military Police (MP) assigned to the Special Reaction Team (SRT), are armed with a number of specialist weapons including the Heckler and Koch 9mm MP5-N sub-machine gun, Shotguns, pistols, and sniper rifles. The SRT conduct annual training events, set by the Provost Marshals Office, which are designed to train Military Police and Criminal Investigators proper procedures when dealing with a hostage situation. USMC SRT MPs don't see themselves as elite soldiers, this might seem to conflict with their aggressive and often violent tactics, but the optimal outcome of any SRT team call-out is one in which no one is needlessly killed or injured. That includes hostages, innocent bystanders, officers and even the criminals themselves. SRT tactics are meant to intimidate and confuse – using deadly force is a last resort.

A typical SRT call-out starts with the on-duty team members out on patrol, training or doing other Military Police work. If an incident occurs on Base which requires their specialist skills the team to assembled. During this time, regular MP patrol officers will have secured the perimeter of the scene and kept it under surveillance. When the SRT team assessable at Provost headquarters, they will be briefed on the situation before loading into their SRT vehicle. This

vehicle transports the team and their gear, and in many cases, it is also equipped to serve as a mobile command headquarters. Whether they use a vehicle or a nearby house or office, the team sets up their command post close to the scene of the incident, but in a safe place.

At the command post, team leaders begin assimilating information. Background checks on the suspect, the layout of the area, known weapons involved, the number and disposition of hostages, potential motives – any information could be useful. At this point, negotiators get in contact with the suspect (if possible) and try to get additional information. If the SRT team is missing some crucial information, such as the specific location of the suspect and hostages in a barricaded house, they will send team members to gather it using surveillance equipment. These recon units usually operate as two-person teams, and they are experts at stealth.

One thing SRT teams have learned over the years is that crazed gunmen don't always wait around for SRT to execute a carefully conceived plan. The suspect could start shooting at officers, killing hostages or make an escape attempt. For this reason, SRT teams develop a few 'quick and dirty' contingency plans as soon as they arrive on the scene.

Given enough time, the team will formulate a more extensive plan based on all the intelligence they have gathered. They will determine if there will be separate teams, where they will enter, the timing of the entry, what ordinance will be used and other details. There may be preliminary steps, such as drilling a small hole in a wall and using a pinhole camera to keep an eye on the suspect or using a distraction to draw the suspect toward a certain location.

Throughout Operation Restore Hope Somalia, MP units were in great demand because of their ability to serve as a force multiplier. Marine force (MARFOR) and ARFOR commanders quickly took advantage of the MP's significant firepower, mobility, and communications and used them effectively as a force multiplier conducting security-related missions as one of their combat forces. Doctrinal missions included security of main supply routes military and NGO convoys, critical facilities, and very important persons (VIPs); customs; detention of local civilians suspected of felony crimes against US force or Somali citizens; and criminal investigative division (CID) support as the JTF's executive agency for joint investigations. MPs responded to a significant number of hostile acts taken against US forces, NGOs, and civilians by armed bandits and 'technicals' and to factional fighting that threatened US forces or relief efforts. They also supported the JTF weapons confiscation policy by conducting recons and gathering information and intelligence human intelligence about the size, location, and capabilities of factions operating throughout the ARFOR and MARFOR AOs. This information included the location of sizeable weapons caches. MPs also had an expanded role in the actual confiscation of weapons by establishing checkpoints and roadblocks along main supply routes within small villages, and within the congested, confined urban environment of Mogadishu. Serving in both a combat and CS role, MPs also participated in a larger, combined arms show-of-force operation (air assault) in the city of Afgooye.

In the Marine Corps of the 21st century, MWDs are highly trained operators, putting their natural abilities to good use protecting Marines in a variety of complex environments. Specifically, MWDs are able to detect improvised explosive devices with their keen sense of smell and can capture high value targets using their powerful nonlethal bite capability. When attached to an already formidable squad or platoon of Marines, these fierce dogs also heighten the unit's intimidation factor toward potential foes.

The Marine Corps relies on German shepherds, Belgian Malinois, and Labrador retrievers to fill its MWD program. The first stop for these motivated pups is Lackland Air Force Base in Texas, where all U.S. MWDs are sent for training. The length of boot camp is based on each dog's abilities, and the instruction focuses on teaching obedience to orders, tracking and attacking, and physical fitness. After completing their basic training, most dogs spend six to ten years in the military before transitioning and retiring around age ten.

In order to tap into these dogs' skills, the Marine Corps relies on military working dog handlers – specially trained law-enforcement Marines that can attach to infantry and reconnaissance units in order to add a nonlethal capability as well as enhance the unit's situational awareness to threats.

After training, Marine Corps law enforcement and special operations units throughout the world receive their dogs and pair them with a handler. In garrison at their units, MWDs train just as all Marines do, regularly going on field operations to hone their skills in both urban and field environments, and even running special obstacle courses to stay strong and agile, all alongside their trusted handler. The process of finding the right handler and dog pair is not an exact science; units will shuffle dog handlers around to get the right combination between the abilities of the Marine and the MWD to support the necessary mission set.

Marine MPs conduct criminal investigations, protect and direct logistical operations, guard prisoners of war and perform police intelligence operations. In Afghanistan the Marine MPs do a lot of main supply route security protecting convoys and doing I.E.D sweeps, perimeter security is a big part of combat for MP's.

Sgt. Andrew Schlake deployed to Afghanistan for about eight months last year. But as soon as he got off the bus at Camp Lejeune, he knew he wanted to go back.

His reason: 1st Sgt. Luke Mercardante and Cpl. Kyle Wilks, both killed last April in a roadside bomb explosion. Both men, like Schlake, were military police.

When the improvised explosive device went off, Schlake said, it was overwhelming, but the Marines reverted to their training – doing what they had learned to defend the convoy, treat the injured and leave no one behind.

Since then, more than 25 Marines have died while supporting combat operations in Afghanistan, many in IED blasts.

Wednesday, Schlake and his new unit – Military Police Company, 2nd Marine Division – practiced what to do when a convoy is attacked by an IED, as well as how to interact with tribal leaders in Afghan villages.

The company will deploy to Southern Afghanistan with 2nd Marine Expeditionary Brigade later this spring.

In the simulated village, Marines sat on rugs under tarps, using a translator to talk to Afghan role players, some of whom puffed on hookah pipes or passed around local pastries.

The scenario was supposed to imitate a first meeting with village elders, said Gunnery Sgt. Chuck MacNeil, the company first sergeant. The 'elders' were playing the role well, he said, demanding a female doctor, water, and money.

"We're training for a different kind of fight," said MacNeil, who deployed for a year to Iraq but has not yet served in Afghanistan. "There is a lot more focus on getting out and talking to the people. ... Counterinsurgency is our main focus, doing it the right way."

The training provided an opportunity for the Marines to practice the 'meet and greet,' working with the Afghans to answer questions they may have and built rapport, said 2nd Lt. Matt Carwile, commander of MP Company's 2nd Platoon.

"This type of training is going to set us up for success," he said. "It is invaluable."

After leaving the 'village,' Marines encountered an ambush on the road. Two bombs exploded simultaneously, followed by gunfire from the woods.

"You're down!" one Marine shouted to the turret gunner in one vehicle.

"Well, get somebody else on the gun," someone else shouted as two men were pulling the 'injured' Marine out of the Humvee.

Gunfire continued as a man called for a medevac and a corpsman worked to 'stabilize' the injured Marine.

"They've got one down up there," the Marine on the radio shouted to the corpsman, shortly before more gunfire erupted.

In Afghanistan, the military police may do any number of things, MacNeil said, such as provide convoy security, work with detainees or train Afghan National Police forces. The situation is more kinetic than Iraq, he said, with more firefights than Marines might encounter now in Iraq.

But like in Iraq, the Marines will adjust and do what is needed, MacNeil said.

That's why the Marines must be prepared, said Schlake, who described his job responsibility as "making sure we all walk out of here unharmed"

"You never know what to expect," he said.

Sgt. Brian D. Mocha, a U.S. Marine and military policeman, uses a military working dog to screen bags for bombs or bomb-making material, at an Iraqi police recruiting drive, June 26, 2006, in Qaim, Iraq. More than 300 local Iraqis from Euphrates River towns near the Iraqi-Syrian border lined up at the Marines outpost in hopes of becoming policemen in one of Iraqis newest police districts. Photo by Cpl. Antonio Rosas.

As early as 1935, the Marines were interested in war dogs. They had experienced the enemies' sentry dogs used in Haiti and in the other 'Banana Wars' in Central America where dogs staked around guerrilla camps in the jungle sounded the alarm at the approach of the Marines.

Marines thought they would have to fight the Japanese in the Pacific. Since the Japanese were well established in the islands and atolls of the central, south, and west Pacific, the Marines knew they were going to be fighting in tropical climates where the vegetation provided jungle-like coverage. In such conditions, dogs would be ideal sentries and couriers. It was no surprise later that the Marine Corps had the first large dog unit in the nation's history to see action against the enemy. More than 1,000 dogs were trained by Marines during World War II.

Unlike other branches of the military where service members become dog handlers after several years of enlistment to become a dog handler in the Marine Corps, Marines go from boot camp to Military Police school and straight on to the dog handling school after a selective process. While at MP school, individuals interested in the K-9 field must be in the top 10% of their class. After writing an essay on why they want to be a handler, they will then go on an oral board to get selected for the K-9 school.

United States Air Force Security Forces are the Military Police, Base Security and Air Base Ground Defence (ABGD) forces of the USAF. Security Forces, or simply 'SF', were formerly known as Military Police (MP), Air Police (AP), and Security Police (SP). The Security Forces

Guarding millions of dollars' worth of aircraft is as important in peace time as it is in war. Photo DoD USAF.

career field has a long, rich history which predates the inception of the Air Force in 1947. The invention of the aircraft and its subsequent military use required a protective force to guard the aircraft and defend the people who fly and fight. In early 1943, the first Army Aviation Military Police Companies were established from existing Army MP units. The USAF Security Forces lineage can be traced to its beginning in WWII due to the tactics employed by the Germans, namely the use of paratroopers and airborne forces to capture or destroy air bases.

On February 12, 1942 the United States approved the allocation of 53,299 African American troops to the Army Air Forces for the sole stipulation of air base defence. These Army Air Force (AAF) air base security battalions were influenced by racial as well as military considerations. Units were deployed throughout the European, Asian, and African theatres and designed to defend against local ground attacks. These units were armed with rifles, machine guns, and 37-mm guns. Of the initial planned 296 air base security battalions, 261 were to be 'black', however, the widening Allied superiority of air and ground had reduced this threat and resulted in a diminished need for this goal and by 1943 inactivation of units formed had already begun. In 1945 all AAF air base security battalions were closed.

The National Security Act of 1947 established the current Department of Defence or DoD and formed the United States Air Force as a separate service. MP units serving with the Army Air Corps before this separation were transferred to the Air Force. The Army-Air Force agreement of 1947 stated that "each department will be responsible for the security of its own installations. In 1948, General Order No. 1 from Headquarters USAF designated those transferred units and personnel as 'Air Police' (AP). On 1 September 1950, the first Air Police school was established.

In June 1950 the Air Force began urgent operations focused on air base defence with the outbreak of the Korean War. A build-up of ground combat forces began. The centre of this build-up was the expansion of the Air Force Air Police from 10,000 in July 1950 to 39,000 in December 1951. Still, one year into the war, the Air Provost Marshal reported that "the Air Force is without policy or tactical doctrine for Air Base Ground Defence. Air Police serving as the cadre of this force were organized and equipped like infantry. Though at times some 32,000 to 35,000 North Korean guerrillas were operating in United Nations controlled territory they ignored US air bases. This would not be the case for USAF Air Bases in the Republic of Vietnam.

On November 1, 1964, between the 12:25 and 12:33 AM, Vietnamese Communist (VC) troops attacked Ben Hoa Air Base with six 81-mm mortars positioned about 400 meters north of the air base. The VC fired 60 to 80 rounds into parked aircraft and troop billets then withdrew undetected and unabated. The attack killed 4 US military personnel, wounded 30, destroyed and/or damaged 20 B-57 bombers. U.S. air bases had become targets and became routine targets thereafter. The VC routinely reconnoitred U.S. air bases for lengthy periods and assessed them for vulnerable points which included terrain, reinforcement approach routes, reaction time of artillery support, and the daily routines of U.S. personnel which included their sleeping and eating times, patrol operations and guard shift changes. However, as good and as exact as their reconnaissance was, their failure and/or inability to chart Security Police patrol patterns became evident in one case when their presence was detected by a USAF Sentry Dog Patrol and a Security Alert Team which lead to their capture. During another incident, nine well-trained and highly disciplined combat engineers, failed to locate Security Police postings on the flight line. The anxious Sappers met their end when they tried to enter the parking ramp by passing directly in front of a SP machinegun emplacement. To a large extent security of bases can be directly attributed to Military patrol dog teams.

The USAF Sentry Dog program was a product of the Korean War. By 1965 the USAF had a pool of sentry dog teams available for deployment to South Vietnam. Nightly at every air base, sentry dog teams were deployed as a detection and warning screen in the zone separating combat forces from the perimeter. Nearly all air base defence personnel agreed that the Sentry Dog Teams rendered outstanding service. Some of which went as far as to say, "Of all the equipment and methods used to detect an attacking enemy force, the sentry dog has provided the most sure, all-inclusive means". In the 1970s the USAF used over 1,600 dogs worldwide. Today, personnel cutbacks have reduced USAF dog teams to approximately 530, stationed throughout the world.

Many dogs that operate in these roles are trained at Lackland Air Force Base, the only United States facility that currently trains dogs for military use.

In 1966, the name of the career field was changed to 'Security Police' (SP) the term was considered descriptive, concise, and uniformly applicable as it combined two main mission elements: Police and Security functions.

In March 1971, the security police career field was split into two separate functions: Law Enforcement and Security specialties. Law Enforcement personnel provided the typical 'police' response to safeguard personnel and property while Security personnel preformed duties associated with physical security, the flight line and weapons storage areas. In 1996, As threats to the world security changed, so did the requirements for security police to better respond to worldwide contingencies and protect

Air Force resources and ultimately laid the foundation for the career field transformation into the current Security Forces.[39]

As threats to the world security changed, so did the requirements for security police to better respond to worldwide contingencies and protect Air Force resources. Specialized fields with single skills could no longer meet AF needs. Under direction from the Air Force Chief of Staff the Security Police reorganized their entire career field. In April 1997, three distinct career fields or Air Force Specialties (Air Force Specialty Code – AFSC) merged to become 'Security Forces' (SF). Security Specialist (AFSC: 811X0), Law Enforcement Specialist (AFSC: 811X2) to include Military Working Dog Handler (AFSC: 811X0A), and Combat Arms Training and Maintenance (AFSC: 753X0).

In 1997, the Air Force activated the 820th Base Defence Group, a Force Protection unit based in, Georgia. The unit is a trained force protection with an Airborne capability. At a moment's notice, the group provides one of expeditionary Air Force's worldwide deployable, 'first-in', fully integrated, multidisciplined, self-sustaining force protection capability.

435th Security Forces Squadron (435 SFS) is a United States Air Force unit capable of overland airlift, air assault, or airborne insertion into crisis situations. The unit incorporates more than 13 different specialties including people with civil engineering, medical, intelligence, investigative, fuels, logistics, personnel, and security skills. It was formerly known as the 786th Security Forces Squadron. In March 2003 the 786 SFS participated in a combat parachute drop into Bashur Airfield in conjunction with the 173rd Airborne Brigade to open up the northern front in Iraq during Operation Iraqi Freedom. The 786 SFS is the first conventional Air Force unit to participate in an airborne jump. The 786th SFS was re-designated the 435 Security Forces Squadron on 16 July 2009 and falls under the 435 Contingency Response Group (CRG) (formerly 86 CRG).

1st Special Operations Security Forces Squadron are upgrading their

---

39 Air Force Security Forces Police: Security Forces K-9, Sentries and Law Enforcement – Composition Notebook, CreateSpace Independent Publishing. 2018.

training to protect high risk aircraft in deployed locations. Handpicked members of security forces squadrons from all over Air Force Special Operations Command are participating in a new training program called DAGRE (Deployed Aircraft Ground Response Element) to upgrade their combat skills to support future AFSOC deployments into contingency areas. During this inaugural 11-week course, security forces Airmen learn advanced combat and shooting tactics, honing unarmed fighting and combat first aid skills. In between their combat courses and tough physical training regimen they are also taking classes at the Air Force Special Operations School in anti-terrorism, counter insurgency, and other specialized courses. This further prepares them for scenarios they will find in Iraq, Afghanistan, and other hot spots around the globe. The training culminates with an 8-mile tactical road march into a scenario where each team will be required to showcase their new skills in an austere environment under hostile conditions.

In January 2006, Brig. Gen. Robert Holmes, Director of Security Forces and Force Protection, stated "We want to make our airmen more proficient, and to do that, we need to adapt. We're going to change our training, our tactics and our procedures and the Air Force will be better for it." General Holmes calls these transformations a 'refocus' on how Security Forces train and fight. General Holmes elaborated, "We're not in the Cold War anymore; we have to alter our mentality and our practices for today's reality. Because of the nature of the threat, our airmen are fighting the global war on terror on the front lines, and we owe it to them to provide training, equipment, and resources to be effective. Essentially, Security Forces will focus on preparing for their warfighting mission at forward locations, as well as security at a fixed installation. Our Airmen are going 'outside the wire' to conduct missions and are proving successful in keeping people safe." General Holmes also said one of the transformation goals is bringing security forces back in step with standard Air Force 120-day deployments. General Holmes explained, "Right now our folks are going out for 179-day rotations. Our airmen need time to reconstitute and train. So it's important to get them in line with the rest of the Air Force. We aim to do just that." Overall, General Holmes said the changes would make Security Forces more effective and relevant to Air

Force needs in the face of the current changing nature of warfare.

In September 2010, the Air Force announced it was increasing all combat deployments to 179 days beginning in 2011. Lt. Col. Belinda Petersen, a spokeswoman for the Air Force Personnel Centre, said the increase in deployment duration is an effort to "improve predictability and stability for airmen and their families." Peterson added, by revising the policy, airmen affected by the change will also 'ideally' get more time at home. The dwell time for those airmen is expected to increase from 16 to 24 months. Despite these 'improvements', Security Forces, civil engineers, contractors, and intelligence are among the busiest in the Air Force, with six-month deployments, followed by only six months at home.

On March 2, 2011, Senior Airman Nicholas J. Alden, 25, of Williamston, S.C., assigned to the 48th Security Forces Squadron at Royal Air Force Lakenheath, England, and Airman Zachary R. Cuddeback, 21, of Stanardsville, Va., assigned to the 86th Vehicle Readiness Squadron at Ramstein Air Base, Germany, were shot and killed by 21-year-old Kosovo native of Albanian descent named Arif Ukaat at Frankfurt International Airport, Germany. Ukaat's relatives in Kosovo tell the Associated Press he's a devout Muslim and German federal prosecutors said they suspect he was motivated by extremist, Islamist ideology. A U.S. law enforcement official says the shooter shouted "God is Great" in Arabic, as he opened fire. The Air Force says most of the airmen attacked were part of a Security Forces squad passing through Germany, on their way to a deployment in Afghanistan. In addition to the two dead, two other airmen were wounded.

President Obama stated the incident is a "stark reminder of the extraordinary sacrifices that our men and women are making all around the world to keep us safe and the dangers that they face all around the globe."

Missile Security Force Duties

One of the most vital security operations the USAF Police provided is the guarding of the Air Force missile bases that oversee Minuteman missiles. An extensive security task force that requires 24/7 alertness and seriousness securing 150 Launch Facilities that contain the world's most powerful weapons. The security force is assigned to a missile complex cover anywhere from 10,000 to 13,000 square miles.

Given the responsibility of providing state of the art security to the Minuteman weapon system, the security forces are provided with some of the most serious weapons to accomplish that task, including Humvee mounted with M60 machine guns, heavily armoured BearCat vehicles and Bell Huey UH-1N helicopters. The Huey UH-1N is an integral part of the mobile fire team and are always present when a valuable weapon systems component is transported to or from a Launch Facility. These helicopters are utilized if a Launch Facility has been breached, and an elite ready reaction security team needs to get there quickly.

Apart from equipment the Air Force Missile Security Force also employ military working dogs to add to the security layer. These Military Working Dogs are also trained to detect explosives and other dangerous ordinance. The dogs are highly versatile, highly skilled working set that are an invaluable component in providing the utmost of security and safety.

With the current 2022 threat to world peace caused by the Russian invasion of the Ukraine these Security Police are tasked with and are given the immense responsibility of assuring the safety and security for the world's most powerful weapon, the Minuteman III missile.[40]

---

40 Article: *Defenders of the Force; The History of the US Air Force Security Forces 1947–2006* by James Lee Conrad and Jerry M. Bullock.

Canada

Canadian MPs guard convoy during a stop in Afghanistan.

At the outset of the First World War, the Canadian Army consisted of a tiny 'Permanent Force' or Regular Army and a large Non-Permanent Militia. There was no organized Corps or Regiment of Military Police in the Army, a few units had a Regimental Police or Provost section consisting of a dozen or so men under the command of a Provost Sergeant. Camps and Garrisons had locally appointed personnel functioning as Military Police; however, discipline was primarily a Regimental concern, through the normal chain of command.

Soldiers temporarily assigned to Military Police duties were expected to be locally recruited, often from gentlemen of large physical stature, who might or might not have civil police experience. Camp Police are mentioned briefly in various Militia publications prior to 1914. Major General William Otter's *The Guide: A Manual for the Canadian Militia* describes very briefly, the duties and identification of military police. Generally, the duties of Camp Police were to maintain order, regulate civilian tradesmen, provide escorts for defaulters, and to enforce sanitary regulations.

In September 1914, a small detachment of Military Police accompanied the First Contingent of the Canadian Expeditionary Force to England. Captain E.S. Clifford D.S.O. was appointed as Assistant Provost Marshal for the First Contingent. A section of Military Police consisting of a Warrant Officer and 9 Privates was with Divisional Headquarters. 1st Infantry Brigade Headquarters had a section of 4 Military Mounted Police. Upon arrival in England, the detachment underwent training with the British

Military Police. During the First World War, Canadian Military Police appear to have adopted British methods, organization, and equipment.

The Canadian Military Police Corps (CMPC) was authorised on the 15th of September 1917. The initial establishment was set at 30 Officers and 820 Warrant Officers and NCOs. Only trained soldiers were to be selected and they were required to serve a one-month probationary period before being transferred. Applicants were required to have exemplary service records; most having served with existing Military Police units. The CMPC School was formed at Rockcliffe near Ottawa in June 1918. The first commanding officer of the school was Major Baron Osborne. The basic course was of three weeks duration, upon successful completion of the course Privates were promoted to Lance Corporal.

The following is an excerpt from the Report of the Minister, Overseas Military Forces of Canada, 1918:

> *"The selection of personnel for Provost Service is a matter of great importance, even more so than in the case of policemen in civil life. The Military Police must be tactful, intelligent, and determined."*

Today the Canadian Forces Military Police Group (CF MP Gp) is a formation of the Canadian Forces that groups Military Police members employed in policing duties across the Canadian Forces; in short MPs are tri-service. You can be an MP on a Ship or Air Base or Army establishment. Canadian Military Police are unusual in that they are classified as Peace Officers in the Canadian Criminal Code, which gives them the same powers as civilian law enforcement personnel to enforce law on Defence property anywhere in the world. They have the power to arrest anyone who is subject to the, regardless of position or rank under the *National Defence Act*.

Although MP jurisdiction is on military establishments across Canada and throughout the world, any civilian accessing these areas falls under MP jurisdiction and are dealt with in the same manner as any civilian policing agency. If in fact a crime is committed on or in relation to DND property, CFMP have the power to arrest and charge the offender, military or civilian, on or off DND property.

The Canadian Forces Military Police Group is comprised of the following subordinate units.
Land Force Military Police Group (LF MP Gp)
Air Force Military Police Group (AF MP Gp)
Naval Military Police Group (Naval MP Gp)
Military Police Unit Borden (MPU Borden)
Military Police Unit Ottawa (MPU Ottawa)
Special Operations Forces Military Police Unit (SOF MPU)
Military Police Services Group (MP Svcs Gp)
The CF National Investigation Service (CFNIS) and
The CF Military Police Academy (CFMPA).

The Canadian Forces Provost Marshal (CFPM) is the Canadian Forces Military Police Group Commander, supported by the Deputy Commander who manages the day-to-day operations.

The Canadian Forces Military Police Group was established in November 2007 to group Military Police units that did not otherwise belong to the environmental commands (Army, Navy, and Air Force) or operational commands (Canada Command, Canadian Expeditionary Force Command, Canadian Operational Support Command, and Canada Special Operations Forces Command).

Left: MP provides ground security to a CC-177 Globemaster III in Bamako, Mali, 2013. Right: Military Police patrol the CFB Halifax dockyard, 2019. Photo: DND.

On April 1, 2011, the Canadian Forces Military Police Group was restructured to its current establishment, with the environmental and operational commands policing assets now under the full command of the Canadian Forces Military Police Group Commander. The Military Police Security Service and the CF Service Prison and Detention Barracks are now part of the Military Police Services Group, while the CF National Investigation Service and the CF Military Police Academy remain directly under the Canadian Forces Military Police Group structure.

The land force MP group is a Military Police formation with the mandate to provide policing services to the Army. The formation is comprised of a Headquarters (HQ) in Ottawa, and four subordinate units: 1 Military Police Regiment (1 MP Regt) with headquarters (HQ) located in Edmonton, 2 MP Regt with HQ located in Toronto, 3 MP Regt with HQ in Sackville, and 5 MP Regt with HQ in Valcartier.

The Naval MP Group is a Military Police formation with the mandate to provide policing services to the Navy. The formation is comprised of a Headquarters in Ottawa, and two subordinate units: Naval MP Unit

Esquimalt, and Naval MP Unit Halifax.

The Military Police unit Borden has the mandate to provide policing services to Canadian Forces Base Borden/Canadian Forces Training Support Group. The MPU Ottawa is a Military Police unit with the mandate to provide policing services to Canadian Forces Support Unit Ottawa.

The Special Operations Force Military Police unit has a mandate to provide policing services to the Canadian Forces Special Operations Command. The HQ is located in Ottawa.

Military Police Services Group is a Military Police formation with the mandate to provide MP operational support to Canadian Forces operations, be they domestic, continental, or expeditionary. The formation is comprised of a HQ in Ottawa, and three subordinate units: the CF Close Protection Unit located in Ottawa, the Military Police Security Service, and the CF Service Prison and Detention Barracks. The CF Protective Services Unit (CFPSU) is a high-readiness, specialized and expert protective service organization capable of conducting a broad range of special protective missions and tasks at home and abroad in support of defence missions.

The Military Police Security Service (MPSS) is as a unit of the MP Svcs Gp seconded to the Department of Foreign Affairs and International Trade (DFAIT). The role of the MPSS is to provide security services to specific Canadian Foreign Missions and related properties under the direction of the appropriate Head of Mission. These services include protection of classified and administratively controlled material and equipment, Canadian personnel and property. The performance of these duties includes the execution of instructions for the protection of Canadian Foreign Service Missions and their personnel in emergencies.

The MPSS employs over a hundred Military Police personnel. The

MPSS personnel are located at the unit headquarters, in Ottawa, and at 47 Canadian Embassies, High Commissions, or Consulates around the world.

The first embassy to employ MP personnel as Military Security Guards was Beirut in 1976. The MSGU was declared an official unit of the Canadian Forces in 1990 and was officially renamed the Military Police Security Service in 2009.

The Canadian Forces Service Prison and Detention Barracks was originally established as one of several military detention centres, the CFSPDB, located at Canadian Forces Base Edmonton, is now the sole, permanently established military corrections facility remaining in the CF. The roles of the CFSPDB include: to provide imprisonment and detention services for Canadian Forces service detainees, service prisoners and service convicts; to adjust detainees and prisoners to service discipline, and prepare them to resume an effective role in the Canadian Forces; to return prisoners to civilian life, where appropriate, with improved attitude and motivation; and to provide subject matter expertise and guidance in support of Canadian Forces disciplinary programmes and deployed prisoner of war/detainee operations.

Inmates at the Canadian Forces Service Prison and Detention Barracks serve sentences that range from 15–90 days of detention, to sentences of imprisonment up to two years less a day. Inmates serving a sentence of 14 days detention, or less, may serve their sentence at a local Unit Detention Room.

The Canadian Forces National Investigation Service (CFNIS) was established in 1997 with a mandate to investigate serious and sensitive matters related to DND and the Canadian Forces. It performs a function similar to that of a Major Crime unit of the RCMP or large municipal police agency. The CFNIS was created to address lessons learned through our experiences in Somalia, the Former Republic of Yugoslavia and on other difficult deployed missions. The creation of the CFNIS also fulfilled recommendations made by the Dickson and Belzile commissions that the Military Justice System required an investigative agency that was independent of the chain of command.

The CFNIS investigates serious or sensitive service and criminal offences against property, persons, and the Department of National Defence. It has authority and jurisdiction over persons subject to the Code of Service Discipline, wherever Canadian Forces are established or deployed throughout the world, regardless of rank or status.

The Canadian Forces National Investigation Service is commanded by a Commanding Officer who reports directly to the Canadian Forces Provost Marshal. Regardless of the circumstance or environment, the members of the CFNIS remain under command of the Commanding Officer CFNIS. The independence that results from this command relationship enables the CFNIS to conduct thorough investigations without fear of influence from any command element.

The Support Detachment provides specialized investigation services. Such as computer forensics, polygraph services, physical and technical surveillance, and other unconventional services.

While the Canadian Forces National Investigation Service Regional Detachments are co-located with other military bases, the CFNIS personnel work independently from the normal military chain of command. They receive direction and report directly to the CO CFNIS.

The Canadian Forces National Investigation Service has maintained a presence in every major CF deployment since 1997. The CFNIS has repeatedly demonstrated the value of their independence, investigative expertise, and ability to function under the most austere conditions.

The Canadian Forces National Investigation Service is comprised of members of the Military Police. The members are selected for these positions and typically have a broad variety of experience both in Canada and with deployed CF Missions. Section 156 of the National Defence Act and Section 2 of the Criminal Code of Canada define the powers of military police. Their investigative training is on par with any major police agency in Canada. They receive training at the Military Police Academy at CFB Borden, through the Canadian Police College in Ottawa and through a variety of partnerships with domestic police agencies and our military allies.

The members of the Canadian Forces National Investigation Service remain subject to the Military Police Code of Conduct and are subject to oversight by the Military Police Professional Standards organization as well as a Civilian Oversight Panel: The Military Police Complaints Commission.

Requests for Canadian Forces National Investigation Service investigations come through regular military police organizations, but CF members and DND employees can lay complaints, or communicate directly with regional offices or individual CFNIS members.

Charges, through either civilian or military courts, can follow investigation and documentation of complaints that fall within the CFNIS mandate. Investigators receive dedicated, independent advice from military prosecutors throughout the course of their investigations.

Canadian MPs have to be able to fight and patrol in Arctic snow, the Afghan desert, or the domestic urban environment.

The CFNIS works in close cooperation with other military police units and civilian law-enforcement agencies. Other countries with an independent military investigative capability include the United States, United Kingdom, and France.

CFMPA was established 1 April 1999 when the Intelligence Training Company was detached from the former Canadian Forces School of Intelligence and Security. At this time the unit was transformed into a distinct Military Police/Security training establishment.

The primary mission of CFMPA is to provide career and specialist training to Regular and Reserve Force members of the Military Police Branch and security-related training to non-Branch personnel of the Regular and Reserve Forces. CFMPA also provides training to personnel from other government and law enforcement agencies and to foreign nationals under the Military Training Assistance Program.

Operation CALUMET is Canada's support to the Multinational Force and Observers (MFO). The MFO is an independent peacekeeping operation in the Sinai Peninsula. Canada has been in the MFO since September 1, 1985. Approximately 55 Canadian Armed Forces (CAF) members make up Task Force El Gorah. They are based in South Camp and Forward Operating Base North of the MFO, in Egypt. Military police officers have been a part of the Canadian group since March 2015.

From March 2015 to March 2019, they had the police and security duties in the North and South camps of the MFO. This included traffic control, patrols, investigations, inspections, and searches. They also worked to stop crime and run general security within both camps.

As of March 2019, the CAF continues to fill the following positions: MFO Provost Marshal, Force Military Police Unit (FMPU) Sergeant Major and Lead investigator. These key leadership positions provide guidance to the FMPU to ensure that good order, safety and discipline within the MFO are not compromised.

Military Police Unit for Operation IMPACT, at Ali Al Salem Air Base, Kuwait, on May 4, 2020. Operation IMPACT is Canada's training mission in the Middle East. Members of Operation IMPACT's Military Police Unit role are to help protect CAF personnel abroad, conduct police investigations and escort VIPs.

The requirements for Military Police services to domestic and international operations are varied. These services include, among others, crime prevention, patrols, traffic control, police liaison, evidence collection, biometric collection, forensic analysis, investigations, counter-IED analysis, physical security surveys, Information Technology surveys, threat risk assessments, close protection, detainee handling, service custody and training of indigenous forces. In 2020 Canadian MPs have seen deployments overseas and at home aiding civilian police during Covid control missions.[41]

Operation IMPACT is part of Canada's whole-of-government approach to the Middle East. The Canadian Armed Forces (CAF) mission to build the military capabilities of Iraq, Jordan and Lebanon, and set the conditions for their long-term success by enhancing regional stability and promote the rules-based international order. Over the past several months, the regional security environment has shifted considerably due to the COVID-19 global pandemic, but the Canadian Training and Assistance Teams in Jordan and Lebanon have been able to enhance their military and security capacities through mentorship and training. A Military Police Unit with detachments in Kuwait and Iraq provides support to all CAF operations in the region.[42]

Canadian Military Police Dogs

Canada Forces (CF) for such a reasonably large modern Defence Force involved in many United Nations operations and modern conflicts such as Afghanistan has used MWD on a very limited scale. Canada did not use dogs during the Second World war officially however some Regiments had mascots and some prisoner of War

41 https://www.cmpa-apmc.org/
42 https://www.cmpa-apmc.org/news

Camps in Canada often had local guards' own dogs used in a sentry role unofficially.

A dog program was started in May 1963 in preparation of going in a joint nuclear program with the Americans in Europe. The first group of 18 handlers was trained by the Americans (with some German instructors) at Kreuzberg Kaserne in Wiesbaden Germany. Kennel facilities were built at the Canadian Forces base in Zweibrücken Germany for 18 dogs. (20 kennels) The first contingent all came to this base with no scale of issue for this type of operation, so a lot of ingenuity had to be used as well as some midnight shopping and fast talking carried out to get the operation up and running. The second wave of handlers were trained again in Wiesbaden and returned to the base in Baden Germany. They had a much easier time of it though as the Canadian MWD teams were gradually getting a scale drawn up for rations and equipment identified.

In 1967 Canadian dog handlers went to Lahr Germany to set up a dog kennel facility as they were taking over this base from the French Air Farce and closing the Zweibrücken base. In the late summer, early fall, all dogs and handlers from Zweibrücken were housed and operational in Lahr. In 1970 Lahr was phased out of nuclear weapons and some of the dogs and handlers were moved to Baden. The dog program was completely phased out in 1973 when Canada ceased to have operational nuclear weapons in Europe.

The nuclear capability roll was in joint custody (Canada/USA) and that NATO had a big say in the operation and management of the MWD program. Canada used German Veterinarian who did routine physicals once a month or as need be if a need for urgent medical treatment. Any major medical problems were handled by US Vets in Wiesbaden.

As Canadian MWD handlers rotated through the program to replace those returning to Canada some worked with the Americans in a training capacity and assisting the resident veterinarian. At Wiesbaden there were kennel facilities for 568 dogs. All buying of dogs for the program for Europe and SE Asia (Viet Nam) was done from this facility as well as the training of handlers for these venues.

It should be noted that these were sentry dogs who were trained to alert and if need be, attack when released. They were always worked on lease in times of poor visibility (dense fog and hours of darkness) as in some cases the area was heavily wooded and of course darkness on the perimeters.

For many subsequent years Canada has not employed dogs in the Military, however the CF has returned to a former proven tool from the past and re-implemented a canine program. A focus on proven policing programs showed that once established, canine units prove to be one of the most efficient and cost-effective police resources available and they continue to be one of the fastest growing tools for militaries and police. Alas, they are down to one dog, and it is unknown if a canine program will continue.

Today Canadian Military Police routinely work within the civilian criminal and military justice systems and are recognized as peace officers in the Criminal Code of Canada. With over 1,250 full-time members, they form one of the largest police forces in Canada. Military Police provide around-the-clock service to the military community in Canada or around the world, including areas of armed conflict or natural disaster. In 2020 the Military Police Branch of the Canadian Armed Forces celebrates its 80th anniversary. The Branch can trace its unbroken lineage back to the creation of the Canadian Provost Corps on 15 June 1940, which has been adopted as its official birth date.

EUROPE

Germany

German MPs are involved in all NATO operations and are one of the first options of choice when deploying German troops overseas.

The history of Germany's military police dates back for many hundreds of years, certainly to at least the 14th Century. A Royal edict of 1312 apparently also gave the then 'Marshall' absolute legal power which made him a figure that generated more fear than all the devils and witches that seemed to be an obsession of these times. The roots of the modern military police in the German armed forces however can be traced back to the 'Proffoss' of the 16th Century, and the creation of the *Reitendes Feldjägerkorps* by Friedrich II in 1740. The title 'Profos' (Provost) entered German usage from France in the 16th Century with a later document from the 17th Century describing the Provosts tasks as punishing disobedient soldiers and dealing with "freebooters, robbers, vagabonds and those who carried forbidden weapons" and what were termed 'lazy rogues'.

The Provost became, in effect, judge jury and executioner in one, with his mounted Knights as his 'enforcers'. The primary duties of the *Reitendes Feldjägerkorps* were to control traffic, to carry important messages, and to protect members of the royal family. Springing from this band was the *Feldjägerkorps zu Fuss* (1741) which served both in the Napoleonic Wars and the Franco-Prussian War.

Initially, it would be various Cavalry-type units which would carry out military police-type duties, but in the early 19th Century, Prussia created a distinct military police formation and in 1813 the '*Gendarmerie im Felde*' (literally Field-Police or 'Police in the Field') was formed.

In 1850, the Prussian-Austrian conflict threatened to open over the Prussian rite of passage to Hesse-Cassel, troops were mobilized including the military police was formed for about 1 year. When the war broke out between Austria and France and 1866 in the German civil war. In July 1870 came the order for mobilization for the war against France. Two military police detachments took to the field after a victorious war ended in 1871, they were demobilized.

These early incarnations of the *Feldgendarmerie* came into being on an ad-hoc basis through mobilizations of the German army as a whole, most notably in the wars of 1866 and 1870.

Several German states had their own military police forces, most were raised only during conflict and then disbanded immediately afterwards. In 1816 the Bavarian state established Military field police known as gendarmerie. In Peace they garrisoned Bavaria. Cash in transit and high-ranking personalities were also accompanied by the gendarmerie.

An edict stated that *in times of war in enemy territory our troops had to be kept under control by gendarmerie patrolling on horseback the occupied territory.*

With the outbreak of WW1, 33 *Feldgendarmerie* units each of around 60 NCOs and men were formed with drafts of men from the civil Gendarmerie and other suitable soldiers, again many of whom were experienced Cavalry NCOs. By the end of WW1, a total of 115 *Feldgendarmerie* units plus five cavalry squadrons for special missions had been formed. In total by the end of WW1, around one third of military policemen had been drawn from the Gendarmerie, and the remainder drafted from other Army formations, predominantly the Cavalry.

The most iconic symbol of the Feldgendarmerie was the Gorget plate or Ringkragen worn around the neck when on duty, as these WWI soldiers display.

After World War I during the period from 1919 to 1939 all military police units were disbanded, and no police units existed in the post-war Weimar Republic. Garrison areas were patrolled by regular soldiers functioning as military police.

Prior to mobilisation before the outbreak of World War Two, Germany had no full time permanent Military Police force. When MPs were needed units were created by temporarily assigning personnel from the civilian Police. On mobilisation, these same experienced policemen were called upon to create the first of the Army's *Feldgendarmerie* units. Initially, they wore their original Police uniforms, and were identified as Military Police, solely by the wear of an armband on the left sleeve. It was in green cloth with the legend *Feldgendarmerie* machine woven in yellow rayon thread.

The *Feldgendarmerie* was formed on the mobilisation of the German Army in 1939. Its members were, in the main, experienced former civil policemen. The start of WWII opened the floodgates for numerous police formations to form and characterized the sometimes-chaotic hierarchy of the German armed forces. Again, civilian police units would form the basis of many Army units as well as a number of Waffen SS divisions too which at least two well-known commanders Sepp Dietrich and Kurt

Meyer of the 12th SS were serving as policemen prior to joining the military.

The German Military Police *Feldgendarmerie* above all others have received an infamous reputation during the Second World War for brutality. Some deserved some not. Military police from this era were deemed as particularly harsh, given almost extraordinary powers to apprehend and punish in a summary manner deserter. Punishment of the type most often involving execution. During the campaign on the Eastern Front during WWII desertion was not uncommon and extraordinary circumstances called for extraordinary measures.

The Feldgendarmerie received full infantry training and were given extensive police powers training subjects included Criminal code, general and special police powers, reporting duties, passport and identification law, weapons drill, self-defence techniques, criminal police methodology, and general administration. Courses lasted one year, and failure rates were high in 1935 only 89 soldiers graduated from an initial intake of 219 candidates.

One of the reasons the German Military Police had such a reputation for brutality was in part confusion of who did what in association to their name. Simply put, there were multiple Police units under the Nazi Regime many of them were military units.

Even at wars beginning some Police units were transferred wholesale into the Military one example was in the 1930s, Herman Goring, after having observed Soviet airborne infantry manoeuvres, became committed to the creation of Germany's airborne infantry. He ordered the formation of a specialist police unit in 1933, devoted to protecting Nazi party officials. The unit carried out conventional police duties for the next two years, but in 1935, Göring transformed it into Germany's first dedicated airborne regiment. The unit was incorporated into the newly formed Luftwaffe later that year and training commenced. Göring also ordered that a group of volunteers be drawn for parachute training. These volunteers would form a cadre for a future *Fallschirmtruppe* ('parachute troops'). In January 1936, 600 men and officers formed a *Jäger* and an engineer company. Likewise, throughout the war the Luftwaffe had its own Military Police formats including units within the *Fallschirmtruppe*.

To add to confusion the civilian regular uniformed Police (*Ordnungspolizei* or *Orpo*) which was established as the centralized organization uniting the municipal, city, and rural uniformed forces and eventually embraced virtually all of the Third Reich's law-enforcement and emergency response organizations had to release men to the military. In 1939 15,000 members of the *Ordnungspolizei* were drafted and placed together with artillery and signals units transferred from the Army to form the Polizei Division. These men were not enrolled in the SS and remained policemen, retaining their Orpo rank structure and insignia. The Division was equipped largely with captured Czech materiel and underwent military training with spells on security duties in Poland. Within the Division staff there was a motorcycle troop of Military Police Troops.

In January 1942, the division was moved to the Volkhov River sector, and on 24 February it was transferred to the Waffen-SS; its personnel changing their Police insignia to that of the SS. Becoming the *SS-Polizei Division* in 1943 remained in Greece until August 1944 before being recalled to face the advancing Red Army at Belgrade. It was again involved in heavy fighting and suffered many losses. By September 1944, much reduced SS-Polizei Division of about half its strength was forced back to Pomerania where it saw more action attempting to hold the Soviets. Moved to Danzig, it was trapped by the Red Army and after a dire battle it was shipped across the Hela Peninsula after a brief rest, what remained of the SS-Polizei Division fought its way across the Elbe river, surrendering to the Americans.

To add further confusion between 1939 and 1945, the Ordnungspolizei also maintained separate military formations, independent of the main police offices within Germany. The first such formations were the Police Battalions (*SS-Polizei-Bataillone*), for various auxiliary duties outside of Germany, including anti-partisan operations and support of combat troops. Specific duties varied widely from unit to unit from one year to another. Generally, the SS Polizei units were not directly involved in combat. Some Police Battalions were primarily focused on traditional security roles of an occupying force while others were directly involved in atrocities. Due to their insignia many people incorrectly thought these were Military Police formations.

Feldgendarmerie units were generally given occupation duties in territories directly under the control of the Wehrmacht. The duties policing the areas behind the front lines, ranged from straightforward traffic control and population control to suppression and execution of partisans and the apprehension of enemy stragglers. When combat units moved forward out of a region, the *Feldgendarmerie* role would formally end as control was then transferred to the control of the SS.

But by 1943 as the tide of war changed for Nazi Germany, the *Feldgendarmerie* were given the task to maintain discipline in the Wehrmacht. Many ordinary soldiers deemed to be deserters were summarily executed by *Feldgendarmerie* units. The *Feldgendarmerie* also administered the *Penal Battalion* which were Wehrmacht punishment units created for soldiers convicted by court martial, the sentence deferred instead. They wore the same uniform and gorget as their Army counterparts but had an addition cuff title indicating they were military police. Generally, they conducted the same policing role, such as controlling rear areas, but they also conducted counter-insurgency operations against Jews, partisans and those deemed to be 'enemies of the Reich'.

These SS units had a severe reputation for being strict enforcers of military law. Nicknamed *Kopf Jäger* 'Head Hunters', they also tracked down and punished those deemed to be deserters.

In January 1944 as the Red Army began to advance on the Eastern Front, the power of the *Feldgendarmerie* was superseded by the creation of the *Feldjägerkorps.*

Answering only to the German High Command O.K.H its three regiments were founded to maintain discipline and military cohesion in all branches of the Wehrmacht. *Feldjägers* were recruited from decorated, battle-hardened officers and NCOs. They had the military authority of the OKW to arrest and execute officers and soldiers from either the Wehrmacht or the SS for desertion, defeatism, and other duty violations.

A battalion was subdivided into smaller-sized *Truppen* which were attached to each division or corps. A *Gruppe*, a section sized unit, were then assigned to specific field or local commands. *Feldgendarmerie* sections would also be temporarily assigned to special operations, such as anti-partisan duties. A typical *Truppe* attached to an Infantry or Panzer Division would have up to three officers, 41 NCO's and 20 enlisted men. They would operate with motorcycles and motorcycle combinations which were armed with MG34 machine guns, Field cars such as the Horch 4x4 and 3-ton Opel truck and a small number of armoured vehicles as a means of transport.

At the end of the Second World War, the skills of the German Military Police were quickly appreciated by the British and Americans who used several entire companies of fully armed Feldgendarmes (military police) and Feldjäger (special military police) as auxiliaries to assist their own hard-pressed police formations. In the chaotic conditions of the immediate post war period the experienced manpower provided by these troops was of great help to the occupying authorities.

Elements of the *Feldjäger* were the last German troops to lay down their arms after WW2. When troops in the South of Germany surrendered to the Americans, the US forces realised that with huge numbers of German troops surrendered or attempting to surrender, the *Feldjäger* could be of great use in maintaining order. General Kesselring agreed to put his *Feldjäger* at the disposal of the US Army; and for several weeks after the cease-fire the *Feldjäger* – fully armed and equipped – remained on duty.

Their tasks included overseeing German adherence to the cease-fire; maintaining order among German troops; maintaining order in occupied areas; controlling traffic; and collecting individual stragglers. The *Feldjäger* finally laid down their arms as late as 23 June 1946.

On rare occasions, allied troops found themselves being directed by German MP even though they had surrendered, and the allies had won. This caused the odd problem or two and the odd allied soldier was punished for disobeying the German MP directions as they had come from the allied Command staff. Areas like 'out of bounds' and 'no parking' were common tasks allocated to the German MP and the holding areas for surrendered German troops.

Feldgendarmerie der Luftwaffe – Air Force

During the early part of the war, there was no need for the Luftwaffe to maintain its own force of Military Police, its field units being very limited in size. With the creation of a considerable number of Luftwaffe Field Divisions and of course the massive *Fallschirmpanzerkorps* Hermann Göring, the Luftwaffe decided that its units should field their own military police.

The organisation, structure and size of the Luftwaffe Feldgendarmerie units followed the army model. Initially, the *Feldgendarmerie* of the Luftwaffe was considered as part of the Divisional Supply and Support elements and wore the light blue *Waffenfarbe* associated with these troops.

The Navy Police *Marineküstenpolizei* (MKP) was formed in 1940 with a draft of personnel from the *Wasserschutzpolizei* (WSP), much in the same way as the Feldgendarmerie was originally formed with drafts of personnel from the civil *Gendarmerie.* The subjugation of a number of countries (Norway, France etc) with extensive coastlines meant that a naval equivalent of the Military Police would be needed. Its areas of responsibility included the security of rivers and river mouths, protection of fisheries, controlling order and discipline of personnel onboard ships whilst in port and also of naval land units in coastal areas. It was a very small branch however, and generally consisted of a small number of NCOs attached to the office of the local harbour commander (*Hafenkommandant*) rather than based in independent units with their own command structure like the *Feldgendarmerie.* Members of the WSP who transferred to the MKP adopted naval ranks but with the suffix 'der MKP', thus a police *Oberwachtmeister* would become a Feldwebel der MKP. Again, as with the *Feldgendarmerie* where for an interim period, former civil police personnel could be seen wearing a mixture of both Gendarmerie and Army clothing, in the newly formed MKP many former WSP personnel wore their original police uniforms, often with the addition of the Kriegsmarine.

The Feldjäger is the military police of the Bundeswehr, literally meaning field huntsmen or field Jäger, has a long tradition and dates back to the mid-17th century. Their emblem is the historic Order of the Black Eagle.

Today the *Feldjäger* are the Military Police of the German Federal Armed Forces and are responsible for all three services – Army, Air Force and Navy. The *Feldjäger* have nine battalions in peacetime of which eight are under command and control of Divisions and Military District Commands, and one is under command of the Ministry of Defence. In times of defence, one additional battalion of reservists will be activated for each division or military district.

Military police in the modern Bundeswehr are not called *Feldgendarmerie.* In fact, the original intent was to call the MPs *Militärpolizei,* literally military police. However, state officials protested as the law enforcement function in the brand-new German constitution had been given primarily to the states, not the federation. The word *Polizei* (Police) was jealously guarded by the states, so the Federal Defence Ministry searched for a new designation and adopted *Feldjäger* which was a traditional Prussian regiment with some military police type functions.

Shortly after the Bundeswehr (or German Federal Defence Force) was founded in 1955, the Bundeswehr Military Police and Headquarters Service School was established in Sonthofen at a castle-like installation in the picturesque Bavarian Alps. In 2001, the German Department of Defence decided to move the school from Sonthofen to Hannover.

But it was clear from the outset that this move would involve more than just a simple relocation; the leaders agreed that the move represented an opportunity to build the most modern school in the German Bundeswehr. The German government spent about 90 million Euros (currently the equivalent of about 135 million U.S. dollars) to achieve that goal. By 2009 the school was finally equipped with the latest in classroom technology and holds realistic military police and headquarters staff training across the full spectrum of operations. In addition, the school leads the way in developing advanced distance learning programs and courses. All military police career courses (ranging from advanced individual training to pre-command courses covering all *Feldjägertruppe* (German Military Police Corps) missions are taught here.

Military Police duties are, in peacetime are performed by 34 Military Police stations (MP Companies) employed in area covering operations that cover the entire of Germany. Each company is assigned an area approximately 120km x 120km on average. The peacetime strength of an MP station totals 81 soldiers. These MP stations operate around the clock in the same way as the civilian police. The military police force has authority over all branches of the German armed forces and defence administration. It is their task to police of the army they carryout investigations, security missions and traffic and discipline enforcement. For any foreign missions which the Bundeswehr is involved in the Military regularly make use of military police units to support multinational units.

In the performance of security tasks Military Police be used to prevent crimes against the army and to eliminate unlawful disturbance of the functions of the armed forces. They can also be charged with the protection of allied forces. Military Police are also used in passenger and accompanying protection of vulnerable members of the armed forces. Hedging operations centres in command posts of large organizations Apart from maintaining and restoring the discipline and military order. The Military Police are the central point of contact for all soldiers who need help.

One task as a MP is the monitoring and control of military traffic. This is in line with the statutory regulations of the European Union to monitor compliance with the provisions concerning the transport of dangerous goods by road. They work closely with the police. The inspections are intended for road safety and the prevention of threats the armed forces. This includes the following tasks:

- Identify and explore roads
- Recording of traffic accidents with Bundeswehr involvement
- Military traffic controls
- Accompany and control of military and high-volume transports hazardous
- Participate in planning and monitoring the military road
- Military control of dangerous goods
- Setting up a Vehicle Check Points
- Regulate the traffic in the voltage and defence case, as may be necessary for the fulfillment of the defence contract

Military Law and Order Operations with the aim to supervise, maintain and restore military law and order by performing, MP patrols, train and railway patrols, AWOL and POW operations, support at military courts and support of legal authorities, recording and investigating traffic accidents, employment during military ceremonies. Military police missions abroad under the auspices of the United Nations include not only the monitoring of behaviour of German soldiers in the areas of deployment but MPs also work closely with local authorities and agencies with security responsibilities, this includes the investigation and prosecution of crime. To perform these tasks, military police soldiers conduct numerous house searches to find illegal weapons and, monitor checkpoints and explore and identify streets and spaces to be used in convoy protection tasks. They take on tasks such as 'people and escort' for people at risk such as counsel staff officers.

In support of the military police force operations, they can call on the support of specially trained service dog teams.

Service dogs were first trained as protection dogs and then were specialized as sniffers to search for explosives and narcotics. Currently German Military Working Dogs are deployed in all German overseas operations. Post WWII German troops until recent times had not had many International tours of duty due to public opinion. Nowadays the Bundeswehr area regular partner in United Nations lead operations. Military Dog handlers are in Afghanistan and the Balkans assisting in Mine detection, Explosive Detection, and general assistance to Police operations.

German Military Police Dog Handler as part of KFOR. MWDs in Kosovo are used as Base security, General Police support functions including Riot Control, Tracking offenders and general deterrence and specialist roles such as EOD.

Belgian

Operation Vigilant Guardian was launched in January 2015. This mission is part of the fight against terrorism on Belgian territory. Military Police are amongst a larger defence force that provides support to the Federal Police to monitor and secure sensitive sites.

The Military Police Group *Groupe Police Militaire* performs military police duties on behalf of all four components of the Belgian military. The group is headed by a Colonel and has over 188 members in five MP detachments. Until 1995, the Belgian Gendarmerie was, besides its civilian policing tasks, responsible for Military Police duties. The Military Police Group staff is located in the Queen Elizabeth Barracks in Brussels various detachment cover the regions of the country.[43]

The Military Police force carries out the following missions: Maintenance of order and discipline: Consists of monitoring, maintaining and, if necessary, re-establishing discipline and military order. This also involves controlling stragglers and refugees in times of war and guarding and escorting prisoners of war. Traffic regulation: Includes traffic monitoring and regulation to ensure the flow of military movements in accordance with plans. This includes route reconnaissance and marking, convoy and oversize vehicle escort and river crossing control. Traffic accident investigations is also a part of the job. Security missions: Prevents and deters any threat to or attack against the personnel and property of the armed forces. The Military Police force protects, for example, the Palace of the Nation and the Parliaments and Councils of the Regions and the Communities, headquarters, and classified conferences. MPs also provide VIP motorcycle escorts and honour guards, perform close protection missions, and escort classified documents and money transports.[44]

In 2003, duties relating to refugees and deserters in wartime were transferred from the then disbanded Gendarmerie to the MPs. Members of the former 4 and 6 MP Companies were merged into the new MP Group, along with some Gendarmes previously assigned MP-related duties.

Belgian MPs are identified by black armbands with the letter's MP in white block letters, worn on the left arm and Red brevets.

---

43 Before and during World War Two, personnel from the Belgian Gendarmerie performed military police duties for the Belgian Army personnel that escaped to Great Britain.

44 https://www.mil.be/armycomp/unit

MPs carryout many missions that generally people associate with Special Forces, such as high-risk entry or hostage rescue. Image supplied by MPPG.

The Belgian Military Police has taken part in multinational peacekeeping missions such as Afghanistan, Kosovo, and the Congo. Image supplied by MPPG.

Military Police conduct VIP security to Belgium's heads of state visiting dignitaries and high-ranking defence staff. Image supplied by MPPG.

During missions abroad, Military Police contribute to the restoration of peace. Together with their international partners, they also ensure the stability of the environment in which they are deployed. Currently units are carrying out missions in Mali, Niger, and Afghanistan. These missions take place within the framework of NATO or the United Nations. On a daily basis, Military Police carry out surveillance and security missions in strategic places in support of the Civilian Police which contributes to the security of the population in the event of an internal threat such as terrorist attacks.

The canine MP units is relatively new to Belgium. The first four-legged MP was called *Layka*, she performed so well the in Jun 2020, the two MP Dog Teams have finished their training. the Commander of the Military Police Group stated the Military Police Group will welcome eight more dogs over the next few years. The tasks of the MP dog vary considerably: control of buildings, ordinary interventions and detection of people, support to soldiers on mission. A dog handler can only start the course with a dog after having successfully completed his MP training.

The Belgian Military Police consists of two different units, the Military Police Group (MP Group) and the Military Detachment Palace of the Nation (MDPN). The latter was established to ensure the surveillance of the Palace of the Nation and the Cabinet and the Official Residence of the Prime Minister under the direction of the Military Commander of the Palace of the Nation.

Within the Military Police (MP Group), since 2019 the Force Provost Marshal (FPM) has coordinated the planning of MP activities, develops the MP support matrix and coordinates MP activities with national and international commands and organisations. The FPM is responsible for the formatting and review of all MP-related concepts, doctrines, guidelines He can also investigate complaints against the Military Police and deal with sensitive files at the request of military authorities.

There are several detachments of Military Police throughout the country each MP detachment is responsible within their zone for the maintenance of the order and discipline of the military and security around the respective military domains. In addition, they provide support for military traffic control and road control on which the military vehicles are used. In the case of incidents involving the military, they intervene to carry out the first findings. In addition to their regional MP assignments, the respective MP detachment must, also support the MP groups national assignments.

The Belgian Military Police must always operate within the framework of Belgian law, the MP contributes to the overall security by implementing various security functions such as general security, physical security, close security of persons (VIP) and the security of information, equipment, funds, and sensitive arms transports escorts. The Modis operandi of the Military Police is taking all necessary measures and carrying out all actions necessary to prevent or avert any threat or attack against protected persons and property. Since 2017, the MP Group has developed a K9 MP project that should result in 8 full-fledged Dog Handler MP teams by 2021.

Although the Military Police is not regarded as a police service of public power, in carrying out its duties abroad, in the course of a crime or a misconduct, it will take all precautionary measures which impose itself and shall inform the competent judicial authorities, as well as the competent hierarchical chief thereof. In general, if the military escapes the control of their direct chiefs or at the request of the latter, the Military Police may support the commander's action and contribute to the surveillance, retention and, if necessary, restoration of order and discipline,

Even though MPs do not have authority in civilian situations due to the complex traffic situation in Belgium with multiple NATO gatherings and numerous VIP visits the MP transport unit are heavily engaged in public traffic control.

Since 2003, the MP Group has participated in numerous foreign missions, including: NATO mission in Afghanistan (Kabul, Baghram, Kunduz and Mazar-e-Sharif), the UN mission in Lebanon (Naqoura, Shama, Tibnin and At-Tiri), the EUTM Mission in Central African Republic, the UN Mission in Mali, the UN mission in Republic Democratique de Congo, NATO missions in Greece, Poland, Lithuania, and Estonia. The MP Group is also asked externally to provide courses to the Gendarmerie in Tunisia and Niger, to MPs of the Czech Republic and Ukraine and also provides instructional specialists to the NATO training institution in Madrid.[45]

45 Information supplied by the Belgian Military Police Association 2020.

Like many MP units across the world Belgium have established Military working Dogs.

UNITED KINGDOM

The Royal Military Police

RMP conducts CPP of a high-ranking officer.

Britain's Royal Military Police claims to have a tradition of service to the Crown and Nation longer than any regiment or corps with an antecedence stretching back to at least 1241, when Henry II appointed one William of Cassingham as a Military 'Sergeant of the Peace'. He and his Under-Provosts were the ancestors of the modern Royal Military Police.

As the Provost Marshal's office gradually assumed more and more duties of a policing nature within the Army, he was provided with State-paid troops, referred to in Henry VIII's day as Provost Companies the term still used today to describe a formed body of Military Police.

The first recorded Provost Marshal in English history of whom there is a personal record, is one Sir Henry Guldeford (or Guylford) appointed in 1511. The Provost Marshal was responsible for maintaining discipline within the English armies together with the King's personal security. He

was also described as the 'first and greatest gaoler of the Army'.

Britain's first standing military police force came into being in 1813, when the Duke of York, Commander-in-Chief of the British Army proposed the formation of a Staff Corps of Cavalry to be attached to the Adjutant-General. Commanding Officers of Cavalry Regiments were then ordered to submit the names of soldiers to serve in this new unit, detachments of which were allotted to each division of the Peninsular Army, similar to today's Provost Companies, which allocated to every manoeuvre and logistic brigade.

Wellington asked for a Provost Marshal to be appointed to hang looters and by the end of the Peninsular War the Provost Marshal controlled 24 Assistant Provost Marshals. The Assistants were also authorised to hang offenders and eventually each division had its own Assistant Provost Marshal. Until a uniform was approved, members of the Staff Corps of Cavalry were identified by a red scarf tied around the right shoulder of their original uniform, which while some consider this to have been the origin of the famous 'Red Cap' of the Royal Military Police and its forebears, it was certainly the most likely precursor of the 'MP' armband (and now the Tactical Recognition Flash), which identifies the modern Military Policeman or Policewoman.

Although disbanded in 1814 at the end of the Peninsular War, following Napoleon's defeat at the battle of Waterloo the Duke of Wellington re-formed the Staff Corps of Cavalry to police the occupying British Army in France. Later, in the Crimean War, a Mounted Staff Corps comprised of almost 100 troopers from the Police Constabulary of Ireland, with some recruited from the Metropolitan Police, was established to prevent the theft of supplies and to maintain discipline in camps. This 'Corps' was disbanded with the cessation of hostilities.

On the 1st of August 1882, a sister Corps to the MMP was formed for special service in Egypt – the Military Foot Police (MFP). The Foot Police were recruited entirely from men recalled to the Colours, who had served with the Metropolitan Police Force. The MFP were authorised as a permanent Corps on 2nd July 1885, with an establishment of 1 sergeant-major; 13 sergeants; 17 corporals; and 59 privates. The end of the century saw the Military Police with a strength of just over 300, with detachments at all the garrison towns in United Kingdom, permanent detachments in Cairo and Malta, and an honourable active service record in Egypt and Sudan, and in South Africa during the Second Anglo-Boer War (1899–1902) where the majority of both the MMP and MFP would serve eventually.[46]

The First World War (1914–18) The total Military Police strength at the outbreak of war was 508 all ranks – immediately increased to 761 with the recall of all reservists, many of whom had been civil policemen. By 1918, Corps strength was over 25,000 all ranks and battalions of famous regiments such as the Honourable Artillery Company, the Oxfordshire and Buckinghamshire Light Infantry and the King's Own Yorkshire Light Infantry were used to supplement provost duties. The Military Police served in all major theatres of war and in addition to Provost there were also Traffic Control Companies, Docks Police, and a Special Investigation Branch. During the First World War the Military Police began to be employed on operational tasks: route control; host-nation liaison; and straggler control tasks they still perform today.

In 1927, the MMP and the MFP were amalgamated to form the Corps of Military Police (CMP) with an initial strength of 508 all ranks, the same as the combined strength of the two units before the war in 1914.

In the 1930s CMP was radically reorganised: in 1935 Provost companies and sections were formed with fixed establishments, in 1937, a Field Security Wing (the 'Green Hats') was formed, although it was transferred to a new Intelligence Corps in 1940, some 800 Automobile Association scouts joined the Supplementary reserve of the CMP between 1938 and the outbreak of war; and again in 1938 direct enlistment from civilian life into CMP was allowed for the first time.

During the Second World War, the Corps expanded from its pre-war peacetime establishment of 4,121 to over 50,000 by 1943, seeing service in all theatres starting with the British Expeditionary Force to France in 1940. The Military Police were present on every battlefront and in every country where British Troops fought or were stationed, earning a reputation for bravery and devotion to duty, as reflected in the WW2 Roll of Honour, which list 912 names, and the 229 operational awards

---

46 https://rhqrmp.org/rmp_history.html

which were won. Military Police carried out difficult and valuable work, establishing the tradition of being 'first in, last out' on the battlefield. The Military Police were present on every battlefront and in every country where British troops fought or were stationed. The ever-smart Redcaps directing traffic often under fire and where they were increasingly seen as a symbol of steadfastness and of fair play, contributing to maintaining law and order, goodwill, and morale among the soldiers of the United Kingdom, the Dominions and the Empire, as well as the citizens of war-torn Europe and the Far East.

Paratroop MPs

The 1st Airborne Provost Company was formed in 1942, and despite the 'police' role, the men had to through the same rigorous training as other paras in order to earn their wings. Following brief service in Tunisia, the men were dropped into Sicily; as part of the invasion force, they quickly reverted to soldiers rather than policemen as the landing was heavily opposed the men jumping from the gliders and attacking the enemy. After the surrender of Italy, the men resumed their MP duties, policing the red-light districts and bars.

During the battle of Arnhem many people do not release the role of the Military Police there. No.1 section took over the police station in Arnhem to house German prisoners. As the Germans attacked the small band of men were left to defend the police station. Surrounded by German troops who were unaware of their presence they lay low, looking for opportunity to link up with the rest of the British force. On 19th September the Germans realised they held the police station and assaulted it, capturing the men inside, although three managed to escape. At the Ginkel Heath drop zone No.2 section had a similar role of watching over captured Germans. However, they were forced to retreat to Oosterbeek. The men were fighting for survival, and all of them were either killed, wounded, or captured. No.3 section landed at Wolfheze and were involved in the defence of the Hartenstein hotel, along with No.4 section (attached to Divisional HQ) until they withdrew.

Many specialist units were also raised, and it was in 1940 that 19 volunteers from the Metropolitan Police Criminal Investigation Department were drafted to form a Special Investigation Branch (SIB) to serve with the BEF. The SIB RMP task then, as now, was the investigation of serious crime involving military personnel or Service interests. In 1941, the Vulnerable Points Wing (the 'Blue Hats') was formed with men of lower physical categories to patrol and guard key installations and infrastructure. In 1942, the Auxiliary Territorial Service for women formed a Provost Section. Later, a Ports Provost Wing (the 'White Hats'), with 9 companies was formed for service overseas.

At war's end, General Sir Myles Dempsey KCB KBE DSO MC paid the following tribute: *"The Military Policeman became such a well-known figure on every road to the battlefield that his presence became taken for granted. Few soldiers as they hurried over a bridge which was a regular target for the enemy, gave much thought to the man whose duty it was to stand there for hours on end, directing the traffic and ensuring its rapid passage".*

In 1946 in recognition of its outstanding war record His Majesty King George VI graciously granted the 'Royal' prefix to the Corps of Royal Military Police (RMP) in recognition of its outstanding wartime record. CRMP was chosen to avoid confusion with the Royal Canadian Mounted Police or RCMP.

Since 1945, the RMP has served in every theatre and campaign undertaken by the British Army since 1945 including the Falkland Islands, the Gulf, Rhodesia, Rwanda, Bosnia, East Timor, and Kosovo. For example, during 1952–1960 in Kenya the British Army was conducting operations during the Mau Mau Uprising. An RMP unit was based in Nairobi.

Several RMP units were involved in the Aden Emergency (1964–1967) the 24 Brigade Provost Unit RMP (Falaise Barracks, Little Aden),Port Security Force RMP (based at HMS Sheba until 1967),Joint Services Police (Army Navy and Airforce) based at HQ P&SS Steamer Point until 1967. During the troubles in Northern Ireland which started in 1969, four members of the RMP have lost their lives.

The United Nations Peacekeeping Force in Cyprus (UNFICYP) was established in 1964 to prevent a recurrence of fighting between the Greek Cypriots and Turkish Cypriots and to contribute to the maintenance and restoration of law and order and a return to normal conditions. After the 1974 Greek coup-d'état and the Turkish invasion of Cyprus, the UN Security Council extended and expanded the mission to prevent that Cyprus dispute turning into war.

RMP have served with the Force Military Police Unit (FMPU), from the outset. The FMPU is 1 of only 2 multi-national subunits within UNFICYP, the other being the Mobile Force Reserve. The FMPU is commanded by a RMP major who is both OC FMPU and Provost Marshal. 7 other members of the RMP form the spine of the 25 strong unit. Other contributing nationalities are Argentina, Hungary, and Slovakia. The British contribution to FMPU is now the longest enduring operational commitment for RMP.

The Falkland Islands War

In 1991, British forces as part of US-led coalition forces invaded Kuwait and Southern Iraq as part of Operation Desert Storm. RMP units involved were the 203 Provost Company RMP - 7th and 4th Armoured Brigades (1 (British) Armoured Division). This unit was a composite of various RMP units from the UK and Germany plus the 174 Provost Company RMP – Force Maintenance Area. The RMP suffered one fatality.

During 1994 the British Army deployed units to Bosnia as part of the

United Nations Protection Force, which was later superseded by IFOR and then SFOR. These included 111 Provost Company Coy RMP – Force Military Police Unit (FMPU) support. Elements of 24 Airmobile Brigade Provost Unit (156 Provost Company, based in Colchester, England) provided the British Force Military Police Unit (FMPU) for UNPROFOR (UK Operation Grapple 5) between Oct 1994 and April 1995.115 Provost Company RMP provided the British Force Military Police Unit (FMPU) for UNPROFOR (UK Operation Grapple 7) between August and December 1995 and then reverted to its unit designation of 4th (UK) Armoured Brigade Provost Unit RMP as part of IFOR until April 1996. RMP personnel have also been involved in the European Union Force which took over in 2004.

On 12 June 1999, the UK sent 19,000 troops into Kosovo as part of KFOR. Lead units of the force, included Royal Engineers and RMP, had to deal with booby traps in road tunnels before the Force could advance into Kosovo. In many cases they have been the first to arrive and last to leave, and currently there are over 150 RMP personnel deployed on operations across the globe in the Balkans, Iraq, and in Afghanistan.

Today the Royal Military Police comprises over 1800 Regular and Territorial Personnel they RMP exist in order to deploy, they are distinct from their civilian counterparts as they have unique operational tasks that have no equivalence in civil society. The RMP deploy as part of the field army, both at home and overseas, in support of the full spectrum of national and multi-national, joint, multi-agency conflict, conflict prevention and post conflict operations. On joining the RMP everyone undertakes General Police Duties (GPD). GPD provide Garrison Policing, provide a 24 hr manned Police Station in larger garrisons, and support the military on operations.

Whilst other agencies can and do investigate crime committed by or against members of the Defence Department, it is the Service Police alone who have the unique capability to deliver the full range of policing functions, throughout the spectrum of conflict, at home and abroad. The policing capability required by the Army in the UK, Germany and other overseas Stations is provided by the RMP.

The RMP powers of arrest (in addition to those conferred on every civilian by civil and common law) are established within the Army Act of 1955, and can be exercised anywhere in the world, as service personnel are subject to English criminal law wherever they serve. The Act provides that a person subject to Military law, which includes all civil offences (Sect 70), found committing or alleged to have committed an offence against the Act may be arrested by a Provost Officer, or a person exercising authority under a Provost Officer. It also allows for a civilian to whom the act applies to be arrested and processed by the military police. These powers are extended to all service personnel by the Naval Discipline Act and the Air Force Act.

The RMP do not charge offenders, nor do they have responsibility for the prosecution process, they do not detain in custody and are not constables. When the RMP investigates a case, a series of reports will be produced to keep the chain of command informed of the process, allowing them to take any necessary action.

The policing skills utilised by the RMP in Station maintain the skills required on operations. Whilst the environment the RMP work within may change dramatically on deployment, the policing skills required are the same. There is an inextricable linkage between policing operations at home and on deployment, and all skills must be immediately transferable.

The investigations conducted on operations must be the same high standard as those conducted at home producing professionally complied case reports that show due regard to the laws of evidence and the Service Police Codes of practice. In high intensity conflict and on peace support operations the investigative procedure is the same; it is only the location that changes.

The Special Investigation Branch (SIB) of the RMP deploy along with the regular RMP companies across the globe, providing specialist investigative support to the Field Army. In high intensity conflict they continue to police, investigating a myriad of offences that range from murder to fratricide. The high-profile nature of these investigations often draws great media and governmental attention. The SIB like all members of the Army work in all environments.

In addition to investigative support the RMP also have a distinct operational role to undertake. This is to regulate, to protect and to inform. The RMP on operations are enablers as they regulate the battlefield and move the Army forward and rearwards, in war and in support operations.

Whilst some RMP companies are attached to the fighting Brigades others work in the complicated rear and divisional areas. The RMP are required to make sure the Army gets to where it needs to be.

Inextricably linked to this is the information provided to commanders. The RMP will advise on the use of routes, the movement of stragglers and refugees, and the movement of high-profile Prisoners of War. They will also provide protection for high profile Military Commanders (Close Protection).

In post conflict operations the RMP role often expands, and they have historically found themselves as the only police force within a foreign country. In recent years (Kosovo and Iraq) they have found themselves as the only police force, required to police a foreign nation, and assist in the regeneration of the local Police Force.

The RMP role in a society where Law and Order has collapsed involves more than investigations, it requires the RMP to establish and train the Indigenous Police and in some cases completely rebuild a Police Force. Whilst the International community's provide civilian police officers to undertake this role in the latter stages, it is the RMP who are the first police on the ground post conflict. It is the RMP who have the soldierly and policing skills required to undertake this in very hostile situations. In Iraq the RMP are still heavily involved in this complex role.

In 2006 the Battle of Majar al-Kabir as it would be known was the result of a growing distrust between the British military and the local people of the south-eastern region of Iraq over house searches and confiscation of personal weapons that locals felt were crucial for their self-protection.

Despite a signed agreement between local people and British forces stating that the British would not enter the town, the 1st Battalion

Parachute Regiment started patrolling Majar al-Kabir on 24 June 2003 the day after the agreement was signed by both sides. The British thought the agreement was to stop the weapons searches that involved going into the houses of local inhabitants.

At first, angry locals stoned the Paras whilst being encouraged by anti-British rhetoric being chanted from microphones on minarets in the town. The Paras used rubber bullets to try and bring the situation under control, followed by conflicted reports about who fired the first live shots; this led to street battles. Six Royal Military Police were in the police station at Majar al-Kabir. In March 2006 an armed mob descended on the police station and the soldiers were brutally murdered.[47] The six RMP were killed by an angry mob of up to 600 people whilst maintaining a defensive position within the police station. They did not fire a single round before they were killed. An inquest into the Red Caps' killings in March 2006 found that the men had been given antiquated radios and inadequate ammunition.

Royal Marines & Naval Police

Elite Royal Marine Commando MPs and Royal Naval Police still work side by side, especially during garrison duty.

The Royal Marines Police is responsible for providing garrison policing services; law enforcement and crime prevention as well as general security advice to the command and includes a SIB section for the investigation of serious crime.

---

47 Last Round: The Red Caps, the Paras and the Battle of Majar. Cassell. 2006

The Royal Marines Police is a unit of the Royal Navy Police. The RM Police is responsible for providing garrison policing services – law enforcement and crime prevention as well as general security advice to the command and includes a Special Investigation Branch (SIB) section for the investigation of serious crime. Perhaps one of the world's most warrior elite policing units as each RM Police personnel are recruited from within the trained strength of the Royal Marine Commandos. Following completion of a first posting to a rifle troop in a Commando.

They are posted to the Headquarters support unit of 3 Commando Brigade.

In military operations, the Royal Marines Police Troop provide military police support for all phases of operations and peacekeeping operations including co-ordinating vehicle movements out of the beachhead, marking the main supply routes and providing convoy escorts. It also conducts general police duties and provides close protection for the Brigade Commander.

Personnel are eligible to undertake the close protection courses run by the Royal Military Police. Royal Marines Police personnel are also attached to other units. In 2009 the RM Police was absorbed into the Royal Navy Police, although it still exists as a distinct unit.

The Royal Navy has always, in one way or another, had the need to maintain order and discipline. When at sea, historically, the Captain was the king's representative, his rule was kept by the First Lieutenant who was assisted by a person known as the 'Ship's Marshal', who was supported by a number of Ship's Corporals. Ship's Marshals were abolished and replaced by the Master At Arms (M.A.A.) rate, which was introduced in about 1699. A tradition that continues right up to the present day. The RNP have jurisdiction over members of the Royal Navy subject to service discipline, as well as having reciprocal powers to deal with service personnel of the other two branches of the Armed Forces.[48]

The Royal Navy Police was known as the Royal Navy Regulating Branch until 2007, when the service was renamed the Royal Navy Police in a change brought about by the Armed Forces Act 2006. Members are, however, still known

48 https://www.legislation.gov.uk/uksi/2007/1861/contents/made

as 'Regulators'. Up until 2018 the Royal Navy Police recruited internally, from within the service, requiring candidates to have reached the trained strength in their initial branch, before serving for four years and qualifying for advancement to Leading Seaman rank within that branch. However, from 2018 it has been possible to apply directly as a civilian. The trade badge for regulators is a crown (worn in a wreath by masters-at-arms).

When undertaking General Police Duties (GPD), regulators will wear either combat uniform or senior rates (petty officer and above) wearing long-sleeved shirt and tie, and ratings wearing short sleeve white shirt with open neck and black trousers. They will also wear a black stab vest, or high-visibility equipment vest or both, or hi-visibility jacket marked with 'RN POLICE' or 'ROYAL NAVY POLICE' and a dark-blue beret.

RAF Police

RAF Police wearing MP flash during international operations for ease of recognition.

Air force police or sometimes known as 'Air police' refers to certain units that are part of a country's Air Force that performs the same role as Army military police. In addition to law enforcement some Air Force Police units have a force protection and airfield defence role such as in the UK, New Zealand, the United States and Australia.

Duties can include canine patrols of bases, VIP protection of aircrews and dignitaries flying on their assets, the guarding of facilities and base entrances, defence of an airfield in the light Infantry role. Many have investigation units (SIB) for the investigation of major crimes on bases.

In the RAF Police, you will protect personnel and vital operational equipment, both in the UK and on operations overseas, from criminal, terrorist, and other threats. At the beginning of your career, you will carry out both unarmed and armed patrol duties and react to a wide range of policing incidents where you will often be expected to use your own initiative to resolve sometimes stressful situations. There will also be early opportunities to become an RAF Police dog handler.

Later on, you may be employed on special (criminal) investigations or provide specialist security advice and assistance. Other opportunities exist to undertake activities such as close protection (bodyguard) duties protecting senior military officers; providing forensic support to investigations; and working closely with other police and security organisations. RAF Police are expected to have a high level of integrity and be physically robust enough to deal with the challenge of police duties.

Following completion of your recruit training at RAF Halton in Buckinghamshire, you will start a 23-week specialist training course at the Defence Police College at Southwick Park in Hampshire. Here you'll learn the essential skills needed to do your job, including your duties and responsibilities, criminal law, how to conduct investigations, interview techniques, driver training, arrest and restraint techniques and enhanced military skills and weapon training. You'll also have a week of adventurous training.

RAF Police non-commissioned officers and warrant officers are noticeable by their white-topped caps (giving rise to their nickname of *Snowdrops*), which they have worn since 1945, and by black and red flashes worn below their rank slides (known as Mars Bars). RAF Police commissioned officers wear the standard peaked cap of all Royal Air Force officers, although they wear 'Mars Bars' in the same way as RAFP NCOs. Unlike their British Army colleagues in the Royal Military Police, RAFP personnel do not wear a distinctive red beret when wearing camouflaged uniform, although they do wear the same 'MP' badges, the internationally recognized symbol for MP personnel.

Originally established in 2001 to provide support to two simultaneous military policing operations (one warlike, one non-warlike) it comprised two regular Squadrons and one Auxiliary Squadron. Since this time, it has trained and been resourced to provide a function similar to that of an RMP Provost Support unit. However, in 2006/2007 a decision was made to reduce the establishment to one regular squadron and one reserve squadron.

TPW's first major operational deployment was in Iraq 2003, where

No. 1 Sqn, TPW operated as a full sub-unit under command of CO 5 RMP, as part of the Joint Force Logistics component and was the first full MP sub-unit to deploy to the theatre. OC 1 Sqn was Sqn Ldr Girvan Stewart, his 2i/c was Flt Lt Gavin Outteridge, and they were joined by the WgWO, WO 'Tosh' Thomas, Wg QM FS Kev Huggins, and FS Fred Dawson as FS Ops.

The primary role of 1 Sqn during major conflict operations was Policing on the military road-route network linking the air and Sea Ports in Kuwait to the front line. This included route reconnaissance and signing, escort of troops and supplies along the road network, traffic policing and counter-terrorist patrolling. In 2003, the entire UK joint force was moved into and out of theatre with no own force's fatalities in 1 Sqn's Area of Responsibility.

Additional duties undertaken within the standard MP roles of regulation, protection and information included Air Transport Security (ATSy) duties at coalition airheads, enforcement of discipline e.g., patrolling areas out of bounds to UK forces in Kuwait, and close protection for UK Air rank officers. TPW now performs similar tasks in both Iraq and Afghanistan.

In 2006 the majority of TPW's deployed commitment was taken over by the Auxiliary Squadron, who completed a 11-month mobilization in July 2007.

The Royal Air Force Police also has its own Special Investigation Branch (SIB) for the investigation of serious crime. This is effectively the RAF's version of a civilian police CIB who, like them, operate in plain clothes. This is known as the Specialist Police Wing (SPW) and is split into four geographical regions covering the United Kingdom and Germany. This section of the RAFP is also responsible for forensic investigation through the RAF's own Forensic Science Flight.

The RAFP also has a tactical, deployable squadron, known as the tactical provost wing (TPW). Their major role is forward policing and 'line of communication policing' (LoCP) in conflict zones. TPW was heavily involved in operation telic and are still heavily involved in operations in Afghanistan.

A Tongan marine, teams up with a RAF Police colleague, to provide security as part of Camp Bastion's Force Protection Wing. Photo: Sergeant Corrine Buxton RAF, Crown Copyright/MOD 2011.

Some RAFP members are also trained in close protection (CP) and carry out CP duties wherever required, ensuring the safety of VIPs and other dignitaries in hostile territories.

The RAFP operates a large Police Dogs section, with detachments at many RAF stations. These dogs are referred to as Air Dog followed by their name, (Air Dog Rex, for example). RAF Police dogs and their handlers currently support overseas operations in theatres such as Iraq & Afghanistan, in both patrol and specialist search roles. As well as their usual German Shepherd dogs, more commonly known as Alsatians, used for the 'attack' role, Labradors and Spaniels are well utilised for their expertise as 'sniffer' dogs for drugs and explosives.

With the recent establishment of the Military Provost Guard Service (MPGS) on RAF stations to undertake armed guarding and security tasks and the introduction of the RAF Force Protection Organisation in 2003, the RAF Police have been subjected to large-scale reductions in personnel and a major realignment in the way the branch supports global RAF tactical operations and joint military manoeuvres. In April 2005 as part of *Project Darwin*, the former RAF Provost & Security Services (P&SS), located at RAF Henlow in Bedfordshire, was renamed as the Headquarters Provost Marshal (RAF) (HQPM) (RAF). The Air Commodore relinquished his office as Provost Marshal (PM(RAF) to a provost Group Captain before taking up his new appointment as Assistant Chief of Staff Force Protection, Commandant General RAF Regiment &

Air Officer RAF Police. The change at the top was brought about to allow the Air Commodore to concentrate on directing the wider aspects of Force Protection, whilst allowing the Group Captain to independently manage all police investigatory functions. While the Air Commodore remains the figurehead of the branch in his capacity as Air Officer RAF Police, he has no remit to investigate or influence criminal or security matters. Although the new PM(RAF) is tasked to report through the Air Commodore to the Air-Officer-Commanding No 2 Group (HQ Air Command) in respect of normal police and security matters, he retains direct access to the Chief of Air Staff (CAS) in respect of investigative affairs. As part of the restructuring, the Specialist Police Wing (SPW), under the command of a wing commander was formed, to take over the functions previously carried by P&SS and comprises three single-capability squadrons; RAF Special Investigation Branch (SIB), Counter-Intelligence Squadron (CIS) and Security Services Squadron (SSS). The SSS in its entirety is based at RAF Henlow with HQPM (RAF), along with the nucleus and command structure of the SIB and CIS, while elements of expertise from the SIB and CIS are established at three dispersed units:

HMS *Caledonia* (Scotland), RAF Cranwell (Lincoln) and RAF Halton (Buckinghamshire), to provide prompt professional specialist support to RAF unit commanders. Plans are currently in hand to divide RAF Police resources within the UK into three wings: General Police Wing Five squadrons, Specialist Police Wing three squadrons and Tactical Police Wing three squadrons. The establishment of the RAF Police stands at approximately 200 commissioned officers, and 1,500 other ranks.

Since November 2005, all RAF Police training has been carried out at the Defence Police College at Southwick Park in Hampshire, an establishment shared with the Royal Naval Provost Branch and the Army's Royal Military Police. In addition to initial police training for new recruits and provost officers, specialist post graduate courses are offered in respect of Air Transport Security training, Special Investigation training, Crime Scene Forensic training, Counter-Intelligence training, and Computer Security training. Other specialist police and security training courses, such as the Home Office Detective training course, continue to be conducted at other service or civil police establishments around the UK, while basic and specialist training courses for dog handlers are conducted at the Defence Animal Centre, Melton Mowbray.[49]

No 1 (Tactical) Police Sqn based at Royal Air Force Honington provide the Royal Air Force with a highly trained combat policeman able to provide policing and security in all environments. They are able to deploy alongside their RAF Regiment counterparts providing them protection in dealing with captured personnel and handling evidence. Alternatively, they are equally as happy deploying to provide security to RAF aircraft around the globe and providing policing and security to RAF ceremonial events.[50]

In 2018 the RAF Police as part of a force protection unit deployed a training team in Nigeria for a few weeks to the Nigerian Air Force, teaching them various specialist skills and how to deal with various situations. The RAF Police tuition included the vulnerability of Air Power; the complexity of the environment; the external and internal threats to an airbase; and how to mitigate those threats through a range of active defensive, tactical Policing and Security measures developing a range of skills that can be employed, from conflict management and stop and search principals. The second phase enabled the Nigerian Air Force Police to learn about the protection of their critical assets and the role of Air Transport Security, both aspects being key to enabling successful and effective Air Operations. RAF Police personnel also serve with joint

---

49 Stephen R. Davies, *RAF Police Operations in Europe 1918–2005: An Illustrated History of the RAF Police Since 1918*, 2007.

50 http://www.rafpa.com/news.html

units overseas such as Gibraltar, Cyprus, and the Falkland Islands, and on exchanges all over the world.

Military Working Dogs are great force multipliers, one dog is worth 30 men patrolling open spaces and can detect intruders up to a kilometre away.

In 2005 the British Royal Air Force Police had been working with dogs for 60 years forming a very special and successful relationship.

Chances are, if you told anyone you were in the RAF Police, they would invariably want to know all about your dog, assuming that every member of the branch is issued with one on appointment; such is their notoriety.

In 1942, at the height of World War II, Lieutenant Colonel Baldwin formed the Ministry of Aircraft Production Guard Dog School (MAPGDS) at Woodfold near Gloucester, turning out professionally trained RAF dog handlers which in turn released hundreds of men for war duties who had previously been employed as guards. In 1944 the MAPGDS was absorbed by the RAF Police and re-titled as the RAF Police Dog Training School.

In 1949, the RAF Police Dog Demonstration Team appeared for the first time at the Royal Tournament in London and became an instant public success. In 1957 the first annual RAF Police Dog Championship Trials were held at Netheravon. In 1969 the Dog Demonstration Team covered 8,000 miles around the USA and Canada giving 65 public performances in 23 cities and became a favourite at every venue. The RAF began training dogs to detect illicit drugs in 1970 and later trained dogs to detect firearms and explosives. Soon after, HM Customs & Excise began using RAF Police drug detection dogs against smugglers. In 1991, in line with defence reviews, RAF Police dog training merged with the Royal Army Veterinary Corps at Melton Mowbray and the Defence Animal Centre was formed.

To some, the life of a RAF Police dog handler may seem glamorous, but in reality, the job demands a lot. The men and women who volunteer, do so because they love the challenge of working with dogs even though a considerable amount of their time is given up to the training and welfare of their charges. In 60 years, the Royal Air Force Police have earned a glowing reputation both at home and abroad for their high standard of training dog teams and for their highly professional use of dogs for patrol duties as well as in specialist roles.[51]

During part of the Afghanistan deployment a crack squad of specially trained RAF Police took charge of the UK forces' dog unit at the Contingency Operating Base in Basra. In a first for the Royal Air Force, the Henlow-based team will assume control of the dog section, providing crucial support to ground troops. This role is usually an army responsibility. This comes back to joint training and interoperation abilities allowing such moves. As part of their role the RAF Police team provided force protection dogs to control crowds during operations, and sniffer dogs to locate arms caches and take part in roadside check points to combat illegal gun and drug running in some areas of southern Iraq. It is the first time that RAF Police dog handlers have been responsible for the joint Army/RAF dog unit on operations in Iraq to protect the Contingency Operating Base.

They will take over responsibility from the Royal Army Veterinary Corps (RAVC), whom they have been supporting since 2006. In addition to the patrol teams, specialist dog teams from the Theatre Military Working Dogs Support Unit search vehicles at control of entry points for concealed weapons and explosives. They also provided protection to Army teams mentoring the Iraqi Army and Department of Border Enforcement.

Flight Lieutenant Karim Coslett, Officer Commanding TMWDSU, said: "My handlers and I are relishing the challenges that lie ahead and are confident that this new and exciting capability for the RAF will play an important part of force protection of current and future air and land operations for years to come."

---

51 Steve Davis. *RAF Police Dogs on Patrol: An Illustrated History of the Deployment of Dogs by the Royal Air Force,* Paperback, 2006

The teams are currently undertaking a full range of pre-deployment training and will exercise alongside their RAVC colleagues and members of the Army and RAF Regiment.

Squadron Leader Jeff Brock, HQ RAF Police, said:

"The reorganisation of the RAF Police under Project Darwin 2 in April 2008 has meant that, for the first time, the RAF Police has had greater flexibility to manage its resources more efficiently in support of the homeland task.

"As a consequence, we are able to deploy whole Formed Units such as TMWDSU rather than individual augmentees in support of deployed operations."

The work undertaken by RAF Police dogs in theatre is invaluable and they are considered a key asset for the Commander. Providing specialist arms explosive search capability and Force Protection, they act as a Force Multiplier, allowing the Commander greater flexibility with their personnel whilst delivering maximum effect on the ground. In some situations the MWD team can do the same amount of work as ten personnel.

RAF Police Dogs provide an essential Force Protection component to military operations worldwide. Since 1945, RAF Police Dogs have been employed in the protection of RAF Airfields and Military assets, the recovery of evidence, public order, used in the detection of drugs and on anti-terrorist operations. On an operational front, RAF Police dogs have served or are currently serving in: Ghan, Misera, Singapore, Aden, Hong Kong, Northern Ireland, Falkland Islands, Bosnia, Kosovo, Diego Garcia, Gibraltar, Cyprus, Kuwait, Saudi Arabia, Iraq, and Afghanistan.

Most people that may have come into contact with a RAF Police Dog have done so while it was patrolling one of the UKs Military Airfields. Signs displaying Warnings that they are on patrol can be seen on perimeter fences. There is of course much more to the RAF Police Dog Section than the image of an aggressive guard dog protecting Britain's Frontline fighter Squadrons. Even though the Defence against sabotage has always been a vital part of their work. As in all deterrent claims which by virtue of their success they cannot be given a true figure the RAF Police Dogs must have saved the UK Defence budget hundreds of Millions of pounds over the years.

In March 2009 In a first for the Royal Air Force, they have assumed control of the dog section, providing crucial support to ground troops in Iraq. They will take over responsibility from the Royal Army Veterinary Corps (RAVC), whom they have been supporting since 2006.

Royal Air Force Police and patrol attack dog played a vital part in protecting air assets, personnel, and the air base at Basrah International Airport.

Because of the quarantine restrictions in the UK, MWD have to spend six months in Cyprus, after every tour of duty. The RAF Police Dog handlers wore Army Military Police MP arm flashes for ease of Coalition force recognition. An RAF Police dog handler, working with a German Shepherd force protection dog in Afghanistan.

After six years of UK presence some of the last British troops that left Iraqi soil were four-legged, from the Royal Air Force who handed over to their American canine counterparts. Military working dogs played an important security role during the drawdown of UK troops from Basra, they have been at the centre of the action, sniffing out explosives and pounding paws on patrol.

NORDIC COUNTRIES

Finland

Finish SRT unit conduct high risk entry techniques to practice hostage rescue missions.

The *Sotilaspoliisi* ('Soldier Police') are the military police of the Finnish Defence Forces. Their emblem is a black armband on the left shoulder with the letter's 'SP' in white. SPs have no power over civilians except inside military zones and installations. However, SP's can be used as temporary manpower when the regular police are undermanned. For example, during the 2005 Helsinki athletics championships military police conscripts were placed all along the running tracks through the city to prevent the large numbers of spectators from obstructing the runners. In these cases, they are given a limited amount of power over civilians, as the regular police needed the extra support to handle the large influx of tourists. As military police conscripts are trained with basic police techniques, they are suitable for usage in instances such as these in Finland. In times of peace their tasks include the protection of individuals, their warlike operations include seeking out and destroying hostile special-purpose forces as well as handling prisoners of war.

Military police are taught the skills and knowledge, which may well be compared to the police or security guard training. The aim of training is to provide knowledge and skills, capable of producing high-quality personnel and military police units during peacetime.

As training progresses, the military police serve as security officers in the garrisons. However the aim is to produce a fighter.

Military Police dog handlers are selected for the brigade operational requirements. Military Police dog handlers require to be of good physical and mental condition. This role is regarded as elite within the MPs.

The Military Police School instructs officer candidates and regular military police courses and conducts research and development of military police training and equipment as instructed by the General Staff. Military police courses vary as many soldiers are conscripts Officer training is 330 days and for enlisted military police is 285 days.

Finnish MP's provide security for installations, but they also do personal security, anti-partisan ops, checkpoints, and counter strikes behind enemy lines. They are trained for crisis/war time employment, guarding/policing the garrisons is sort of a secondary duty. They are more like a large SWAT team than ordinary police. Maybe they are a sort of an elite if you compare them to some other nations where most MPs are actually just the police force within the army, and you have special detachments of MP's doing this SWAT type role. But in Finland as a conscript force there is a lot of stuff that ordinary soldiers do that would be considered elite in another army due to their small size their soldiers require to be multi skilled.

Finnish Air Force Police SPs Guard an F18.

Denmark

MPs are frequently identified by having both long arm weapons and pistols.

The military police (MP) in Denmark are police units within the armed forces branches. Each branch has its own MP corps, although they often work together and wear similar insignias.

MP personnel typically wear either specific display dress uniforms with white MP shoulder markings or the branch-common daily battle dress uniforms with a red beret.

MP personnel generally do not have any legal authority towards civilians in non-military places, but only towards military personnel as towards everyone on military installations (also publicly accessible places such as the Holmen naval base in Copenhagen), in the buildings housing the Ministry of Defence, royal palaces (like Amalienborg Palace) and parts of Christiansborg Palace. On some occasions, MP personnel can provide support to the civilian police for certain tasks but will only have slightly more legal authority than civilians, similar to the police home guard.

The modern era of Danish MPs started on the 4th of May 1945, when Field Marshall B. L. Montgomery issued the decree namely the decree about the unconditional surrender of the German forces. Nothing happened immediately with the Danish Armed Forces, they had been closed down during the German occupation, but soon the Armed Forces were back on their feet again. By the 18th of February 1947 the Chief Command issued an order to all Danish forces to detach personal to form a Military Police force of 80 men, some officers, and non-commissioned officers.

The demands made on the picked men, were quite tough, both concerning political observants, personal qualities, manner, and appearance.

In 1947 His Majesty King Frederik IX signed a law, which authorized the Ministry of War to issue an order to the Armed Forces to form an occupying force for duty in foreign countries. The Danish Military Police were dispatched to North Germany, at Lundtofte airport, and were quartered in a camp of huts their first of many overseas deployments.

Danish armed forces have been deployed to the streets of the capital to guard potential terrorist targets, as well as the German border, to aid police with their duties. It is the first use of troops in Copenhagen since WWII.

On Friday a total of 160 soldiers, bearing automatic weapons and special insignia, were sent to assist police at the German border and to watch locations in the capital vulnerable to terror attacks, the local media reported. These include several Jewish institutions, such as the Great Synagogue in central Copenhagen and the Israeli embassy, as Jews observe the Yom Kippur holiday.

The Swiss Military Police

MPs in Switzerland are among the few fulltime professional soldiers in this predominately conscript army. Image supplied by Swiss consulate.

Switzerland's land-locked situation coupled with its long tradition of neutrality has left it with unique military problems. As Norway, Denmark and Holland learned to their cost in World War Two, neutrality in itself is not enough to protect a small country against its more powerful neighbours if the latter regard invasion as strategically necessary. Despite having no natural enemies, Switzerland with its commanding position in Southern Europe might be considered a legitimate target in any future war and for this reason has always maintained a highly effective Army. The Army and Air Corps, which are incorporated into a single force concept, consist of 1,500 regular servicemen supported by 18,500 recruits called up in each February and July to undertake 17 weeks basic training. Thereafter the recruits transfer to the Reserve and are liable to report for three weeks refresher training between the ages of 20 and 32; for a further fortnight between the ages of 33 and 42; and for a final 7 days' training over a two-year period between the ages of 43 and 50. Reserves keep their weapons at home to facilitate mobilisation in an emergency, as a direct result of which a staggering 625,000 soldiers, including 45,000 officers, 110,000 NCOs and 3,000 women auxiliaries can be called to arms within 48 hours of a crisis. However, dedicated the Reserves, they are only able to fight within their own parameters.

The military police of Switzerland are organised in four military police zones. For example, MP Zone 2 handles troops in cantons: Basel city, Basel landscape, Aargau, Solothurn, and Berne (the yellow area of the map). In addition, they take over the representation of other military police zones, if they are not in operation. MPs can be tasked to support the cantonal police forces in situations where civilian police resources are insufficient, such as catastrophes or large-scale unrest. In this case, the military serves under cantonal civilian responsibility and command.

Swiss military police uniforms are based on those of the Swiss armed forces. This includes Service Dress and camouflage dress. Military police wear distinctive collar badges on both the Service Dress uniforms and on their camouflage dress. A badge is also worn on their berets. A badge also appears to be worn on the arms of the MP. A distinctive band is worn around the helmets of military police, and it is also believed that a white brassard with a black letter 'P' is worn. Unlike regular army personnel, military policemen also have a grey uniform in order to provide distinct identification.

VIP protection is a vital role. All MPs in Swiss army are full-time professionals. Photo supplied by Swiss consulate.

The Military Police is responsible for law enforcement on military property and for all incidents where military personnel or equipment is involved. Furthermore, the military police provides protection of Swiss representatives abroad and is in part responsible for the guarding of embassies and foreign VIPs in Switzerland, as well as maintaining personal security for members of the Swiss Federal Council. In addition, the Swiss Explosive Ordnance Disposal Centre is a branch of the MP for the disposal of Unexploded Ordnance and also participates in various operations around the world.

The professional MP units comprise 758 officers and are divided into four Regions, each consisting of two companies and additional groups specialised on criminal investigations and training. In addition, there are two militia MP battalions with a head count of roughly 2000 men.

The MP are uniquely, armed with SIG Pro side arms and SIG 553 assault rifles (compared to the standard issue SIG P220 pistol and SIG 550 assault rifle). Professional MP units drive patrol cars similar to those of the civilian police, but also use Piranha and Duro APCs.

Swiss MPs in charge

In May of this year, Lieutenant Colonel Stéphane Theimer took over the function of Force Provost Marshal of the Kosovo Force, making him the highest military policeman of the multinational force under NATO leadership in Kosovo. For several years now, the position of Force Provost Marshal has been alternately filled by representatives from Switzerland and Austria every six months.

The military police in the operational area consists of women and men from different nations: from Switzerland, Austria, and Poland (as with the IMP), as well as from the USA, Slovenia, and Italy. The responsibility of the military police does not end at the borders of Kosovo, but also extends to other areas in which KFOR soldiers move. "North Macedonia and Greece are important logistical supply routes for KFOR. Accordingly, we have to be ready to intervene in these areas, if necessary," explains Lieutenant Colonel Theimer.

The responsibility of the military police does not end at the borders of Kosovo, but also extends to other areas in which KFOR soldiers move. "North Macedonia and Greece are important logistical supply routes for KFOR. Accordingly, we have to be ready to intervene in these areas, if necessary," explains Lieutenant Colonel Theimer.

Norwegian

MPs in Norway during wartime operations would play a vital role in organizing militia groups to defend roadways, bridges and passes.

The Norwegian Military Police was established on 10th September 1940 in Dumfries, Scotland during the WWII. During the establishment of the Norwegian Army in Great Britain a Military Police Platoon was organized within the Army Brigade in 1942. Small Military Police units were also established at Norwegian Navy and Air Force units around Great Britain. A bigger Military Police unit was established in 'Little Norway' Canada where the Air Force had their flight academy during the WWII.

The Norwegian Military Police did not see any combat action during WWII but had their hands full when policing during the liberation of Norway especially in Oslo, the Norwegian capital.

During May 1945 the Allied Command created a joint command with American, British, Norwegian MP and civilian police in Oslo which was operational until August 1945. By 1946 the Army Military Police had established themselves around bases and garrisons around the country. The same year the Air Force and the Navy established their first MP units on Norwegian soil.

The Norwegian Military Police was almost closed down during 1947, but Norway's participation in guarding Occupied Germany stopped these plans. The first MP Company (Military Police Company 471) followed the army brigade to Germany in September 1947 and served together with different brigade contingents until 1952 with Military Police Company 522 as the last one. After the withdrawal from Germany in 1952 the Norwegian armed forces established Brigade North in Northern Norway. Within the Brigade a Military Police Platoon served there until the creation of Division 6 and the establishment of the Military Police Battalion in 1995, which is still operational.

After the Second World War, Norwegian Military Police have served in different conflicts around the world under either UN or NATO command. This has included Egypt, Lebanon, Congo, Somalia, Saudi Arabia, and the Balkans. Norwegian Military Police have also been stationed in Belgium, France, Italy, and other countries.

In Norway, military police are service members of the Norwegian Army, Royal Norwegian Navy or Royal Norwegian Air Force. Since about 2002, all are trained at Sessvollmoen Camp. MPs in the Army are assigned to the Military Police Battalion, located at Bardufoss, Troms county. The first battalion commander and Provost Marshal of 6 division Norwegian Army was Maj

M Langvik, the current Battalion commander is Lieutenant Colonel Jan Henry Norvalls. The battalion consists of approximately 50 officers and NCOs, and 150 privates and corporals. Norwegian MPs first go through a six-month selection/educational period, before being assigned to the battalion or to regimental duties with other units for the remainder of their twelve-month service. Norwegian MPs do not have authority over civilians, except on or in the vicinity of military installations, vehicles, or other property or under martial law. They do have authority over military personnel, including in certain circumstances reservists, anywhere, including when such personnel are off duty.

The *Heimevernet* ('Home Guard') also has MPs in its ranks MP-tjeneste (Military Police service). Usually each District (regiment) has one or two platoons, consisting exclusively of former regular or conscript military police personnel.

Norwegian MPs wear a red beret and a red lanyard around the left shoulder extending to the left front pocket. Only personnel currently serving as MPs are allowed to wear this. When on official duty, they also wear the MP armband, which is black with 'MP' in red letters. It was previously worn on the right shoulder, but is now worn on the left shoulder, following NATO practice. They can also wear white webbing, or a number of items for special duties, like high visibility vests for traffic duty, or as mounted personnel while performing motorcycle escort for the Royal Family or their official guests, etc. The Norwegian Military Police do not have their own uniform insignia and use the transport wheel as part of the Transport and Logistics Corps. The internationally known crossed 'Harpers Ferry' pistols of the US Army Military Police Corps have however been in use since 1940 as the patch of the Norwegian Military police, though in different layouts.

Army canine units *Hundetjenesten* (K9 unit) are also assigned to the MP battalion, but the personnel in such units are not necessarily MPs. Such personnel do not hold military police authority, and do not wear the MP insignia.

The Norwegian Military Police have the authority to conduct investigation of breaches of both military and civilian law, and in general must maintain law and order inside the armed forces. They have no other powers over civilians than ordinary members of the public, except inside, or in the immediate vicinity of military installations. More serious cases, like narcotics, are handed over to civilian police for investigation.

The task of the Home Guard is to protect the local population and the essential functions of society. This includes helping to maintain Norwegian sovereignty, national crisis management, the reception of allied reinforcements and contributing to the safety and security of society.

Many of these tasks are mostly relevant in the coastal zone and can best be carried out through integrated Home Guard operations in which the land, naval and air force Home Guard work together. The Inspector General of the Home Guard is responsible for force production to man the Home Guard's war structure, making use of the territorial district staffs, schools, and competence centres for this purpose.

In Norway today the Military Police are small, but effective units serving at army garrisons, naval bases, or Air Forces Bases around the country. Downsizing the Norwegian armed forces is changing the Military Police as well, and there are ongoing efforts to restructure the Military Police's peace support units and combat support units. For the time being the Norwegian Military Police (Army) wartime strength are: 3 battalions, 6 independent companies and 3 independent platoons. Air Force and Navy MPs have up to platoon strength in their units. National Guard MP has up to company strength. The Norwegian Military Police wartime personnel strength is:

Army Military Police (Wartime) 2500 officers and soldiers
Air Force Military Police (Wartime) 240 officers and soldiers
Navy Military Police (Wartime) 120 officers and soldiers
National Guard Military Police (Wartime) 850 officers and soldiers
Total Wartime strength: 3710 officers and soldiers.

Norwegian Military Police soldiers and officers are trained at three different MP schools: army, navy, and air force. Norwegian personnel also attend the UN Military Police Course which are conducted at the Danish Army Logistics School at Aalborg, Denmark.

A Norwegian military police officer stands guard during a live-fire capabilities demonstration as part of exercise Cold Response.

Military Police Rangers *Militärpolisjägarna*: The Swedish Army's Military Police (MP) Rangers are a relatively new unit. These specially selected MPs are trained to conduct counter SOF missions near Swedish Army installations. The main task of the military police rangers (MP-rangers) is to hunt down and neutralize the threat of enemy sabotage forces. This task resembles the one that the Air force Rangers and the Marine's Base Security have with the exception that the MP-rangers do not have an assigned base or area of operation but can be sent anywhere they are needed at the moment.

The MP-rangers are trained like the 'ordinary' military police, and have the same authority, but they are more extensively trained in regular combat and search while the 'ordinary' military police handle more police business within the military forces and anti-sabotage at a specific place. All military police are highly trained in law and police authority and of its practical use. Much is, for obvious reasons, kept secret about the MP-rangers and not much about their equipment, weapons, or organization have been released. Known, though,

is that the MP-rangers use the world's best tracking device, the dog. A MP-ranger squad consist of eight soldiers and two dogs: Squad chief, an assistant squad chief, two dog handlers, two marksman, one medic and one radio operator.

Swedish Armed Forces Military Police Unit

As a neutral country Sweden maintains a very active and well-equipped force. The MPs are no exception with a large percentage of them being fulltime servicemen as opposed to conscripts.

Sweden's stated policy of neutrality does not guarantee its immunity from the scourge of international terrorism. To deal with this potential threat the Swedish government maintains a variety of specialized, and high classified military and paramilitary units. Nordic countries have combined in recent times for joint exercises and operations. The most important job of the military police is to maintain order and safety within this Nordic Battle Group. There are five different nationalities included in this unit, which may seem like a challenge, but thanks to comprehensive training and a good mix of people the work has progressed without friction.[52]

In modern times the Swedish Army the Dragoons Battalion of the Lifeguards are the only organizational unit in Sweden that trains military

---

52 https://www.forsvarsmakten.se/en/news/2010/11/the-military-police-a-multinational-unit/

police and Military Police Rangers. The Dragoons Battalion have roots that go back as far as 1523, making it one of the world's oldest military units still in service and the only Horse mounted unit still retained by the Swedish Army. Horses are used for ceremonial purposes only, most often when the dragoons take part in the changing of the guards at The Royal Castle in Stockholm. The Lifeguards also provides dog teams the Swedish Armed Forces Dog Instruction Centre raises and trains sniffer dogs to find weapons and explosives and MP guard dogs for security. Along with their handlers, they are trained for rapid response missions, both nationally and internationally.

However, Sweden has a custom of provosts that dates back to Gustavus Adolphus in 1611 whose infantry march to battle with two chaplains, a provost, and his hangman. Left is an image from 1813 of a provost with his symbol of authority and punishment a Roman style fasces.

The Military Police Rangers are a new unit within the Swedish Army. These specially trained Military Police units conduct counter SOF missions near Swedish Army installations. They have received training in tracking enemy SOF units and countering any potential assault that they may be conducting.

The military police battalion must be able to operate throughout Sweden. In 2019 the battalion reconnoitred and become acquainted with the strategically important area around Sundsvall and Härnösand in lower Norrland. The soldiers trained together with the company's dog group and learned where, when and how they can use the dogs for various tasks to be solved. Among other things, they learn different methods for how to follow a dangerous person and patrolled and practiced searching for perpetrators through dense forests.

The military police carry out operations both nationally and

Swedish and Norwegian military police conduct joint exercises and patrols.

internationally. The military police have complete police powers within the Armed Forces. The concept within the Armed Forces is defined geographically, materially and personnel.

Military police are in high demand, both in Sweden and abroad, and can therefore count on a lot of travel at work. Most of the training and education takes place in Kungsängen outside Stockholm. The basic military police training takes place in collaboration with the Police Training in Växjö (Linnaeus University) and gives academic higher education credits.

The tasks of the military police include:

Criminal investigations, Personal protection, Criminal intelligence service, Handling of persons deprived of their liberty and a Traffic service. There are several formations that perform specific functions, however. The 11th Military Police Battalion consists of a personal protection company, two military police companies and an investigation group. The battalion is led and coordinated by a battalion staff with the support of the associated staff and troop platoon. The battalion is staffed with both full-time and part-time soldiers and officers, as well as civilian employees.

The 114th military police company consist for the most part of temporary staff. This means that only a small number of professional officers serve daily at the company. Other personnel consist of reserve officers and soldiers who are part-time employees and work only for limited periods of time.

The 15th military police company consists of full-time soldiers and officers. The company is stationed in Kungsängen but works all over the country and also internationally in countries such as Kosovo, Afghanistan, Mali, and Somalia. The 115th Military Police Company consists of a company command, two military police platoons, a staff squad, and a group of dogs. The military police at the company are specially trained, trained and equipped. Recruitment takes place from the entire Armed Forces and the Police Authority.

The 116th personal protection company are those who work at the personal protection and are specially selected, trained and equipped and recruited from both the Armed Forces and other organizations. Those who are admitted to the company are further trained to then be able to perform their main task – to protect the lives, health and integrity of socially important people.

In addition to the above-mentioned units, there are also military police at the Armed Forces' various garrisons. The military police are subordinate to their regular platoon commanders but are functioned by the Swedish Armed Forces' Military Police Unit. These military police are commonly referred to as 'Garrison MPs' and are found in all types of weapons and these have the same basic training as the military police who serve in e.g., 11th Military Police Battalion.

The investigation team is, as the name suggests, the smallest division within the 11th Military Police Battalion. Since the group was formed in 2011, the group has mainly focused on investigating violations of the law on munitions, theft and receiving linked to internet-related advertisements – both nationally and internationally. The preliminary investigations themselves are not led by the investigation team, but a civil prosecutor does. It is also the prosecutor who is in charge of the investigation and is the one who gives directives to the military police from the investigation group.

Austrian Military Police

In 1955, Austria declared its everlasting Neutrality and made neutrality a constitutional law. The Austrian Military's main purpose since then has been the protection of Austria's neutrality. The main constitutional tasks of today's Austrian military are to maintain order and security inside the

Austrian MPs are some of the most highly trained specialists in the world, it is far from easy becoming one with many years of training.

country and to render assistance in the case of natural catastrophes and disasters of exceptional magnitude. The Austrian Military Police is the branch within the Austrian Armed Forces; its mission is to protect the troops and all military installations and property. Military patrol, plus the protection of persons and is responsible for operations abroad as military police for the security and order within the federal army contingents. The soldiers of the Military Police have the most modern equipment available.

Becoming a MP in Austria is a long and difficult process. Prior to admission to the MP selection course, every candidate has to successfully complete basic training phases1, 2 and 3 as well as the corporals' course. Having passed this selection course, the candidate is admitted to the first semester of the NCO training course at the NCO Academy. The training course covers the 17-week training course for military patrols soldiers (FüOrgEt1) and the 13-week training course for military officers (FüOrgEt2). An intense combat course is part of the training and begins after the selection course. Some of the subjects covered on the MP course include: Unarmed self-defence, Service weapons and ammunition, statutory provisions, Service inspections, Security staff, Investigation Service, Medical services, Transport services, Penetration and access techniques, Basic collection service, Tactics, Personal protection, computer database course, POW Handling, squad leader, Search and Rescue, Driving technique including car and Motorcycle riding, Weapons qualifications on various small arms, Refugee affairs. Evacuation management.

During the second semester the candidate starts MP basic training at the Training Division of the Military Police Command in Vienna. Then after the successful completion of this course he becomes a member of the MP.

To ensure the necessary skills to cover civil police tasks in the context of missions abroad with appropriate legal framework training is completed in cooperation with the Federal Ministry of the Interior and the Ministry of Justice. These modules are included in the individual courses or are run as separate courses such as for specialists. The implementation is carried out by qualified personnel of the Ministry of Justice and the Federal Ministry of the Interior. The final takes place in an examination and an appropriate certification. The following topics are covered:

Law in general; Code of Criminal Procedure; Forensic and crime scene investigations; Traffic Accident Recording and collection; Interrogation techniques; Testimony in court or with the Independent Administrative Senate.

Austrian MP K9 handler are used in the Military and to support civilian authorities during major events or demonstrations.

Finally, only after all this an MP can specialize in different areas, one of them is the specialist Military Dog course. In addition to training the dogs the training of the handler is attached the next greatest importance. Future dog handlers must undergo a 14-day review pre-selection which includes training in the feeding, care and training bases of a dog. In addition, they undergo 24 hours of sleep deprivation and intense physical activity whilst being reviewed by the Army's Psychological Service for their physical and mental resilience. A final test on the knowledge acquired completes this selection process and a discussion on the admission to participation in military dog-training course is made. Military police operations for military dogs cover a wide spectrum from the detection for drugs, explosives, or people and including a full range of application of protection of handler to tracking of offenders.

In his speech, Minister of Defence announced the military police would play a vital role in the future especially in the case of national disasters and to ensure peace and stability at home and abroad. The Military Police was created as an important tool to tackle international problems. The military police missions abroad can close a security gap that exists at the beginning of the mission in the area of operations. The military police take over tasks of the missing local police and to work for their establishment of local law and order. Thus, the military police is an important and valuable contribution to the stabilization of a region in crisis.

Army MPs, assigned to the 529th Military Police Company, 709th MP Battalion, 18th MP Brigade, and Austrian MP view an Iveco Light Multirole Vehicle in 2019, Salzburg, Austria. designated Hussar in Austrian service and mainly operated by military police and patrol units. Photo: U.S. Army photo by Pvt. Agustin J. Lopez.

Currently, there are 372 soldiers in the military police command with 100 members on foreign missions. Currently military police patrol in the Golan Heights, Bosnia, Kosovo and now in Chad. There, they will contribute as part of the Austrian contingent to refugees and aid agencies to provide protection and assistance. Currently, military police officers in the use of premises

Kosovo, Bosnia, and Syria are used. A Military police squad also includes the Austrian contribution to the German ORF Battalion for the Balkans. First time, personal security forces in Kosovo are perceived. For the foreseeable future the Austrian military police will remain with the

Multinational Task Force South in Kosovo and the guide element to all police forces of the Military Task Force (Provost Marshal Office).

Austrian MPs have been used during recent ISIS attack alerts and also during Covid virus alerts to supplement civilian police, especially in guarding State buildings.

The basic shape of the MP badge is a Spanish shield, the base colour is black. The white lettering thereon 'military patrol' and 'MP' refer to the duties of the association in the back at home and abroad. The silver grenade is similar to several European armies as the badge of the military police.

EASTERN EUROPE

Poland

The Polish Military Gendarmerie is a separate, specialized service within the structures of the Polish Armed Forces.

The main tasks of the Military Gendarmerie are focused on enforcement of military discipline, prevention of pathologies in the Polish Armed Forces, detection of crimes and offences, criminal investigations, and prosecution of perpetrators. One important role is the prevention department, which takes a great care in the enforcement of military discipline. Prevention tasks are mainly carried out through patrols, convoys, traffic control and widely performed prophylactic measures.

Gendarmes appear wherever the Polish Armed Forces appear. The Military Police secures the deployment and field exercises of Polish and other NATO troops. They control the transport of military goods and dangerous materials, protect the national and military ceremonies. The military police provides help to the local communities and supports other services during natural disasters, catastrophes, and technical breakdowns.

The formation cooperates with civilian institutions on the central and local levels, moreover it works together with the Police, Border Guard, Fire Department, General Customs Inspectorate, Main Inspectorate of Fiscal Control, Government Protection Office, Interior Security Agency. This cooperation also includes joint trainings and exercises. In recent years, by the direction of the Prime Minister, the Military Police possesses the same police powers as civilian police towards the general public during specific periods of time such as Christmas, New Year Eve, Easter, 1st November and during holidays. Gendarmes together with policemen take care of public safety.

The first Polish Gendarmerie regiments were established in 1812 in Lithuania. In that time Poland was not even present on the map of Europe, but their soldiers fought for the independence of their motherland under the company of Napoleon.

The tasks of the Polish Gendarmerie at that time were arresting fugitives and marauders, escorting duties, transportation of important materials or persons and even exacting taxes. The government of the Polish Kingdom – state subordinated to Russia decided to keep the formation and to organize it similarly to the French Gendarmerie. During the November Uprising gendarmes had the opportunity to prove their patriotism and heroism in active service on the field. Thanks to gendarmes fighting under the command of Lt. Col. Sznajde, Poles were victorious during one of the most famous battles of the November Uprising – 31 March 1831 near Dębe Wielkie. In the January Uprising the gendarmes fought against traitors and representatives of the Russian administration.

The formation also took part in the creation of the II Republic of Poland – first, side by side with the Polish Legions, later during the Russian War. The Military Gendarmerie then counteracted desertion in the Polish lines and prevented the spread of Bolshevik propaganda. In the II Republic of Poland Military Gendarmerie was regarded as one of the most prestigious military formations in the pre-war period.

During the Second World War, gendarmes shared fate of all Poles – soldiers and civilians. They took an active part in September Campaign in 1939. The Military Gendarmerie operated within the structures of the Polish Armed Forces for the Allies and fought under British command at Tobruk and Monte Cassino.

The Polish MP cooperates on permanent basis with other Military Police formations from different countries. This results in meetings being conducted on various levels and undertakings like exercises, trainings and competitions which enhance professionalism. The Military Gendarmerie have established cooperation with the Military Police from: Bulgaria, Croatia, the Czech Republic, Denmark, France, Germany, Italy, Ireland, the United Kingdom, Latvia, Lithuania, Netherlands, Norway, Portugal, Spain, Turkey, Ukraine, and the United States of America.

One of the greatest outcomes of this long-lasting international cooperation was the formation in 2007 of the NATO Multinational Military Police Battalion.

The Battalion consists of the MP from the Republic of Croatia, the Czech Republic, the Republic of Slovakia, and the Republic of Poland. The most important task of the Battalion is to provide police support to NATO operations. Since its creation, the Polish Military Gendarmerie it has participated in peacekeeping and stabilization missions as a part of the Polish Military Contingents. Its soldiers also served on individual positions on observers' missions. Recently, there has been an increase – in quantity and quality – of the formation engagement in solving the world's conflicts. Currently, gendarmes are participating in the peacekeeping and stabilization missions in Afghanistan, Tchad, Bosnia and Herzegovina, Lebanon, Kosovo, and Syria.

In 2006 for the first time in its history, the Military Gendarmerie independently formed Polish Military Contingent. The soldiers of the Contingent, in which the dominant strength belonged to the scarlet berets, watched over the safety of the electoral process in the Democratic Republic of Congo, on behalf of the European mission. The activities carried out by soldiers on the missions were doubtlessly related to the glorious traditions of the Polish army.

The increase threat of organized crime and terrorism has caused the active participation of the Polish Armed Forces in international operations. The need for the Military Gendarmerie type forces capable of ensuring the public order in the sphere of peacekeeping and stabilization missions has increased. It has also caused the grounds for establishing the Military Gendarmerie Specialized Units (MGSU). They are fully professional, specialized and prestigious units created to perform special military tasks. The Military Gendarmerie has established three Specialized Units: in Warsaw, Gliwice, and Mińsk Mazowiecki. The first Military Gendarmerie Specialized Unit was established in Warsaw in 2004. It is the military equivalent of the Government Protection Office. Gendarmes from the MGSU in Warsaw are trained by the instructors from the Special Forces and the Anti-Terrorist police, they perform VIP protection functions for the highest personnel of the Ministry of National Defence and towards the representatives of foreign delegations.

The Military Police possesses its own vehicles adjusted to the various types of activities. Among them there are patrol and intervention vehicles like Dzik II, terrain-intervention commanding vehicle and Land-Rovers, mainly used during foreign missions.

In 2020 Poland has offered to establish the NATO Military Police Centre of Excellence in order to enhance the NATO's military police or gendarmerie interoperability. Poland is the framework nation.

The NATO MP COE is located in Bydgoszcz. The COE's mission is to enhance the MP capability of NATO and its member nations in order to support military transformation, the SNs and other customers, thus improving the alliance's interoperability in the field of MP. The NATO MP capability providers subject matter expertise on all aspects of MP activities, thus improving the alliance's interoperability in the field of MP operations.

Latvian Military Police

Many former eastern bloc countries use western equipment, this Latvian MP complete with red beret could come from any country.

After regaining the national independence of the Republic of Latvia in 1991, integration into the North Atlantic Treaty Organization (NATO) became one of its main foreign policy goals.

Alignment of the structure of the National Armed Forces of the Republic of Latvia (NAF) with NATO standards required the establishment of a separate military unit – the Military Police (MP), which would perform support tasks in peacetime and combat support tasks in war conditions. One of their priorities was to establish an MP unit for participation in NATO-led international operations. In order to bring the structure of the National Armed Forces of the Republic of Latvia into NATO standards, it was necessary to establish a military unit that would perform support tasks for the armed forces in peacetime and combat support tasks during the war. They Military Police were established in 1997. After merging with the Latvian Security Service in 2009, the Military Police is also responsible for security of the Parliament and the President of Latvia. They carry out military discipline and ensuring lawful provision functions with the right to perform investigations and operational activities and prepares Military Police units for their deployment to international missions. It safeguards military and strategically important sites, provides escort and security of military transport columns, military cargoes, as well as of state and foreign officials. The Military Police provides for the exchange of classified materials between the state institutions of Latvia, institutions of NATO member states and other competent foreign institutions.

Latvia has undergone training with multiple armed forces to both to achieve a NATO standard and to ensure operational uniformity. MPs have been training with the Michigan National Guard and 2018 marks the 25th anniversary of the Latvian-Michigan National Guard's involvement in this partnership program. Today Latvia is part of the NATO multinational battle group which is currently led by Canada and consists of more than 1,300 troops from Albania, the Czech Republic, Italy, Poland, Canada, Slovakia, Slovenia and Spain, who rotate on duty in Latvia, participating in exercises with the National Armed Forces, thus improving interoperability. with regional allies to be able to respond to the challenges of the security environment.

The Latvian Military Police have ten service dogs at this time. These operate in support of Provost operations with dogs typically trained to search, track, defend handler and attack work.

MP soldiers have participated in the peacekeeping mission in Kosovo since 1999. In addition, the first MP unit was deployed in Iraq in 2003. MP soldiers are always well-prepared for their work on these missions; thus, their input is always highly appreciated.

The Latvian National Armed Forces (NAF) Military Police Squad

Latvian military police are a full-time part of the NATO Reaction Forces. One of its areas of responsibility today in 2020 is providing highly trained close protection officers to guard NATO officials.

began its tour of duty as part of the eighth rotation of the NATO Response Force in 2006 were 34 military police officers and two national support element soldiers from the Supply Command operated in the Turkish-led international military police unit until for twelve months. As part of its operational involvement, the Military Police Squad conducted traffic management and security operations in its area of responsibility, as well as ensuring the legality of operations. Its assignment was to reconnoitre existing roads within the sphere of operation of its main force, investigate road accidents, escort convoys and heavy equipment in transit, and undertake the guarding and escorting of senior officials.

Lithuanian

Lithuanian MPs are an elite force within the armed forces.

Military Police are a law enforcement institution operating within the National Defence System of the Republic of Lithuania and are part of the Lithuanian Armed Forces.

Military Police are directly subordinate to the Chief of Defence of the Republic of Lithuania. Main tasks of Military Police include preventing of crimes and other breaches of legal acts, investigating and disclosing offences, enforcing law and order in military territories and in the Armed Forces and ensuring the security of military traffic.

The Military Police is a law enforcement institution operating within the National Defence System of the Republic of Lithuania and is a part of the Lithuanian Armed Forces.

The Military Police Law outlines the Military Police's competence, functions, and tasks as well as organizational procedures, rights and responsibilities of military policemen and relationship with other law enforcement institutions.

Functions of Military Police include implementation of measures to prevent crimes and other breaches of legal acts, recording and control of crimes and other violations of legal acts, investigation of committed crimes and other breaches of legal acts. Keeping with procedures outlined in legislation Military Police carries out search of soldiers suspected or accused in crimes and violations of other legal acts, deserted or missing soldiers as well as pretrial investigations in cases that are in the competence of Military Police under the legislation on penal process, in cases stipulated in legislation, carries out the orders of interrogators, prosecutors, judges and courts. Military Police maintains military discipline and order by patrolling, security of military transport, escorting of military transport convoys, as well as guarding of key military objects, guardhouses.

Military policemen participate in multinational operations and exercises. They already participated in international missions in Bosnia and Hercegovina, missions in Iraq, multinational exercises 'Amber Hope', 'Baltic Challenge', 'Baltic Eagle', 'Strong Resolve', 'Rescuer-Medceur', where they maintained security of military transport and public order.

Any person serving in the National Defence System or having served in the compulsory military service, after passing an established selection process can be accepted to Military Police.

On 22 October 1998 in the (Seimas) Parliament of the Republic of Lithuania the Military Police Law of the Lithuanian Armed Forces was adopted which served as a basis for the establishment of military police. In 1999 Maj Dainius Janėnas was appointed as Commander of Military Police. In 2000 Vilnius and Kaunas Garrisons were established, in 2001 Klaipėda Garrison was founded. On 22 October 2004 Military Police colours were adopted – like many nations they are red.

Military police dogs have been recently introduced to supplement manpower.

The K9 section is part of the Military Police and is tasked with use of military dogs to improve the disclosure and prevention of criminal acts and other law violations. Military dogs are trained in searching for narcotic substances, explosion devices, weapons, guarding service facilities, carrying out search and rescue work, suppressing riots and tracking.

The Lithuanian Military Police have established very high standards for their Military Working Dogs and in addition to the above specialist roles dogs are also employed in defending persons or objects under guard against attack, conducting convoy escorts, detaining a person escaping from custody or detaining a person suspect in committing a criminal act or outrage against public order or breach of disciplinary order in a military territory.

Estonian

Sõjaväepolitsei are the Military Police of the Estonian Defence Force. The Estonian MP organization was created in 1994 and is today divided into tactical (patrol) and investigative units. MP tasks include investigation of serious disciplinary cases and some armed service-related crimes, supervision of military discipline within the Forces, military traffic control and various security tasks. Within conflict/crises areas such as in Afghanistan, the MPs provide close protection of the Estonian national representative and other visiting VIPs. When on regular patrol assignment, Estonian MPs wear a black Brassard on their right shoulder, with the letters *SP* in silver.

Additionally Conscript based reserve-MP Platoons are employed in the Guard Battalion every year. The Guard Battalion (official name *Northern Défense District Guard Battalion*) is a battalion of the Estonian Defence Force specialized in urban warfare. It is based in Tallinn and consists of the Infantry Company under the command of a Lieutenant and the Military Police Company also under the command of Lieutenant. The battalion was previously known as the Infantry Training Centre Independent Guard Battalion. Being the capital's main garrison, the Guard Battalion also has the duty of carrying the watch over the presidential palace and overseeing security of diplomats and political guests.

Estonia has been a member of the European Union since 2004. A strong, united and internationally influential Europe is in Estonia's best interest. Estonia contributes to the development of the European Union's military and civil crisis command capabilities. Estonia has also been a member of NATO since 2004. Membership in the collective defence organisation ensures military security, allowing Estonia to participate productively in international security co-operation as well as representing the most certain guarantee of Estonia's national defence. Estonia has sent many different units and specialists to crisis areas: infantry, military police, staff officers, medics, EOD (Explosive Ordnance Disposal) specialists, air traffic controllers, military observers, transport maintenance officers and cargo handlers. In 2011 there will be around 200 Estonian Defence Forces members in various operations at any given time. Estonia began its military involvement in Afghanistan in 2002 in the US-led Operation Enduring Freedom. Estonia has participated in the NATO peace support mission in Kosovo since 1999. Estonia stood in the ranks of the international coalition in Operation Iraqi Freedom from 2003–2008. In addition to membership in the EU and NATO Estonia has been a member of the United Nations (UN) since 1991. Estonia considers co-operation within the UN to be necessary for maintaining international peace and security by fulfilling development goals, protecting peace, and combating international terrorism. Estonian Military Police are usually at the forefront of any international deployment.

Romanian

Romanian MPs are well equipped and trained and frequently deploy on international operations as a lead element.

The Romanian Military Police (*Poliţia Militară*) is the military police of the Romanian Armed Forces. It was formed in 1990, immediately after the 1989 Romanian Revolution, although the Romanian Gendarmerie (also re-established in 1990) performed military police duties between 1850 and 1949.

The duties of the Military Police are similar to most MPs around the world, this is not surprising with more and more countries jointly training together. Their tasks therefore include to control military personnel and documents, to control and maintain discipline in places/crowded areas frequented by military personnel and to eliminate any conflicts between military personnel or military personnel and civilians, to maintain the security during military exercises/parades, to prevent the illegal introduction of devices/materials/substances into the military units/bases, to apprehend deserters in cooperation with the Police, Gendarmerie, Romanian Intelligence Service and other agencies, to maintain the security of the military detainees and to undertake search and rescue/evacuation missions, together with the Romanian Inspectorate for Emergency Situations/Gendarmerie/other Romanian Ministry of Interior forces, of civilian/military persons, in case of earthquakes, floods, or other disasters.

The history of the Romanian Military Police is close related to the history of Romanian gendarmerie, being a sort of part of it. It should be noticed that at the origins the gendarmerie was set up as a part of Ministry of War. Therefore, the archaic term of 'troops' police' could be found starting with 1850 in army's structure but the born day of the military police should be considered 5 November 1893. At that day King Carol I has promulgated the *Law of Villages Gendarmerie*. As a part of these corps, the Military Police branch should:

- *act as judiciar police*
- *search and arrest AWOLs and unobedient troops*
- *arrest all military personnel without military documents while on leave*
- *searching for armed gangs, considered dangerous*
- *repel the attacks against guards*
- *repel the attempts of prisoners to escape*
- *search for illegal depots of weapons and ammunition*
- *inform the population about mobilisation*

In 1908, 1911 and 1913, new laws and regulations regarding the activity of gendarmerie were set up in order to increase the efficiency of it. To avoid any confusions, the new *Law of Gendarmerie* promulgated on March 24 1908, brought the following specification:

Article. 6: *The Gendarmerie corps are a part of the Army. The dispositions of military rules and orders are applicable except some specific situations because of its mixed organisation – both civilian and military – and specific tasks.*

Article. 7: *The officers will be recruited from the army's personnel. The nominated persons will be assigned to gendarmerie troops by the order of the prince who will release a High Royal decree.*

The same law stated that: *During military operations the gendarmerie will act as Military Police in order to manage accurately the military traffic, the escort of prisoners and to assure the security of main objectives and installations".*

In 1913 –1916 there were made some modifications regarding the MP organisation and strength. New assignments were made especially related to the security of some important economical areas (oil fields) and factories (mainly those factories who were producing military equipment and machinery).

During the WW I the MP corps participated alongside other forces performing MP specific tasks including combat missions and providing assistance to civilian populations. In 1917 the gendarmerie was reassigned to Ministry of War at Ops. These detachments were led by infantry officers their strength consisted of 27 gendarmes/MPs.

On July 1 1931, the gendarmerie has placed again under Ministry of Interior command, until September 12 1940. At the start of WW II as part of Axe's troops, the gendarmerie/MP performed following main activities, preventing terrorist activities, guarding civilian and military installations; law enforcement; – repel the attacks of enemy's airborne and paratroopers and surveillance of anti-Nazi parties.

The Law #264 from April 22 1943 stipulated that: *The gendarmerie is a military corp. The main mission is to assure the activity of civilian and military police cross country. It is subordinated to Ministry of War but could perform activities when the minister of Interior asks for that".*

Starting with August 23 1944, the Romanian Government decided that it is better for the country to leave the Axe and be a part of Allied troops. Therefore, the Romanian Army started to fight against the Nazi and their sympathisers. The main objective was to take back the region of North Transylvania – Vienna Treaty – and liberate Hungary, Czech and Slovakia.

Main mission accomplished by MP structures/units were to identify enemy soldiers, to find their ammo and weapons depots and neutralise them; to block/restrict the enemy movements, to disarm the squads/ small groups of enemy's soldiers; to perform searches and arrests of enemy troops or pro-Nazi; to arrest and annihilate the pro-Nazi partisans from Transylvania and to find and destroy pro-Nazi or Hungarian propaganda. Meanwhile, other gendarmerie/MP units acted as light infantry, performing specific activities, or fighting in close combat.

After the WW II, the Gendarmerie was reassigned to Ministry of Interior, Military Police disbanded, and the personnel were sent to other structures.

In 1947, the communist regime established some separate branches as parts of Ministry of Armed Forces to deal with military police matters. As a result, there was set up a Law and Discipline branch, a Guide and Control of Military Traffic branch, a Military Justice, and a Military Jail unit. These structures and in order not to interfere with the communist political goals, each branch was assigned to different department, breaking the chain of command – and making them inefficient.

In 1990, after the Revolution against communist regime the Ministry of National Defence decided to unify all the branches mentioned above in a single structure entitled Military Police with the # B3/0907 Order to establish MP units the 265 MP Bn, 286 MP Coy, 282 MP Coy, 295 MP Coy, 302 MP Coy under the chief of Land Forces. In 19199 due to further reorganisation of Romanian Land Forces, some MP Coy were transformed into MP platoons and squads and some of them were reassigned to logistic or combat support units. Starting with 2006, 4 MP-Guard Battalions were set up. Main mission is to guard sensitive military HQs and installations. The strength of these Battalions is about 3000 personnel.

International missions have included Bosnia and Herzegovina (2000 – 2004) A Romanian military policemen platoon (23 members) was detached in Bosnia and Herzegovina, since July 2000, as part of the SFOR (until December 2004), as well as part of the EUFOR (since December 2004). Their main missions are to patrol within local police and to maintain public order.

Iraq (2003–2006) Subunits of the 265th Military Police Battalion were detached since July 2003, in Nasiriyah, Iraq, under the operational command of the Italian troops in Iraq. They participated mostly to reconnaissance missions, as well as VIP protection and traffic control. The mission ended in August 2006.

The 265th Military Police Battalion is the largest and most important Romanian Military Police unit of the Romanian Land Forces. It was formed in 1993 and has its headquarters are located in Bucharest. The battalion is often deployed to Iraq on peacekeeping missions. In December 2006, the unit received modernized Humvees that replaced the ARO's still in service.

The *Voennaya politsiya,* Russia's military police

One of the (many) problems of the Russian military has been its lack of a proper military police force, and the extent to which this has encouraged or at least done little to stop rampant criminality, including the brutal hazing of troops Instead, the Main Military Procurator's Office (GVP) largely has to work through unit command structures (which are often more interested in concealing than revealing crimes) and the Commandant's Service, which is largely a guard and traffic-control service and again under local commanders.

Although this is a relatively new concept for Russia many developed countries have military police. Countries in Europe and America that came across hazing in the military realized the need to establish such a body to maintain law and order in military units. At present 44 countries, including former Soviet republics, the Baltic States, Georgia and Armenia have military police.

As far back as 2006, Vladimir Putin, when he was President, insisted that special units must control how the army and navy honour law.

In October 2010, Defence Minister Anatoly Serdyukov and Chief of the General Staff Makarov announced that by 2012, Russia would have a proper military police force initials being VP standing for *Voennaya politsiya*, some 20,000 strong. The dedicated VP will not only act as a check on the corrupt and exploitative officers who are still such a drain on military resources and morale, they will at last provide – assuming they get the support and powers they need – a force able to check the criminality of the Russian military.

A key problem will be addressing the stand over tactic many recruits face from more senior members of their units, which not only blights lives, but also undermines discipline and solidarity within the military. The key problem has been not just that it is culturally entrenched but also that it has been implicitly (and sometimes directly) sanctioned by many commanders. After all, with relatively little training in modern man-management and a lack of the experienced NCOs who are so vital to maintaining discipline in Western armies, bulling allowed them an informal means of enforcing their authority, sanctioning brutality by a cadre of more experienced trustees who get their kicks out of bullying the rest, so long as they also enforce their officers' instructions as well as indulging their own whims.

The creation of the VP will help combat these practices, by creating a separate force able and willing to investigate military offences. It should also be able to address the general problems of corruption, embezzlement, and exploitation. The unit will be commanded by Lt. General Sergei Surovikin an able officer who has a series of key appointments on his resume, including having been briefly the head of the General Staff (GOU). He also served in a Spetsnaz unit in Afghanistan in the last stages of the war and was a commander of the elite Moscow-based 2nd Taman Guards Tank Division's mechanized infantry battalion during the hard-liners' 1991 coup.

The establishment of military police could be useful when taking into account the experience of other countries where this has led to a fall in the number of crimes against servicemen, a similar military police in Ukraine has led to the fall in the number of crimes against servicemen by 40 percent. The duties of military police officers must be engaged not only in patrolling and escorting detainees but also conduct investigations like ordinary police. The creation of the VP is hoped to create a new control mechanism over the military (admittedly a good thing in itself) rather than begin a cultural change within it that could, eventually, create a democratic, cohesive, and more transparent military.

Being rapidly reintroduced into the Russian Military Order of battle are MPs, no country in the world can do without them. The Chief of Military Police is the First Deputy Minister of Defence.

The Army's Military Police provide an important function in the full spectrum of Army operations as a member of the Manoeuvre, Fires, and Effects division. The Military Police provides expertise in police, detainment, and stability operations in order to enhance security and enable mobility. The Army's Military Police can be utilized in direct combat and during peacetime.

2019 Russian soldiers walk past a Russian military police armoured vehicle at a position in the north-eastern Syrian city Kobane on Oct. 23, 2019. Photo: AFP.

Russian military police began patrols on part of the Syrian border quickly moving to implement an accord with Turkey that divvies up control of north-eastern Syria. Turkish and Russian forces jointly patrol a strip 10-kilometers (6 miles) deep along the border.[53] This was the first time Russia had deployed military police abroad. The experiment was clearly considered a success, and Moscow is now deploying battalion-strength scratch military police units created from several constituent elements but with no particular ethnic identity. Four battalions numbering 1200 men were operating in Syria, their primary missions are providing security for Russian facilities and personnel, and manning checkpoints and observation stations monitoring the border between Russia, Iran, and Turkey.

Using military police allows Moscow to send soldiers able to fight if need be although their primary role is not to be front-line grunts. Russia is considered in many countries in essentially negative terms, as an agent of anarchy on the global scale. However, the use of forces such as the military police which also have a potentially positive, even humanitarian, role is considered a way in which the Kremlin can balance deploying hard power assets with maintaining a soft power capacity.[54]

There is a separate Military Police traffic unit. The Military Automobile Inspection (Russian acronym ВАИ) is the military traffic police service, and its name is in direct parallel to the country's civilian traffic police, which is called State Automobile Inspection.

"The main tasks of military traffic police are: Road safety in the Armed Forces; monitoring compliance with military and civilian personnel of the Armed Forces of the legislative and other normative legal acts of the Russian Federation on issues of road safety in the army, with the use of vehicles of military units on public roads; ensuring the movement of troops (forces) on public roads and paths columned, organization of road traffic police patrol on a military vehicle traffic routes of military units; State registration of vehicles of military units; conducting state vehicle inspection of military units, as well as guaranteeing access drivers and vehicles of military units to participate in traffic.

---

53 https://www.militarytimes.com/flashpoints/2019/10/23/russian-forces-deploy-at-syrian-border-under-new-accord-with-turkey

54 Prof. Mark Galeotti is a senior researcher and the head of the Centre for European Security at the Institute of International Relations Prague.2017

Formed only in 2011, the military police force is now 20,000 strong. With the distinctive red beret, they fill a long-discussed need in addressing crime and indiscipline within the ranks. Their growing role in Syria shows, they do represent a different face of the Russian army, and a potential instrument of a robust kind of soft power.

The military police offer Moscow several specific advantages. The units are disproportionately made up of professionals, making it easier to form contingents for overseas deployment, as they must be volunteers by law. It also means that the valuable experience they are gaining especially useful for such a new force is not going to be bled away quickly by conscripts ending their terms of service.

During Russian Empire a Special Corps of Gendarmes took the functions of Military police, until 1917.

Soviet era

The Soviet Armed Forces did not have any units technically named 'military police'. Two separate agencies handled military police duties on a day-to-day basis.

The *Komendantskaya sluzhba* or 'Commandant's Service' of the Soviet Army wore a yellow letter 'K' on a red patch on the sleeve to indicate their membership of this service – the *de facto* army police. A second organisation called the Traffic Regulators existed within the Rear Services. Traffic Regulators served to control military highway and motor vehicle traffic. Traffic Regulators also wear a white painted helmet with red stripes to indicate their status and either an armband or patch with the Cyrillic letter 'P'

The idea to create military police in Russian Federation came from the second President of Russia, Vladimir Putin, who authorized his then Defence Minister, Sergey Ivanov to establish such an organization. In 2005, human rights ombudsman Vladimir Lukin wrote a special report about abuse in the armed forces and proposed measures including the creation of military police.

On 21 April 2010, when Minister of Defence Anatoly Serdyukov announced further steps to establish military police, pursuant to the President's directive. Russian President Medvedev was a strong proponent of the creation of military police; one of its main objectives would be to combat Dedovshchina or hazing.

Chief Military Prosecutor Sergei Fridinsky said Russia's military police will be instituted in two stages: first, the integration of the relevant Defence Ministry services and second, granting the new agency investigative functions. According to Russian media reports, up to 20,000 service members may be assigned to serve as military police.

Czech

Like Poland the Czech Military Police represent their country in many international operations, they are highly capable and frequently are in charge of US and UK MP units during UN missions such is their professionalism.

After 140 years of a conscription service system being exercised in the historical Czech lands, the country has abandoned this practice. From the beginning of 2005 it has been building a professional career soldier system. It is part of a fundamental reform of the Czech military that was launched in 2002 which also involved downsizing, organizational changes, modernization of equipment and reshaping the locations of garrisons and sites within the republic. In 2006, the military achieved initial operational capabilities and stabilization of its forces. The full operational capabilities are set to be reached before the end of 2012.

The Military Police Corps was set up on 21 January 1991. Within the provisions of the Czech Law No. *124/1992 Dig.* The Military Police are responsible for police protection of the armed forces, military facilities, military material, and other state property controlled by the Ministry of Defence of the Czech Republic. The Military Police are a full-time professional force. The Military Police are headed by a Provost Marshal who directly reports to the Minister of Defence. The structure is based on a territorial principle. The Military Police subordinated headquarters are located in Prague, at Stara Boleslav, Tabor, and Olomouc.

Unlike many of the worlds MPs who wear red, as of 1 July 2003, Czech Military Police officers were equipped with accessories in black, including their distinctive feature – the black beret.

Military Police officers are assigned directly to military units, and they also form part of military contingents and units or detachments of the Armed Forces of the Czech Republic on foreign deployments and within NATO structures.

The Military Police officers served within contingents/units of the Armed Forces of the Czech Republic on foreign operations in Iraq and in the Balkans, and from March 2007 to 2011 its MPSOG (Military Police Special Operation Group) also served in southern Afghanistan in the Helmand Province. At present MPs, serve in Kosovo, NATO missions, and within units of Czech ISAF Task Force in Afghanistan till recent times.

At the beginning of January 2007, the Armed Forces of the Czech Republic concluded their training mission of the Iraqi Police Force at the Shaibah base close to Basra. The mission, saw 12 contingents of Czech Military Police rotated, it began in December 2003.

In December 2003, Military Police deployed in the southern part of Iraq and participation in the Iraqi Zone Stabilisation Force operation (IZ SFOR). Based on the UN Security Council Resolution No. 1546, the operation was renamed the Multi-National Force – Iraq (MNF-I) as of 19 July 2004, and it has been known as the Operation Iraqi Freedom since.

The first Military Police Contingent in the operation was more than 80 personnel located about 18 miles south-west of the City of Basra at the Shaibah Base. This operational sector is under the command of the British-led Multi-National Division – Southeast. At the outskirts of a former airport, the Military police have built up a functional and safe base for themselves.

The primary task of military policemen was to supervise local police, help train its members at the Police Academy at Az-Zubayru and at police stations, it also contributed to police support of the Division. Czech Military policemen served in three-month rotations.

Since March 2005, the Czech MP Contingent was increased by six soldiers, who served in the command structure of the Multi-National Security Transition Command in Iraq, and the NATO Training Mission in Iraq. These soldiers were located in Bagdad.

A unit of 35 Czech military policemen from Czech Special Operation Group of the Military Police has been serving in Helmand Province within British Brigade since April 2007. Czech military police also mentor the instructors at the National Police Training Centre in the Afghan Province of Wardak, they supervise the organisation and plan their training at the Police Academy. The task aim is to support and build a command corps to prepare key staff in the NPTC. The Czech Military Police personnel mentoring at the Afghan National rotate each six months. A second MP unit is part of the France-led international team of mentors. Commander of the French Contingent is at the same time commander of the international team, that Portugal and Romania MPs also participate in.

Additionally, there are 12 military policemen at the MP Command HQ at Olomouc, MP Protection Service Command, and from the MP Command Headquarters in Prague. The Czech military police are a highly trained professional force. One way they accomplishing this status is by conducting exercises and training with various other NATO units. One exercise is called BLACK BEAR, a Military police exercise, and is the coordination of activities of all national units of the NATO Multi-National Military Police Battalion (NATO MNMPBAT) in performing their tasks. The service members of all participating parties form individual sections of the Battalion Staff. The fluent and well working decision-making process of the Staff is the basic prerequisite for fulfilment of tasks that are ahead by individual platoons.

Tasks during the exercise fully reflect the requirements for the supposed operational capabilities of the Battalion during war. Military policemen from the Multi-National Battalion will be engaged in among other things public order during civilian disturbances, setting-up check points, investigation of crimes, and engagement in patrols within area of deployment and in the protection of convoys.

The exercise scenario also includes supervision of local police stations and providing support for local civilian police. This support is not only of a material nature but also is increasing the professional capabilities and readiness of both parties. The Goal of the exercises are to train NATO military policemen of all four countries of the Battalion in interoperability to ensure police protection on stabilization operations. The lead nation for the multinational Battalion is Poland at this time.

Today the strength of the MPs is around 1050 personnel (990 soldier, 60 civilians).

The current organisational structure starts with the Chief of the Military Police who is directly subordinated to the Minister of Defence. Under the Chief of the Military Police direct control are the Crime Investigation Service, Territorial MP Commands, Security Service Command, the Traffic Service, EOD and Military Working Dog Service, and the Quick Reaction Force.

The Czech MP provide criminological expertise in support not only of the Military Police but the State Police in the following specializations: Mechanical-imprint expertise; Criminological technical expertise

of documentation (ID and documents); Criminological expertise of data and data mediums; Dactylography expertise. Pyrotechnical expertise; Photographic and video expertise and Ballistics expertise. The military police are in 2019 developing Biometrics and non-Lethal Capabilities.

Military Police officers are assigned directly to military units, and they also form part of military contingents/units/detachments of the Armed Forces of the Czech Republic on foreign deployments and within NATO structures. Participate in the protection and escort the official Czech delegation and Czech citizens overseas and Czech Armed Forces abroad; Protect designated military transport aircrafts when they provide presidency or government flights including military installations designated for these flights; Provide Air Marshal duty when required.

They wear a distinctive black beret.

Slovenian

All MPs have to be highly skilled soldiers first and foremost, many countries require MPs to be Infantry trained for several years prior to applying for an MP position.

In July 1991 the first military police platoon was formed. In May 1992 this platoon was transformed into the 107th Military Police company, and in January 1998 the company was expanded into the 17th Military Police battalion. The Headquarters and a part of the battalion are located in Ljubljana. Other units can be found in eight different locations across Slovenia.

According to its mission the battalion performs military law and order operations, and traffic control. It performs selective tasks associated with the investigation of criminal acts in the Slovenian Armed Forces and provides the security of key defence installations. On order, it deploys to the designated area of operations and performs military police tasks in support of combat forces. In addition to tasks associated with the readiness status and military training, the battalion regularly takes part in the special training for the acquisition of military police authorizations, training for positions as criminal investigators, traffic policemen, explosive experts, dog handlers, and others. In October 2001 the 17th Military Police battalion took an important step towards achieving the interoperability NATO units by commencing the mission-oriented combat training in accordance with NATO standards. The 17th Military Police Battalion is also active in the international arena. They train and prepares military police units that take part in the NATO-led peace support operation 'JOINT FORGE' in Bosnia and Herzegovina.

The coat of arms in the form of a shield suggests appurtenance to the Republic of Slovenia and the military police (MP). The lower part of coat of arms depicts the stylized Slovenian national flag with Mount Triglav as the symbol of Slovenia and denoting its unit´s mission extended to the entire territory of the state. The treetops of Mount Triglav in the upper part of the symbol suggest determination, robustness, and sharpness and the lower rounded-off part symbolizes fairness and legitimacy.

The military police battalion is designed for performing independent military and police tasks and anti-commando and anti-terrorist assignments in military installations. They provide support to other forces on the territory of Slovenia and abroad. In peace support operations, the battalion conducts assignments which are defined by the nature of the particular peace operation.

Members of the 17th Military Police Battalion is composed of several specialists, such as criminal investigators, motorcycle officers, working dog handlers, pyrotechnic experts, and traffic officers.[55]

The first Slovenian Armed Forces service dog used for illegal search of drugs was deployed as part of ISAF in Afghanistan in response to the fifth Slovenian contingent request in 2006.

55 http://www.slovenskavojska.si/en/structure/force-command/special-military-police-unit-smpu/

They remain in Afghanistan on that same mission today where the tenth contingent operates the third dog deployed to that area.

Dogs in the Slovenian Armed Forces first appeared in 1991 during the war of independence of Slovenia. At that time, some members of the then territorial defence force led the call for the use of Military dogs. The dogs were normally used to protect important buildings, warehouses and transparent point as guards. At the official end of the Revolutionary War the 1st special brigade was set up for training dogs and guides primarily for the 1st BR and the Military Police (SV).

The Military Police cooperate with civil police dog unit in Slovenia and with various dog sections in other armies within Europe. The Slovenian Armed Forces 17th Military Police Battalion since 1994 has had a composition of service dogs at section level strength. Their function is to perform military police working dog duties, namely crowd control, tracking and bite work.

In 1998, the Unit for the breeding and training of military dogs was placed under veterinary service SV. The dog school is located in the south of Slovenia. In 2005 a new centre was built with a capacity for accommodation 50 dogs. Within the canine centre is a modern veterinary clinic responsible for the health of all service dogs and is tasked with the breeding of service dogs. Today the dog training centre conducts training for specialist search (drugs, explosives) and general Police dogs for the needs of the military police. Units with their handlers and dogs (searching for mines) have been in Afghanistan continuously for the past five years in the of Herat province. Training of handlers and dogs are trained for the following specialties:

Searching for drugs or explosives. Protection of facilities. For search for missing persons (SAR) used by the specialist Mountain unit and tracker dogs trained to search for downed pilots (escape and evasion).

Their mission upon establishment was inherited from the former territorial defence force in 1991. By 1994 the first group completed training military working dogs trained for general use. In 1999 they started to use dogs to assist police in Postojna. In that same year the first military dogs were trained to search for illicit drugs conducted by the

Centre for the education and upbringing of the Ministry of dogs Home Affairs Podutiku. In 2002 the unit received the first trained dogs to detect explosives completed at the unit for education and breeding of military dogs in Primoz Kočevski River.

17th Military Police Battalion uses nine dogs comprising eight Belgian shepherds and a Labrador. Three for general duties role, three for the detection mines and resources and three for detection of illicit drugs. They are all housed in barracks at Franc Rozman Stane in Ljubljana.

The dogs used as general patrol Military Police dogs must be well socialized very important is their psychological stability as these dogs must work around the general public as well as on military operations. Dogs for general use or defence dogs are used to control law and order at various events, for the intervention in cases of breaches in military areas, for prevention and protection facilities and the apprehension of military or civilian personnel in military zones. They also assist in the arrest, transfer and monitoring of persons who have committed offense. Dogs for specialized use are selected for their high drive instinct They are well socialized, and they are capable of searching in different conditions and terrains and in the presence of various distractions including people.

Dogs to detect mines are trained to detect explosive devices on vehicles vessels at various facilities and anywhere where there is the possibility terrorist activity. Trained for the identification of several types of explosives they indicate the explosive presence by sitting passively.

Slovenia MPs have received training over recent years (2016–19) from the 220th Military Police Company, 193rd Military Police Battalion, Colorado National Guard. This integrated training with Albanian and Slovenian military police includes conducting crowd control and refugee management tactic training. The Colorado National Guard is partnered with Slovenia as part of the State Partnership Program.

In 2019 Slovenian military police members deployed within the 39th Slovenian Armed Forces KFOR Contingent in Kosovo attended training and exercise training participants in response to recent shooting attacks. In cooperation with the military police from other participating

countries deployed in KFOR, they trained in joint tactical procedures, mutual communication, coordinated and safe movement procedures and the disabling of a shooter.

In 2020 the government adopted a motion that gave civilian police powers to the military police so as to allow troops to take over some of the tasks from police officers patrolling Slovenia's border with Croatia due to the coronavirus epidemic.[56]

Story

Although they are geographically an ocean away from one other, military police from the 220th Military Police Company, 193rd Military Police Battalion, Colorado National Guard, integrated with Slovenian, Macedonian and Albanian military police, found that they had much in common while conducting synchronized training during Exercise Immediate Response 16.

"We've been able to work seamlessly and integrate in with the Slovenian Army," Capt. Christopher Breyrle, company commander for the 220th Military Police Co., 193rd MP Battalion, U.S. Army Colorado National Guard. "Our tactics and procedures are very similar." "We were able to incorporate our lessons learned from forest fires, floods and blizzards, into how we can help build a response for the Slovenian Army," he said. Most of the training occurred with multiple nations soldiers working side by side with one another. One training event in particular involved a simulated refugee checkpoint site set up. The Macedonian and Slovenian MP teams controlled notional refugee flow while training on how to correctly handle refugees that are attempting to pass an area and how to react if events do not go as planned.

Sgt. 1st Class Bradley Tune, 220th MPs, described how each country brought prior experiences to the training and thus learned from one another. "We have worked in internment facilities in Iraq and Afghanistan and the Slovenians have experienced a lot of refugee traffic in the past couple of years so that's something we're very familiar with and that they're very fam Although they are geographically an ocean away from one other, military police from the 220th Military Police Company, 193rd

56 https://balkaneu.com/slovenia-military-given-police-powers-at-the-borders/

Military Police Battalion, Colorado National Guard, integrated with Slovenian, Macedonian and Albanian military police, found that they had much in common while conducting synchronized training during Exercise Immediate Response 16.

"We've been able to work seamlessly and integrate in with the Slovenian Army," Capt. Christopher Breyrle, company commander for the 220th Military Police Co., 193rd MP Battalion, U.S. Army Colorado National Guard. "Our tactics and procedures are very similar."

"We were able to incorporate our lessons learned from forest fires, floods and blizzards, into how we can help build a response for the Slovenian Army," he said.

Most of the training occurred with multiple nations soldiers working side by side with one another. One training event in particular involved a simulated refugee checkpoint site set up. The Macedonian and Slovenian MP teams controlled notional refugee flow while training on how to correctly handle refugees that are attempting to pass an area and how to react if events do not go as planned.

Sgt. 1st Class Bradley Tune, 220th MPs, described how each country brought prior experiences to the training and thus learned from one another.

"We have worked in internment facilities in Iraq and Afghanistan and the Slovenians have experienced a lot of refugee traffic in the past couple of years so that's something we're very familiar with and that they're very familiar with," he said.

Ukraine Military Police

The Ukrainian Military Law and Order Service (MLOS) provides military police service to the Ukrainian Armed Forces.

A relatively new force established in May 2002 the Ukrainian Military Police number around 1,800 members. The military police also referred to as the Military Law Enforcement Service abbreviated VSP is a special military service unit outside General Staff control and subordinated directly to the Ministry of Defence.

Previous International missions include Iraq. Members of the VSP were assigned to each of the four Ukrainian contingents, while they were stationed in the province of Wasit, Iraq between 2003–2005. The MPs form three main operational branches plus a training school. These are the 93rd VSP Battalion, Kyiv, the 138th Special Purpose (Counter terrorist unit) and the 307th Disciplinary Battalion.

Historical background

The first gendarmerie-like formation that functionally resemble that of the modern day's units in France and other European countries appeared in present day Ukraine back in 17th century. In 1668 the Ukrainian Hetman (senior political and military leader) ordered the establishment of the Court Guard that consisted of Dragoon and Court Protection Companies and was responsible for the protection of peace and security. The Court Guard was authorized to apprehend those who were causing disruptions or violating law and order. The first historic mention of the National Guard was recorded in 1848 when the government of Austro-Hungarian Empire yielded to the growing pressure of revolution and agreed to create an armed law-enforcement formation in separate territories of its Empire.

During the Soviet period the National Guard was a part of the Soviet Ministry of Internal Affairs and was known under different names.

In 1991 with the Proclamation of Independence, the modern Ukrainian State needed a robust and professional military formation with policing functions capable of protecting the newly independent State against both external and internal threats. To this end the military formation with Law-enforcement functions with direct subordination to the President of Ukraine was created. On the 4th of November 1991 a bill was signed into the Law creating the National Guard of Ukraine. During early years of its existence, the National Guard was directly involved in the Transnistira conflict during the spring and summer of the 1991, helping to defend the border against the spill-over of the conflict to the territory of Ukraine.

In 1999 the Ukrainian National Guard of Ukraine was merged into the Internal troops and Armed Forces of Ukraine. The Interior troops of

Ukraine was a military formation with mostly security guard and convoy missions.

In 2014 following the annexation of Crimea and external intervention in the Eastern Ukraine, there was a pressing need to have a robust and versatile unit both with a military and law-enforcement security formation. The newly formed security formation was again known as 'National Guard of Ukraine'. It encompassed boarder, Civilian and military functions. This type of versatile formation with both military and police functions revealed itself to be the most suitable to deal with threats then facing Ukraine. The military formation with law-enforcement functions was given broader military capabilities and augmented with heavy weapons and armoured vehicles to better confront military aggression.

The National Guard of Ukraine is a military formation with law enforcement functions. It is a part of the system of Ministry of Internal Affairs of Ukraine and is designed to fulfil the tasks related to protection and safeguarding the life, rights, freedoms and legitimate interests of citizens, society and the state from criminal and other wrongful infringements, and also maintenance of public order and public security, as well as to ensure, in coordination with law enforcement agencies, the national security and protection of national borders, stopping terrorist activities and activities of illegitimate paramilitary or armed troops (groups), terrorist organizations, organized groups and criminal organizations.

The military police will be set up based on the military law enforcement units of other NATO Armed Forces. This general structure functions of the military police will include investigation into crimes committed by servicemen of the Armed Forces of Ukraine, military police will be also authorized to conduct search and surveillance activities.[57]

The Canadian Government has been committed to working with the Ukrainian Government and its security forces to strengthen their capacity and defend Ukraine's territorial integrity and its people for many years. Prior to the 2022 invasion Canada lead the Military Police Sub-committee and co-ordinated the Joint Commission's training assistance efforts to the Ukraine's military police. The principal role of the Military Police subcommittee is to coordinate the activities of participating nations

57 Marko Shevchenko, charge d'affaires, Embassy of Ukraine in Canada.

in training and develop assistance to the Ukrainian Armed Forces on matters related to military policing.[58] With the recent Russian invasion of Ukraine, it is currently impossible to say how they are being deployed in 2022 and what their role is today. An army still needs discipline and in war control and direction of traffic convoys is vital. I suspect some members will be fighting on the front lines like Infantry and there would still be a need to MPs to carry out all standard roles.

58 Marko Shevchenko, charge d'affaires, Embassy of Ukraine in Canada

THE PACIFIC

The Royal Australian Corps of Military Police

Prior to the formation of a Military Police Corps in the Australian Army, policing of soldiers and military areas was carried out by Assistant Provost Marshals (APM) along with Officers and NCOs from various units. They worked directly for the Provost Marshall (PM) and assisted them to help maintain the 'good order and military discipline' of troops.

The Provost Marshal – The Army Act of 1881 thus described his duties: 'For the prompt repression of all offences which may be committed abroad, P-Ms with assistants may from time to time be appointed by the Governor of the Colony. The PM or his assistants may at any time arrest and detain for trial persons subject to military law committing offences, and may also carry into execution any punishments to be inflicted in pursuance of a criminal matter, but shall not inflict any punishment of his or their own authority'. As the power of inflicting summary punishment is no longer vested in the PM, he must in future, on the march, or during the progress of operations when he considers it advisable to make an example by the immediate punishment of a man whom he or any of his assistants have taken in the act, or against whom some inhabitant may complain of violence, &c, apply to the nearest CO to assemble a summary court-martial to try the prisoner.

It is interesting to note that the AIF, kept the ANZAC Provost Corps, a corps d'elite. It was regarded to be an honour and a reward for good service to be selected for it'.

In an order from Brigadier General. D.A. & Q.M.G.of the Australian and New Zealand Forces details the strict requirements to become a Provost in the Australian Imperial Foce.

From inception it had been decided that only A class men would be accepted into the new Corps. Also to eliminate the perception amongst other units in the A.I.F., that men joining the new Corps were doing so to evade Active Service. Those men who had not seen service in the face of the enemy were transferred to the Desert Mounted Corps, on completion of their training. Commanded by, Major General H.G. Chauvel CB, CMG., they remained with the Desert Corps, until they had seen service in the face of the enemy, and were capable of taking their place with the ANZAC Provost Corps (APC). After the initial intake, all new recruits must have seen service in the face of the enemy. By 1917, the requirements for entry into the APC were the strictest of any unit in the A.I.F.

Anzacs during World War I initially saw Military Police, particularly British Red Caps as the 'other enemy'. The Australian MPs had a better reputation as most were veteran soldiers having seen combat some highly decorated. The Anzac Provost corps dealt with more than 26,000 Australian soldiers in England for either absence or desertion between January 1917 and December 1918. Some had been absent for so long that they had married, fathered children, and gained acceptance in the community as discharged veterans....One had even joined the local constabulary...'

Between 1916–18 the ANZAC Provost Corps served in Egypt, Palestine, France, Belgium, and the United Kingdom. 12th May 1916, 21 Officers and 589 other ranks, selected from all units of the A.I.F., were marched into barracks Abbassia. Thus, began one month of intensive training in all aspects of military police duties and soldiering. Those men who failed to meet the rigid requirement of the new Corps, were marched out, and returned to their units.

Matters improved somewhat during World War II, when the role of the provosts evolved from being primarily concerned with discipline into a combat support role that involved hazardous front-line service.[59]

The Royal Australian Corps of Military Police is a small, highly trained and professional Corps providing command support and police support to the Army and the Australian Defence Force in peace, crisis and conflict on any operation, anywhere in the world. Military Police personnel provide commanders with an essential element of command and control through the application of the four main Military Police functions of Law Enforcement – Mobility and Manoeuvre Support; Security; and Internment and Detention operations. In short, your role is encapsulated in the Royal Australian Corps of Military Police motto – 'For the Troops and With the Troops'.

The Military Police law enforcement role is a critical component of the Military Justice System whose purpose is to maintain military effectiveness and to maintain the reputation of Army. This law enforcement function is provided in both Australia and overseas. In Australia, a specific Military Police Unit, the Domestic Policing Unit (DPU) operates within Army bases and is responsible for Garrison Policing and the conduct of Minor Criminal Investigations. The Military Police support their commanders by ensuring that the military adhere to defence and civilian laws, conventions, policies, and directives.[60]

While on operations the 1st Military Police Battalion provides law enforcement and administers applicable international civilian law. The Military Police may also be tasked to assist in the establishment, enhancement or re-establishment of civilian laws and/or judicial systems.

On the battlefield the Military Police provide commanders with an essential element of mobility and manoeuvre support, conducting route reconnaissance, route signing, controlling and monitoring traffic,

---

59 The Other Enemy is a first study of Australia's Military Police. Glenn Wahlert relates this history from the origins of this history from the Provosts Marshal in the colony of New South Wales through the formation of the Anzac Provost Corps in 1916 and the end of World war II.

60 Keith Glyde, Author of Badges & Colour Patches of AMF 1915 – 1951

enforcing traffic regulations and movement priority, controlling military stragglers and the movement of the civilian population. Military Police provide support to logistic operations and provide physical and personal security. Military Police are responsible for the internment and detention of captured persons including their collection, processing and registration in accordance with international, host nation, national and command conventions and requirements.

The role of the RACMP is to support The Australian Army and the Australian Defence Force (ADF) in policing, investigating and protecting members and visitors of the Australian Army and the ADF.

RACMP is similar to the civilian police force in that they provide the full range of police duties from the provision of uniformed patrols to deter crime and enforce the law, Close Protection duties, providing 24-hour advice and assistance on policing and security matters, the investigation of offences (the more serious by the Australian Defence Force Investigative Service (ADFIS).

During war or peace enforcement operations the RACMP provide essential support of route marking and reconnaissance, signing, POW/detainee handling and security, VIP protection, processing of Displaced Persons, protection of HQ and staff, maintenance of morale and discipline (policing of troops), manning a Corrective facility, physical security and investigation of breaches to criminal/military law and other duties as required.[61]

Because the Army recruits from every part of society, the types of crime dealt with by the RACMP are the same as those handled by their civilian counterparts, although there is an important difference in that the RACMP police a smaller, far more disciplined population, aged in the main between 18 and 27 years. Similarly, re-offence is minimal because, following conviction by a court martial for a serious crime, the offender is usually expelled from the Army.

The Australian Defence Force Investigative Service (ADFIS), a section of the RACMP which specialises in the investigation of the more serious and complicated military criminal and non-criminal offences. ADFIS is the equivalent of any civil police detective department often referred

61 Major J.M. Symington, PM 2MD – MP Newsletter January 1976

to as the Criminal Investigation Department (CID). Just like the CID, ADFIS investigators usually work in plain clothes and their role is to investigate and detect the more serious crimes committed against or by Army personnel.

One of the mistakes made by people wishing to become an MP is thinking that MPs are like the civil police, and they will be driving around in a police car conducting policing on a daily or 24-hour basis. Whilst this is a part of their duty and role an MP is a soldier first. As such they still have to perform the normal soldier duties, training and activities such as Infantry Minor Tactics (IMT), weapons training, promotion and specialist courses, equipment maintenance and cleaning, fitness training, Defensive Tactics training (riot, unarmed combat, etc), and unit administration.

Being an Australian MP comes with great responsibility as they are expected to conduct themselves above reproach at all times whilst wearing the MP armband and deemed to be trusted to carry out your duties without close supervision. An MP is expected to provide advice, guidance and policing support to Commanders and soldiers at all levels at any time. It is not uncommon for a Corporal MP to advise a commander or higher Senior Officers on Military Police /Law matters.

It's not easy to become an Australian MP you must first be a current serving member of the Australian Defence Force who formally requests a transfer. You must be a current serving soldier of the Australian Army be recommended by Unit CO for employment as MP and undergo psychological and interview testing for suitability of employment as an MP. Once you have passed the MP Interview procedures you will attend the Military Police Basic Course conducted at the Military Police School for eight weeks and covers light convoy protection, Close personal protection operations, Crowd control, Installation security and support to EOD operations.

Battlefield Circulation Control such as traffic control, route reconnaissance, vehicle check points and straggler and refugee control. Training in Civil-affairs Operations includes host nation support in law-and-order operations, liaison with civil/military authorities and all aspects of POW control such as receiving, holding and evacuation. In fact, the scope and nature of the duties of members of the Corps has varied little from formation in 1916 to the present. Rear area duties included town patrols, VIP, hospital and PoW escorts and detention barrack duties. Field duties included route reconnaissance, water discipline, field security (spies, saboteurs, guarding of stores etc), PoW escorts and discipline.

A day in the life

It's late afternoon in Baghdad, peak hour traffic is at a standstill and the temperature is well into the 50s. Just visible through the smog and traffic gridlock are soldiers from Sydney-based 1 MP Bn providing intermit close protection for the Australian Head Of Mission to Iraq. Their convoy, consisting of ASLAVs from 2 Cav Regt and armoured civilian vehicles, weaves its way through the traffic congestion. Their concentration is intense – the six-lane freeway a scene of organised chaos. The role the MPs play in the security detachment is a complex one. Their tasking is wide and varied and has required highly trained soldiers with specialist expertise to deal with a range of contingencies. Before long, the MPs have the Australian Representative Office Staff back in a secure location, and begin to conduct reconnaissance for their next destination, the United Nations Headquarters Baghdad. Observing the MPs working in a high-threat environment such as Baghdad, you get a real appreciation for the amount of training they require. They are always alert and aware of their surroundings and maintain a high standard of drills through constant practice – ready to act instantly. While the MPs focus on the threat and the route ahead, they know full well their training and discipline to serve and protect is what can be counted on.

MP dog patrol team in East Timor preventing and detecting illegal crossing of the border. Photo: RAAFMWDA.

The first Army Police Dog section was formed in 1977. The purpose of this unit was to maintain a high level of security for the Army Aviation Centre in Queensland (Oakey Aviation Centre, 30 km west of Toowoomba is a high security level facility not just because of the current climate of terrorist threats but it is the home of the Armies latest and sophisticated helicopter assets); a role which remains to this day. It was known as the Base Support Squadron Police Dog Unit and boasted a posted strength of 5 dog teams. The members were all volunteers, and came from various Corps.

MWDs underwent many changes over the next decade including several name changes. Members were still recruited from all Corps and retained whatever pay level they had previously been allocated. In 1990 the unit was given a singular identity when they were incorporated into the Royal Australian Corps of Military Police (RACMP). Incorporation into the RACMP provided for all members to receive the same pay level and opened both career progression and posting opportunities. Today they are called the MP Dog Platoon, Delta Company 1 MP Battalion.

To become a Military Police Military Working Dog Handler is not an easy process, firstly you have to be accepted into the Military Police Corps a difficult and challenging process in itself. Once there you must spend at least 12 months performing general MP duties before applying for specialization as a MWD handler. There is then a rigorous selection process (there are always more applicants than positions available) where applicants are tested on their suitability to become a handler. New handlers undergo an intensive 16-week initial basic MWD course then a further 12 months of development training prior to being eligible for full operational status. Training is continuous with regular exercises and weekly sessions.

The operational duties are wide and varied primarily the role is security but due to the flexibility and professionalism of the Army Dog teams the Army hierarchy have rediscovered the reconnaissance capabilities of MWDs which have been displayed by the units' deployments to the Solomon's and East Timor. Like their civilian counterparts, MPMWDs can be used in riot control situations and are an ideal force multiplier with large crowds. In the garrison duty role, they can likewise be used to apprehend criminals with nonlethal force (42 very sharp teeth), track down offenders or search for missing persons. This flexible platoon also has an on-call Search & Rescue (SAR) response, primarily for the Army aviation assets in case of a downed /lost aircraft.

The war time role Support to ADF, incorporates responsibilities including the following: Canine early warning at a facility or in bush on patrol – similar to Vietnam era tracker dog teams, (assisting Infantry with listening posts, clearing patrols and the pursuit of fleeing enemy).

Most RAAF police are dog handlers, there is only a small amount of general patrol and investigators in the mustering. Photo: RAAFMWDA.

The Provost Service within the Royal Australian Air Force (RAAF) began in a very small way during 1930, when service police were first established for unit duties. The first Provost Marshal and Assistant Provost Marshal were appointed towards the end of 1940, but it was not until 6 April 1942 that the RAAF Service Police Unit was properly established and organised. The headquarters of the Service Police Unit was formed in Melbourne with detachments in each State and overseas.

The service was reorganised as the RAAF Provost Unit from 16 January 1961, with Sections in each State except Tasmania, and North and South Sections in Queensland, all reporting to Headquarters in Melbourne.

Commanding Officers of the Provost Detachment Units were known as Assistant Provost Marshals.

In March 1979, the Unit was renamed the RAAF Police Service. Organisational change within the Unit, however, did not become effective until 1 September 1979. At this time, the Unit relinquished control of RAAF Police Offices throughout Australia, with State offices coming under the administrative control of RAAF support units in the respective capital cities, HQ Support Command Unit in Melbourne, and Base Squadrons in both Townsville and Darwin.

On 12 February 1981, Headquarters RAAF Police was disbanded. Command Police Offices were established within the two RAAF Commands (Support Command and Operational Command) in 1981, to assume the quality control function for RAAF Police Offices under their respective Commands. At the same time the previous agency was relocated to Canberra and became known as RAAF Police Records Centre.

On 16 January 1961 the RAAF Provost Unit was formed, establishing a Headquarters in Melbourne, and Detachments in Victoria, New South Wales, South Queensland, North Queensland, Northern Territory, South Australia, and Western Australia. Specialist sections such as Special Investigations Branch, Field Security, Port Detachment, mobile patrols for traffic duty, street patrols to ensure good conduct by troops, and the Compassionate Section were formed.

On 22 November 1962 the RAAF Provost Unit provided security for His Royal Highness the Duke of Edinburgh. The duties included security guarding of the RAAF Royal transport aircraft, crowd and traffic control and security duties associated with the royal tour. Duties since that tour have included security and traffic duties, guarding of all visiting VIP and Royal aircraft, security for President Lyndon B. Johnson, President of the United States and guarding of His Royal Highness, Prince Charles and his party and all aircraft associated with that tour.

On 22 December 1967, No. 14 Security Guard Course began at 7 Stores Depot Toowoomba and graduated on the 24 April 1969. On 12 December 1969 33 Basic Service Police course graduate from RAAF Base Point Cook. Up to 1978 many courses were conducting including the Advanced Service Police Course, Investigators Course, Drug Investigation and Field Security Courses.

The RAAF Service Police were raised in March 1979 and the RAAF Provost Unit was disbanded on 1 September 1979. At the same time, control of RAAF Police Offices was handed over to the Support units at the nearest RAAF base or establishment. Headquarters RAAF Police was disbanded on 12 February 1981.

In 1994 the RAAF Police Dog Handler, RAAF Police and RAAF Police Investigator mustering were amalgamated into RAAF Police. In 1996 the RAAF Police mustering was renamed RAAF Security Police (RAAF SECPOL) which brought with it a change, with the emphasis on Force Protection (FP) rather than Law Enforcement (LE).

Since 1945 RAAF Service Police have served overseas in all theatres of war, as well as UN and peace keeping missions; including Korea, Malaysia, Thailand, Vietnam, the Sinai, Cambodia, East Timor, Afghanistan, and Iraq.

Today the SECPOL mustering comprises two main streams for employment which are Security and Law Enforcement (SLE) and Military Working Dog Handler (MWDH) streams. SECPOL personnel may be involved in physical, personnel and information security, risk management, and support to Airfield Defence operations. Military law enforcement involves the detection and investigation of offences, and the apprehension and prosecution of offenders. Additionally, SECPOL are involved in Emergency Response, which includes the capability to react to such incidents as aircraft and motor vehicle accidents, fire, natural disasters, traffic control and crowd control duties. SLE personnel conduct investigations into minor Service offences and may further specialize as Service Investigators employed in the Australian Defence Force Investigative Service (ADFIS). The operational role of SECPOL requires them to develop and maintain specialized ground defence skills and knowledge needed to perform their duties in an operational environment.

The Royal Australian Air Force has utilized dogs since the Second World War dogs were first introduced into the RAAF during 1943 when, untrained and extremely savage dogs, were placed loose inside warehouses and compounds; tied to aircraft or fixed to long lines in such a manner that they could run back and forth. Later patrol dogs were used by the RAAF Security Guards to patrol vital assets of a Base. They numbered in excess of 300, before settling to the more realistic numbers that are employed today.

Handlers have moved from part-time handlers with primary tasks elsewhere in the RAAF to the professional group that prevail today. Modern day handlers are capable of being employed in a widely changing environment to meet the needs of the modern defence force.

Today, the Royal Australian Air Force is the largest single corporate user of military working dogs in Australia. Its 195 MWD have an important role in the security of high-value RAAF assets at some 12 bases and establishments located across Australia. The RAAF currently has about 180 trained dog handlers on active duty. The next largest operator is the Australian Army. By 2010 over 2,000 dog teams have graduated from the RAAF Security and Fire School at RAAF Base Amberley. Up until recent times the MWD training school qualified both the Royal Australian Corps of Military Police (RACMP) and RAAF Security Police (SECPOL) members. Today the RACMP train their own dogs.

Traditionally the RAAF employed 'Police' dogs for the sole purpose of security. While this type of dog could track using 'wind' scent, it was generally aggressive to strangers, and predominantly used on foot patrols, alone, out of hours, on the flight line. While reasonably effective in a benign security environment, these dogs were not considered suitable for use in Ground Defence Operations. In 1996 a project team was formed to assess the capability of Military Working Dogs (MWD), in particular, working with Air Defence Guards in the Patrol and Surveillance Area (PSA), Close Approach Area (CAA) and Close Defence Area (CDA).

Military Working Dogs (MWD) are now a well-established force multiplier within the Australian Defence Force (ADF). The Royal Australian Air Force (RAAF) being well established in their use and are the recognized ADF leaders in the field of operating MWD. In 2008 the RAAF celebrated 50 years of military working dog training they have played an essential role in the security of air bases since their formal introduction in 1958. MWDs have served in Australia, Butterworth Malaysia, Singapore, and East Timor.

All of these functions form the peacetime role of the Military Working Dog Handler, with the most important of these being to "provide a protective security presence and response capability for ADF assets" under a force protection umbrella. These tasks are carried out by safeguarding ADF equipment, classified matter buildings and installations against theft, damage or destruction by sabotage, by working with a MWD as either a foot patrol or mobile patrol team.

Navy

The role of a Naval Police Coxswain varies significantly between being ashore and at sea, but all contributes to 'Policing the force in support of the mission'. Policing in the Navy involves, but is not limited to, the following duties: General duties garrison law enforcement. Identifying, investigating, and prosecuting breaches of minor disciplinary matters under the *Defence Force Discipline Act 1982*. Investigating serious, complex and sensitive matters for prosecution by the Director of Military Prosecutions.

As a member of the Military Police in the Navy there are opportunities to work in a range of environments including at the Joint Military Police Unit, Canberra where naval police can work alongside their Army and Air Force colleagues as an ADF Investigator. At Navy shore establishments providing support to Unit Commanders or posted to a ship in a key leadership position. In this maritime environment, policing can also involve anti-piracy and the seizure of illicit drugs and weapons.[62]

Military Police in the Navy have a critical role onboard Navy ship as the 'Whole Ship Coordinator'. This leadership position assists the Command Team in the efficient and effective management of the ship's routines and organisation. The Naval MP is responsible for detailing and correlating departmental and personnel activities for the entire ship. This important role enables to the ship to effectively conduct complex and concurrent activities. In Australia Military Police who serve on smaller Navy vessels, like patrol boats, are also trained and employed in navigation of the vessel and also take on the role of primary medical care health provider for the ship's company.

---

62 http://nepeannaval.org.au/Museum/Justice/Naval-Police.html

New Zealand Military Police

The New Zealand Defence Force (Te Ope Kaatua o Aotearoa), 'Line of Defence of New Zealand') consists of three services: Army, Navy, and Air Force. New Zealand's armed forces have played a part in global security efforts. In 2008, approximately 600 NZDF personnel served overseas in the South Pacific, Asia and Middle East areas, a considerable number given the small size of the force. In the New Zealand Defence Force, 'Military Police' refers to elements within the New Zealand Army only. The term 'Service Police' is used to refer to the elements that provide military police services within the Air Force and Navy.

The Corps of Royal New Zealand Military Police provide military policing within the New Zealand Army. Consisting of full-time and part-time service members, the Royal New Zealand Military Police (RNZMP) conduct Policing Operations, Investigation Operations, Custodial Operations, Security Operations and Battlefield Circulation Control domestically (within New Zealand) and when deployed overseas.

Historically the Corps of the RNZMP date from 1915. However, there are links to earlier Military Policing. The Provost Marshal Lineage as the executive representatives of the Provost Marshal of the New Zealand Army, RNZMP can claim the same ancient lineage as the UK's Royal Military Police.

New Zealand (NZ) become a colony of Britain in 1840. Policing within NZ started the same year with the arrival of six constables accompanying Lt. Governor Hobson's official landing party to form the colony of NZ. Early policing was by a colonial police force, part police and part militia. With many of its first officers having seen prior service in either Ireland or Australia, this early force resembled a military police unit. The New Zealand Armed Constabulary Act of 1867 established an organized structure for a group that operated along gendarmerie lines. The Armed

Constabulary took part in the New Zealand Land Wars against Māori opposed to colonial expansion. Still part police and part militia, this organisation can be considered as the predecessor of military policing within New Zealand.[63]

The Police Force Act of 1886 established a single centralized Police Force. At the same time, government moved the militia functions of the old Armed Constabulary to the forerunner of the New Zealand Defence Force called in 1886 the New Zealand Permanent Militia. The New Zealand Permanent Militia, and later the New Zealand Military Forces, did not have a formal military police element. However, during the Second Boer War (1899–1902) individual NZ soldiers served with the British Mounted Military Police in South Africa.

During World War I NZ Military Police served on all fronts where NZ soldiers fought as part of 1 NZEF. They were all mounted, and the MP squadron with the Mounted Rifle Brigade in the Middle East was allegedly the subject of a very favourable report from Major-General Chaytor, commander of the NZ Brigade. After the Armistice, the NZ Military Police were disbanded.

During World War II, the NZ Military Police were re-established. The first detachment of NZ Military Police sailed for the Middle East in January 1940, where they served on all fronts and in all engagements with 2NZEF. Duties mainly included Battlefield Circulation Control, Policing and Investigations. Major E.W. Hayton was awarded the DSO for outstanding Provost Duties at the Battle of El Alamein as Assistant Provost Marshal, while Major R.R.J. Jenkin was commanding the NZ Divisional Provost Company at the same battle. Major Jenkin was later promoted to Lieutenant Colonel and appointed Deputy Provost Marshal in Italy. After the war ended, the Military Police were again disbanded.

On 18 February 1949 the New Zealand Military Police were re-gazetted and re-formed on 24 March 1951. On 18 July 1952, Her Majesty the Queen granted assent for the title 'Royal', and the Corps became the Royal New Zealand Provost Corps (RNZ Pro).

In 1952, a Colonel Commandant was appointed to the Corps. The first was Colonel E.W. Hayton, DSO, ED and on his death in 1957 was

---

63 http://firedognz.weebly.com/rnzmp.html

succeeded by Lieutenant Colonel R.R.J. Jenkin, MBE until 1968. In August 1955 the first peace-time Regular Force Commissioned Officer was appointed to the Corps. This was Captain D.J. McLeod who had first seen service with the Scots Guards and later with the Special Investigation Branch (SIB) of the Royal Military Police.

Captain McLeod was appointed Head of Corps RNZ Provost at Army Headquarters and held this appointment until October 1962 when a reorganization of the Corps took place.

Royal NZ Provost personnel served with the New Zealand elements sent in support of the British response to the Malayan Emergency and in the Indonesia-Malaysia Confrontation. RNZ Pro personnel were also sent with NZ troops to the Vietnam War. On 1 October 1962, the first peace-time Provost Marshal of the New Zealand Army was appointed: Lieutenant Colonel R.H.F. Holloway, OBE, RNZA. Following this, in 1964 the first Regular Force Deputy Assistant Provost Marshal, Lieutenant Burton, was appointed.

RNZ Provost personnel were stationed with 1 RNZIR in Singapore as part of the Far East Strategic Reserve from about 1972 until 1989. They formed part of a multinational Military Police unit, along with Royal Military Police, Royal Australian Corps of Military Police and service police from the Royal New Zealand Air Force and Royal New Zealand Navy. From 1979 until the mid-1980s, RNZ Pro / RNZMP personnel provided security at the New Zealand Embassy in Moscow.

On 18 December 1981, HM Queen Elizabeth consented a title change and a new corps badge. The title was changed to the Corps of Royal New Zealand Military Police. The current role of the RNZMP is to police the force and provide police support to the mission. 'Policing the force' refers to activities focussed internally on own troops, while 'police support to the mission' refers to activities applied on a military force's objectives.

The five functional areas of RNZMP are: Policing Operations, Investigation Operations, Custodial Operations, Security Operations, Battlefield Circulation Control.

Domestically the RNZMP focus primarily on policing operations to prevent crime affecting the military community, and investigations into incidents involving military personnel or property. MP are also deployed on security tasks within NZ when required in the civilian community.

Internationally MP may form part of a multinational MP unit conducting own force policing and investigations or may be deployed as a standalone MP element within an NZDF deployed force. MP also provide Close Protection to Senior NZ military officers and government VIP within military theatres.

The preverbal recruiting sign says A NZ MP is a highly trained specialist that provides police expertise to the Defence Force community or in combat environments. Whether enforcing the law within Defence Areas in New Zealand or investigating criminal actions by insurgents as part of a deployed force, an MP is always busy.

The NZMP roles are varied, they conduct tasks such as: preventing crime in Defence Areas within New Zealand, as a bodyguard to senior military officers overseas, investigating homicides in foreign countries, providing security to high-level conferences, controlling the movement of a deployed force in an operational theatre, training foreign police forces, or more. Military Police only recruit from currently serving personnel. To be considered, a soldier must have served at least 1 year within the New Zealand Defence Force Military Police work and train with New Zealand Police, Air Force and Navy's police organisations and other countries' Military Police forces.

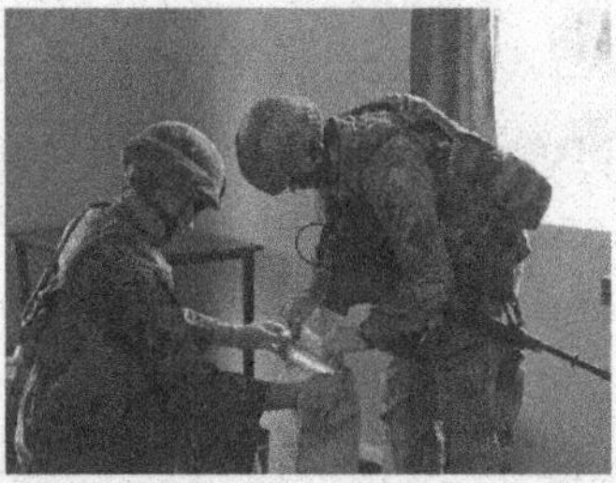

Lance Cpl. Clifford Taylor (right), military policeman with 1st New Zealand Military Police Company, from Wellington, New Zealand, and Cpl. Israel Ponce, military policeman with 1st Law Enforcement Battalion, from Long Beach, Calif., search a house for evidence during tactical site exploitation training in the initial stages of exercise Southern Katipo 2013 at Waiouru Military Camp, New Zealand, Nov. 8. SK13 strengthens military-to-military relationships and cooperation with partner nations and the New Zealand Defence Force.

Service policing within the Royal New Zealand Air Force is conducted

by RNZAF Force Protection. RNZAF Force Protection is the Royal New Zealand Air Force unit responsible for Base Security and Investigations, Ground Defence, Service Policing, Physical Fitness and Core Military Skills. Force Protection traces its lineage back to the RNZAF Police. In 1999 many areas of the Air Force underwent significant change, cost saving and disbandment. The RNZAF Police was no exception and in a controversial move this saw the amalgamation of General Service Instructors (GSI's) with the RNZAF Police. The RNZAF moved away from a sole focused policing role, and a role more suited to ground defence and base security with policing as a secondary service. A name change, in 2000 to encompass the new trade, saw it become 'Air Security Police', the new unit were deployed to East Timor in 1999/2000 and also the Solomon Islands in 2003. A further name change, in 2010 has seen the present name of 'Force Protection', this is to encompass the broad range of skills and different specialties. The unit currently operates under the 'Expeditionary Support Squadron', and has several different specialties which include Physical Training Instructors, Survival Instructors, Military Working Dog Handlers, and Force Protection Operators/Specialists (FPSPEC's). All personnel operate under the 'Force Protection' umbrella but maintain their specialty.

Force Protection is tasked with protecting RNZAF assets and its personnel, military discipline, investigations and general police and security duties. Air Transport Security Missions and VIP flights aboard Air Force aircraft are usually a regular occurrence and exercises overseas has seen many team members of Force Protection travel extensively throughout both New Zealand and the world.

Photo supplied by Alan Inkpen NZDF.

Cry Havoc was the unofficial motto of the Royal New Zealand Air Force Police Dog Sec on, displayed on all badges and plaques of the unit. The Dog Unit was first established back in 1967 when the RNZAF first purchased the P3 Orion Aircraft from the United States. Due to the sensitive nature of the electronic equipment on board these aircraft it was stipulated that additional security measures had to be put in place to prevent unauthorised access to the aircraft. Dogs were chosen primarily for their vastly superior sense of smell, sharpness of hearing and a visual ability to detect even the smallest of movements.

The dogs could work in a variety of conditions and would reduce the manpower required for this task. Thus, the RNZAF Police Dog Unit was established and is still situated adjacent to the main gate at Base Auckland, Whenuapai airfield. Dog Handlers were initially security guards or General Service Hands (GSH).

They had a name and trade change in the 1970s becoming the Royal New Zealand Air Force Police Dog Sec on a sub-unit of the Royal New Zealand Air Force Police Corps, the only Corps uniquely within the RNZAF. All candidates were qualified RNZAF Policemen in the General duties branch before becoming Dog Handlers (DH).

Candidates could also be selected from the RNZMP and Naval Regulating Branch. The Role of the Royal New Zealand Air Force Police Dog Section (RNZAFPDS) was to provide security to Air Force aircraft, sensitive facilities, VIPs, and Tri-Service Support. The Royal New Zealand Air Force maintained the only K9 Unit within the New Zealand Defence Force and as such all members were capable of working in the field alongside Army Units with dog handlers receiving regular weapons and Infantry core training. In particular close co-operation was developed between the Royal NZ Military Police (RNZMP) using RNZAF Explosive Detection Dogs (EDD) search teams and Military Working Dog (MWD) teams for Close Personnel Protection (CPP) and residential security details. Meanwhile the NZ Infantry and New Zealand Special Air Service used the dog section during Escape & Evasion training and SAS selection courses. To this end a large part of the General Police dog course was devoted to tracking in various terrains not just the type found within the confines of an Air Base.

In the 1980s there were several Specialist dog teams in the RNZAF Police, explosive detection dogs (EDD) and narcotic detection dogs (NDD).

Again, it is incorrect of some NZDF sources reporting that the Army Engineers in early 2000 had the first EDDs. In fact, the RNZAF recruited WOFF Mick Martin RAVC-British Army in the late 1970s who went about transforming the RNZAF Police dogs into much more being true Military working dogs in today's sense, able to conduct combat tracking, criminal work, and detection work. He also developed the RNZAF Police dog display team. Mick who had completed several tours of duty in Northern Ireland as a bomb dog handler, also trained and operated the first EDD in New Zealand, many years prior to the NZ Police.[64]

The RNZAF EDDs were used within the military and civilian community to search international airports, aircraft, and other Improvised Explosive Device (IED) emergencies around the Country. For operational and legal reasons all qualified/trained RNZAF Specialist detection dogs were qualified/trained a second time by the NZ Civilian Police Service.

EDD operations were firstly considered to be best used by the Corps of Engineers like in the UK and Australia. However, since the RNZAF were at the time the only animal operators within the NZDF it was decided to place them under Air Force control as they had all the animal husbandry expertise, care and management practices at the time. Today the New Zealand Army Engineers operate the explosive detection dog teams.

Narcotic specialist search dogs likewise due to their Tri-Service employment were exposed after their initial training to work aboard Naval ships, military aircraft, and all defence facilities. These handlers worked regularly with the RNZMP and Naval Regulating Branch. The NDD were mainly used in the Garrison Policing role and were an effective deterrent during random vehicle and barrack searches. NDD operations were conducted covertly (plain clothes/unmarked vehicles) usually in conjunction with Service Investigation on Branch (SIB) operations with command and control directly from the Provost Marshalls Office.

The RNZAF Police Dog School has trained since its establishment, many other Agencies, their personnel and dogs in the General duties and Specialist dog roles. These include the NZ Police, Customs, Avia on Security, Corrective Services, Civil Defence and Red Cross Society (The latter two Departments in the use of Search & Rescue dogs). The RNZAF

64 Interview Sgt Mick Martin RNZAF Dog Master 2019.

Police Dog School has also trained personnel and exported trained dogs to the Armed Forces of Singapore, Fiji, and the Sultan of Brunei.

Today RNZAF handlers and their trained dogs are ready to respond to operations both nationally and overseas, to provide force protection.

The RNZAF Police was originally developed to 'Police' the Air Force with an RNZAF Police Commissioned Officer appointed as a Provost Officer and Non-Commissioned Officers acting on behalf of them. This then provided authority for junior NCO's (Corporals) to provide jurisdiction over service people subject to the Armed Forces Disciplinary Act. RNZAF Police deployed overseas to many conflicts and war zones and were also part of the international military police team at the New Zealand Embassy in Moscow from 1979 to 1985 as well as working in Singapore from 1972 to 1989 as part of the Far East Strategic Reserve. A small contingent of RNZAF Police also deployed to the Iran/Iraq conflict in the late 1980s. They also deployed to Mogadishu, Somalia in 1993 as part of an international military police unit and to support elements of RNZAF personnel and aircraft comprising Hawker Siddeley Andover of 42 squadron and C-130 Hercules of 40 Squadron RNZAF.[65]

Service policing within the Royal New Zealand Navy is performed

by the Master-at-Arms trade. These regular force service members conduct criminal investigation services at sea and ashore, with additional duties also performed while at sea. Security of shore bases is the responsibility of New Zealand Defence Force civilian security personnel. Navy, Military Police are an essential component in the maintenance of good order and discipline, enabling Navy to achieve its mission to 'fight and win at sea'.

Military Police are considered by the Chief of Navy to be the 'Stalwarts of Navy Values', being Honour, Honesty, Courage, Loyalty, and Integrity.

Naval Military Police also contribute to Navy capability more broadly. As with many categories in the Navy, Military Police are trained and employed in a number of roles to achieve maritime capability requirements. Service policing within the Royal NZ Navy is conducted

---

65 Interview (Rtd) WOFF Colin Waite OBE RNZAF Police Flight Commander 2020.

by regular force service members who conduct criminal investigation services at sea and ashore. They also have additional duties to performed while at sea, this could be duties such as being the ships sports officer or moral officer, Customs duties, and border and regulatory work. boarding ships, damage control and whole ship activities.[66]

New Zealand Tri-Service Police for many years, especially over the forma Soviet cold war era have supplied security to overseas embassies such as in Moscow. During this period of time the USSR as it was called then were deemed unfriendly even though NZ had full diplomatic ties with them. The MPs guarded the Embassy secrets and personnel. Postings were of at least 3 months during sometimes much more. Not only was it a potentially dangerous posting, but the weather was also inhospitable and to boot any MP there during the late 1980 to early 1990s had to contend with the possibility of a weather pattern blowing dangerous and hazardous nuclear fallout from Chernobyl. Yet the New Zealand government will not issue these servicemen a medal to recognize their service there. Yet I notice in many other countries that has Embassy guards, a physical and mentally demanding job, reward their MPs for such service.

Naval police stop assault on NZ sailor

Two naval policemen were forced to draw their batons to protect themselves and an injured New Zealand sailor from a menacing gang of youths in a street in Sydney.

The professional way the coxswains acted and controlled the situation has since been praised by the RAN's Investigation Service's LCDR Phil Appleby.

At 2am on March 5 PONPC Bert Tar and LSNPC Stuart McDonald were patrolling Macleay Street, Potts Point, when they saw a serious assault in progress.

The sailors stopped their truck and gave assistance to a man who was being assaulted by four young men using a steel bar.

He was found to be a sailor from the visiting HMNZS *Te Mana*.

---

66 https://www.nzherald.co.nz/northern-advocate/news/northland-woman-carla-marsh-in-military-police-at-nz-navy/W6OAX32D2W4OGBVHK2CZTCRN2M/

In rendering assistance, the coxswains were threatened, and punches thrown at them.

In order to ensure their safety, the pair were forced to draw then extend their tactical batons.

During the incident a crowd of between 30 and 40 people gathered.

As well as calling for assistance by radio for NSW Police the sailors removed the ignition keys from the offender's vehicle.

Three police vehicles arrived, and four teenage youths and a teenage girl were held and taken to Kings Cross police station.

The injured sailor had several stitches put in his head at St Vincent's Hospital. He later returned to his ship.

First female member of the RNZAF Police

Denise Oakenfull always wanted to be a policewoman. After finishing school, she worked in the Police Records department at the Wellington police station. Back in the 1970s you couldn't join the Police until you were 21 and it was recommended to her that she should join one of the defence services to gain experience. Initially Denise joined the Royal New Zealand Navy but while on a driver's course at RNZAF Hobsonville she met her husband to be and changed services to the Air Force. In 1977 the RNZAF passed an order for equal pay and equal rights, this meant females could now re-muster to different trades that were previously closed off to them. Denise straight away applied to the RNZAF Police. Graduating from the three-month police training course in Wigram in April 1978 saw Denise become the first female member of the RNZAF Police. After five and a half years, and the birth of her second child (there were no maternity uniforms in the early 1980s), Denise hung up her uniform and returned to civilian life but her career with the Air Force wasn't finished. Denise went on to be the Instructional Techniques instructor at Ground Training in Woodbourne for six years. For the past 14 years Denise has worked for the United Nations all around the world, from Haiti to Bangladesh, Pakistan, Somalia and Darfur as a Field Security Adviser and Security Trainer. These roles she says wouldn't have come about without her Air Force experience.

MISC COUNTRIES

The Military Police: Corps *Cór Póilíní an Airm*

Irish Military Police Section, 47th Infantry Group of UNIFIL in Lebanon.

Military Police in the Irish Defence Forces are responsible for the provision of policing service personnel and providing a military police presence to forces while on exercise and deployment both domestically and Internationally. During wartime operations tasks include traffic control organisation and POW and refugee control. Like so many MP units the world over the Irish Military Police are distinguished by the wearing of a red beret.

The Military Police enjoy close working relationships with the Garda Síochána the civilian police, at both national and local levels, with the Gardaí providing training in criminal investigation to the corps.

The Republic of Ireland has consistently retained a policy of neutrality throughout her existence. Despite considerable pressure, both internally and externally, she denied Britain the use of strategic naval bases in World War Two and subsequently declined an offer to join NATO, on the basis that to do so would have conflicted with her national aspiration to sovereignty over the entire island. Until recently, Ireland was willing, if only due to geographical expediency, to rely on Britain for her international defence, restricting her own contribution to the provision of a battalion for United Nations service, but the growth in para-military forces over the past two decades has forced a fundamental reappraisal. The MPC was first established in 1922 during the Irish Civil War when they took over military police duties from British troops.

The Corps has three regular army companies and one special-purpose company: The 1st Brigade Military Police Company (Southern Brigade), 2nd Brigade Military Police Company (Northern Brigade). These two brigade companies provide general policing support to each of the army's territorial brigades. The Defence Forces Training Centre (DFTC) Military Police Company is responsible for training and recruitment into the Corps. Finally, the Military Police Government Buildings Company as it suggests provides security to selected high risk government sites and embassy security.

Irish Military police have been involved in the International MP Company of SFOR stationed in Camp Butmir near Sarajevo. The IMP Company provides military security, traffic control, accident investigation, and assists in the maintenance of good order and discipline amongst all SFOR troops in Sarajevo.

The Air Corps and Naval Service now have Military Police Sections dressed in their own distinctive uniforms. The Air Corps Military police company is a small unit that works as a base commander's asset performing their normal policing duties. They are also in control of all access and egress points, along with providing perimeter security to the Air Base and work in close conjunction with Air Corps Fire and Rescue Service and Medical Corp. Prior the Army MPs were posted to Naval and Air detachments. Military Police are armed with the Heckler & Koch service pistol and Steyr AUG assault rifle.[67]

Irish Military police International Missions have included being part of the International MP Company of SFOR stationed in Camp Butmir near Sarajevo. The IMP Company provides military security, traffic control, accident investigation, and assists in the maintenance of good order and discipline amongst all SFOR troops in Sarajevo.

---

67 http://home.mweb.co.za/re/redcap/eire.htm

South Africa

South African Military Police train for terrorist attacks during the soccer world cup.

The SA Corps of Military Police is a corps of the SA Army, but as an integral part of the Military Police Agency, it provides a service to the SA National Defence Force as a whole, but to the SA Army in particular, especially during operational or war conditions. The SA Army is responsible to win the landward battle by the use of its combat forces, but no battle can be won without the full use of its supporting corps. This is mobile warfare and the more movement there is, then the control required of the personnel, vehicles and equipment becomes even more essential.

The SACMP provides such support and is therefore a support corp. This is performed by means of its functional duties and the specialist equipment it has at its disposal. In the fast-developing modern world, more accent is placed on the mobility of forces and the element of surprise. The foot soldier and the cavalryman of the past now fight from RATEL infantry combat vehicles and OLIFANT tanks. The military policeman's horse has likewise been replaced by motorcycles and MAMBA mine-protected vehicles

Traffic control is one of the most important functions of the SACMP, under operational or war conditions. Thereafter follow policing tasks, disciplinary tasks, the management of detention barracks and the provision of general duties (escort duties of VIPs and other tasks). During peacetime circumstance, policing the SANDF increases in priority, with traffic control decreasing in priority

The tasks of the SACMP are people orientated and it is necessary for a military policeman to conform to a certain profile. It is undoubtedly often necessary for the MP to perform unpleasant tasks, such as the investigation of crime and irregularities and the apprehension of offenders. No military policeman must suffer from a prosecution mania but must always be on the lookout to prevent crime. He must keep with the facts of a case and leave the prosecution of a case to legally trained professionals. A military policeman is a special person who must have specific qualities, for which he has been selected and specially trained. The modern military policeman must have a disciplined life pattern and an irreproachable character which can act as an example to be followed – for this reason the motto of the SACMP is *Semper Solidum* – Always Steadfast.

Training and knowledge of his subject is important, but in order to perform his difficult tasks, even when under great stress and under difficult circumstances, it is important that he is part of a team. Knowledge is also born of experience and it lucky that the Second World War provided the SACMP with inter-action with other military police forces. The military policeman must be proud of his profession and of his corps

It is surprising how few people know what the role of the military policeman is. Sgt Perkins of the 198th MP Battalion, Kentucky Army National Guard, described the role of the role and functions of the South African. The functions of the South African Corps of Military include many similar to other countries Such as the maintenance of law, order and discipline and the investigation of crime within the SANDF.

But it has a particular role in traffic control which includes the following tasks: Implementation of the formation staff traffic plan. Planning of traffic control and the regulation of traffic by signing military traffic routes, traffic circuits and the position of points men. Escorting of priority convoys, VIPs, and the protection of the latter.

In regard to the control and handling of people the SAMPs Aid with the control of stragglers and aid with the control of refugees. Detention, control, safe custody, care, handling, administration of military detainees, prisoners of war and civilians' internees which is quite unique.

Taiwanese

Heavily armed and well-trained MPs are amongst other things responsible for the defence of the capital and the President.

The Republic of China Military Police was founded in 1914. When the provisional president of Republic of China, Dr. Sun Yat-sen, took the office in Guangzhou, an internal security unit was established to enforce military discipline among the troops loyal to the Republic of China Provisional Government. This unit was later renamed Military Police and would gradually expands and become present-day Republic of China Military Police. In 1925, under the supervision of then general Chiang Kai-shek, the military police were expanded from a single company to a full battalion and was attached to the Northern Expedition Forces the next year. In the next ten years, the military police gradually expanded into several regiments, and was active in purging the communist elements within the Nationalist government.

During the Second Sino-Japanese War, the Military Police troopers sometimes found themselves clashing with the Japanese despite the fact that they were neither properly trained nor equipped for such combat tasks. In the January 28 Incident, Shanghai and Battle of Nanjing in 1932 and 1937, the Military Police put up fierce resistance against the Japanese forces and suffered heavy casualties. The Military Police were also instrumental in operations behind Japanese line, and in time continued to expand under the direction of Nationalist Military. Military Police were also active in keeping the influences of the communists at bay and were successful at quelling an attempted insurrection by the communists in 1941. The last task of the Military Police in the war was to provide escort to the Japanese delegates to arrange the surrender.

Full scale civil war broke out in 1946 between the Nationalists and the Communists; however, the Military Police were not as active in combat as they once were in the war against Japan. The Military Police were tasked to protect important governmental facilities from sabotages as well as political figures from assassinations. Furthermore, several Military Police regiments were involved in suppressing civil unrests in the newly acquired territories of Taiwan. Following the defeat on mainland, the Military Police headquarters were moved to Taipei, Taiwan in 1950.

In Taiwan in 1970, under the advice from the US Military Mission to the ROC, the ROC Armed Forces reorganized all their regiments into brigades. On 16 March 1970, the Military Police Command formed up four regional commands from the original military police regiments: 201st regional command from the 101st Military Police regiment for presidential guards, 202nd from the 201st MP regiment for capital garrison, 203rd from the 202nd MP regiment in Miaoli, and 204th from the 203rd MP regiment in Tainan City. The overall system has undergone significant changes over the years.

Today the Military Police guard military and certain governmental installations (According to some reports the Military Police are no longer used to protect major military and government buildings. In Taipei some of these duties have been taken over by the Marine Corps.), enforce military law, maintain military discipline, support combat troops, and serve as supplementary police when necessary to maintain public security. The Military Police have five sub-commands and one training centre. The Military Police Command has a Department of Political Warfare and offices of Personnel, Intelligence, Police Affairs, Logistics, Planning, Comptroller, Judge Advocates, and General Affairs. The total number of MPs today is about 12,000.

In general, the Military Police are responsible for a vast array of duties, ranging from enforcing martial law and maintaining military discipline, to providing manpower support for the civilian police force and performing combat duty in times of emergency. However, the MP's most notable role lies in their ability to provide security for certain governmental facilities such as the Presidential Palace, and to carry out counterterrorism and VIP protection operations. In addition, it is also responsible for the defence of Taipei, the capital city and political and financial centre of the Republic of China.

The emblem of the Republic of China Military Police.

The design of the emblem consists of a single pink lotus on top of a plum blossom in the centre, with two curved yellow rice grains flanking the sides. On top of the lotus lies the seal of the Republic of China. The emblem as a whole is highly symbolic. The pink lotus represents MP's pure and untarnished characteristic, reflecting how a lotus flower is grown out of mud, yet is not spoiled by it. The plum blossom connotes the undying spirit and perseverance of the MP; rice grain symbolizes prosperity and peace of the country, while the national seal embodies the MP's loyalty and passion for the country. Overall, the emblem represents the ROCMP as a dignified and righteous force that will serve in the nation's need.

Israel Military Police Corps

Israeli MPs patrol border sectors and man vital entry points.

The Military Police Corps of the serves the Manpower Directorate during peace time, and the Technological and Logistics Directorate during war.

The military police are a Brigade-sized unit of about 4,500, headed by a Brigadier General. It is responsible for various law enforcement duties, including aiding IDF commanders in enforcing discipline, guarding the Military Prisons, locating deserters, investigating crimes committed by soldiers, and helping man the Israeli checkpoints in the Palestinian Territories.

The Military Police Corps is an operational force which aids in anti-terror activities as well as the in the defence of the State of Israel and its citizens. The corps works towards this end by training high-quality personnel to carry out its mission to the best of its ability. Military police officers complete their training at the Military

Police Academy located at the Instructional Base No. 13. The Corps is responsible for numerous aspects of military life, including policing, questioning soldiers suspected of criminal activity, disciplinary problems, military prison bases, traffic, and more.

The Military Police Corps is the IDF's primary operational authority responsible for enforcing law and order, preventing criminal activity, and conducting security-related checks within Israel proper with the goal of aiding continuous security operations, strengthening the IDF's moral fibre, and assisting the IDF in achieving its stated goals.

The Military Police Corps acts as the IDF's leading enforcement authority, conducts operations in cooperation with the Commands, and strengthens the moral fibres of the IDF in accordance with its operations and needs. The military police is an organization heavily reliant on creativity, personal service, and flexibility.

The corps' troops serve with a strong focus on respect, and ethics and professionalism and must behave with integrity and with comradeship, all the while setting a personal example.

The Military Police Corps was formed during the days of the Jewish Brigade. Officers and combat soldiers filled the posts of the Military Police and conducted operations involving minefield detection, control of Home-Front traffic, and prisoner interment during wartime. The unit numbered 39 soldiers and one officer.

The organizational changes in the Military Police began in the fall of 1947, when it was officially made a unit in the IDF Corps. The first commander of this corps was Lieutenant Colonel Dani Megan, who was appointed to the unit along with 160 soldiers and officers. In June 1948, Lieutenant Colonel Magen announced the establishment of a national staff, and of an academy and training camp for the unit. He also announced that every brigade and every regional district would include a military police unit commanded by an officer. During Magen's command another two military prisons constructed and dog training, traffic control and investigation units were formed. A unit to handle draft dodger cases was also formed.

During the early years of the Corps, its troops accompanied combat units, prevented draft dodgers, and oversaw the containment of prisoners and soldiers who disrupted war efforts. In May 1948, the northern military police front was established. This front contained 15 military police officers. Although at first wary of the northern front military police corps, the IDF troops realized that the corps was serving only to assist the combat units and its soldiers in a truly brave and courageous way.

During Israel's wars, the Military Police handled the following tasks: Supervision of transportation, treatment of prisoners of war, supervising disciplinary matters in combat zones, and supervising the entry and exit of personnel in areas and installations.

When a Palestinian vehicle pulled up at the Azaim Crossing point between Jerusalem and the West Bank on April 9, the day of Israel's national elections, the two Military Police officers guarding the site had a feeling something was wrong.

Sgt. Michael Sivan and Sgt. Roman Ambar approached the vehicle and saw that the male driver was behaving in a suspicious manner–he was hesitant, fearful, and acted with insecurity – they said. They diverted the driver to a lane where more in-depth security checks occur.

When they opened the trunk of the car, they discovered two M-16 automatic assault rifles, a Galilee assault rifle, and hundreds of ammunition rounds. The policemen cocked their weapons and arrested the man, passing him on to the Shin Bet for questioning.

"I always had a motivation to get drafted to this role. When these incidents occur and you understand what you did, the motivation only grows. My friend Michael and I handled this incident together throughout, cooperating with a clear objective," Sgt. Roman Ambar told JNS. The ability to quickly identify hidden threats and respond in time is a core part of Military Police training, but it is also a skill that develops over time in the field, a Military Police company commander explained.

Military Police Corps units were stationed all across the country during the War of Independence. Its soldiers were inseparable from those in combat all throughout the war. Military policemen took part in the defence of besieged Jerusalem and aiding in the transport of artillery convoys to Degania as part of the effort to ward off the Syrian assault. Following the war, the IDF built a temporary military prison in north Tel Aviv. Following its closure, the IDF founded what is today known as Prison No. 4.

From a Military Police standpoint, the IDF laid the groundwork for the Sinai Campaign by the end of 1955 when it founded the Military Police Headquarters in the Southern Command. The military policemen who took part in the operation nearly reached the front line and were exposed to units of Arab infiltrators.

The forces began marking territories with signs and combed the towns of the Gaza Strip in search of weapons out of concern they would be used against IDF soldiers. Another problem the policemen encountered during the war was the issue of jailing prisoners of war. At the time, the IDF did not set up a body that would assume responsibility for prisoners of war. Thus, the matter was passed on to the Military Police, which built camps in the north and south of the country. These jails held 5,500 prisoners of war during the course of the war. Due to the need for an additional holding facility, the IDF built Prison No. 6.

At the outbreak of the six-day war, Military Police forces began to advance to their forward positions as specified in the 'Red Sheet' order. Just as in the Kadesh Operation, the Military Police were deployed alongside combat soldiers. At every road junction of territory which the IDF advanced over, the IDF erected a Military Police station. On the Southern Front, 10 divisions of combat soldiers were integrated with 10 Military Police offices. The policemen were tasked with enforcing discipline as well as rules governing dress appearance of soldiers and reservists. Within 10 days of the war's conclusion, the Military Police placed road signs throughout the Sinai Peninsula. In addition, the Military Police oversaw the incarceration of prisoners of war and dealt with escorting convoys throughout the country.

With the dawning of the day of fast, the IDF instructed the commander of the Military Police Company, Ya'akov Danai, to distribute draft orders to his soldiers. During the Yom Kipper war, Military Police forces were responsible for transporting the bridgeheads which were used to cross the Suez Canal.

In addition, Military Police units functioned as any other infantry unit. During the war, the IDF assigned the Military Investigating Police one of the more difficult and sensitive tasks – the search for missing soldiers in the Sinai sector and the Golan Heights. Through continuous, painstaking work, the unit managed to uncover and solve many cases.

Military Police units were attached to all of the IDF's combat formations during the course of Operation Peace for Galilee. Each unit, which was deployed on a scale of a reinforced company, was an inseparable part of the active forces on the front. The Military Police dealt primarily with escorting convoys into Lebanon, directing the forces, placing directional signs on the territories, incarcerating prisoners of war, and other functions.

The Military Police corps is divided into five sectors which carry out the enforcement of IDF law.

The law enforcement sector is responsible for enforcing the discipline and proper image of the soldiers. They also operate to ensure proper driving by IDF soldiers and are responsible for catching deserters and the like. The unit also works very hard to curb the dangerous trend of hitchhiking by IDF soldiers, through filing reports against the offending soldier. The troops operate undercover in order to more effectively locate and arrest those who are AWOL and to return them to their service in the IDF where they can be rehabilitated. The unit was successful in reducing the number of deserters from the IDF by 50 percent. The unit uses advanced technological resources such as F-6 cameras, gauge lasers for immediate and accurate measurements, state of the art digital cameras, motorcycles, and motorbikes.

This Investigation unit is responsible for all criminal and traffic related investigations inside the IDF. They operate in order prevent criminal activity, thereby strengthening the ethics and morals of the IDF and the quality of life for those serving in it.

The investigation unit is responsible for enforcing the law in the IDF for the soldiers and professional military people that are suspected of various wrongdoings. The unit primarily deals with the cases involving drugs, theft, fraud, corruption, unwarranted murders, and traffic accidents involving military vehicles. The military police corps investigation unit is split into three different branches: North, South, and Central (each with their own base).

The Central Unit for Special Investigation (Yamlam) conducts high profile cases. The highly secretive and classified unit deals with drug and weapons trafficking, sexual harassment, and the like.

The Central Military Police Unit (Yamar) handles cases of a less serious nature then the Yamlam unit. Both units are commanded by an officer of Colonel ranking.

The military police corps is exclusively responsible for the IDF prison bases – Prison 4 and Prison 6 and serve as jail instructors on those bases. The purpose of the bases is to contain prisoners in a lawful manner. Before 2006, the military police corps was responsible for confinement of one thousand security prisoners who were then transferred to GSA prisons.

Sgt. Micharl Sivan (left) and Sgt. Roman Ambar, who discovered the weapons' vehicle that was trying to cross into Israel on April 9, 2019. Photo: IDF.

This division was created in 2004 to allow the military police corps to conduct security checks at checkpoints along the Green Line in a more improved manner. The division is constantly expanding and will eventually include security checks at checkpoints nationwide. These checks are conducted to confront terrorism attacks, weapons smuggling and infiltration and collaboration between terrorist organizations. The security examination system is divided into two units, Toaz and Erez. The Toaz unit operates in the Central Command, defending the state of Israel and preventing terrorist operatives from infiltrating Israeli territory in the Judea and Samaria region. The Erez battalion operates in the Southern Command and control checkpoints in the Gaza District. It also works to prevent infiltration of enemy operatives into Israel territory and to curb weapons trafficking through security checkpoints.

The intelligence system of the military police corps is responsible for gathering information, detective work, evaluation, investigation and distributing intelligence pictures to the whole corps. The intelligence system is deployed in all units of the corps and operates in a clandestine manner. The assessment NCOs evaluate the situation using intelligence gathered about deserters including their societal, economic familial pressures. During the investigation the intelligence system is used to observe and track all suspicious behaviour. The collected evidence is assessed by an NCO in order to paint a fuller picture of the situation and to be able to predict the actions of the suspect. There is also an intelligence department located in the prison bases in order to track suspicious activities amongst prisoners and to prevent the occurrence of violent uprisings.

Military Police Command Unit: one of the three regular, non-reservist law enforcement units (390, 391 and 392), headed by a major in an emergency. In the central command, this unit (391) is not subordinate to the Command Law Enforcement Unit.

The military police are responsible for security check at the crossings along the seam line.

The purpose of the crossings Brigade – Brigade 'Taoz' and a regiment of 'cedar' is to protect the State of Israel, its citizens and residents, in preventing terrorist beyond the area of Judea and Samaria and Gaza Strip West Bank while keeping the length of life of Palestinians. The ability to quickly identify and respond to hidden threats is a core part of Military Police training, but it's also a skill that develops over time in the field.

India

MPs in Indian are used in peacetime as additional police.

The corps of military police traces its origin to the days preceding World War II. In

July 1939, one Indian provost section along with one British section were formed to raise force 4 provost unit, which was part of 4 Indian infantry division. Indian section was raised out of other ranks from 7 and 11 cavalry regiments. The recorded date for raising of first Indian provost unit was 28 August 1939. The provost units similarly raised, soon proved their worth in the fast-moving campaigns of north Africa and Burma thereby prompting the government to formally sanction the formation of corps of military police (India) on 07 July 1942. It was, however, in the aftermath of World War II that the corps of military police (India) truly won their spurs.

In 1947, the 'corps of Indian military police' shed its historical British connection and was re-designated as the 'corps of military police'(CMP). This date is celebrated as the corps raising day. After independence, the corps has served with élan and proved its mettle while contributing to the maintenance of the highest standards in the Indian army. The corps of military police boasts of a regimental centre and school in the picturesque surroundings of Bangalore. While initially the manpower for provost units were drafted from other regiments, in 1963, the corps of military police started direct recruitment for the corps. The regimental centre has since then been training recruits to take on the responsibilities of military policemen, after imparting a rigorous training of 65 weeks.

Apart from basic military training, every military policeman is imparted provost, signal and driving and maintenance training before he finally passes out of the training centre to join his assigned unit. The officers in the corps of military police are posted from all arms.

After the 1971 war, the corps was closely associated with the onerous task of looking after 90,000 prisoners of war for more than a year. The military policemen have also had the honour to serve with distinction, as part of the un mission forces in various theatres, around the globe. The members of the corps of military police are the most visible faces during national functions and army events. The tall, smart, and immaculately turned-out personnel of the corps of military police are the pride of Indian army during important ceremonial events.

The first provost marshal of the Indian army was brigadier Forbes and the first commandant of corps of military police centre and school was major Dutton, MC. In recognition of the dedicated and distinguished service rendered, the president of India, presented 'colours' to the corps on 24 April 82.[68]

The role of the Corps Military Police is to assist the commanders in maintaining and preventing breaches of good order and discipline, while the functions of corps is to assist commanders in the maintenance of discipline. Execution of sentences awarded by courts martial or under army act section 80. To assist in the control of movement of men, material, and vehicles, both in peace and war. To assist in the enforcement of security precautions. Custody and handling of prisoners of war and Control and handling of stragglers and refugees in war. They are also tasked to provide pilots, outriders, and escorts for designated VIPs in both Indian and overseas. They maintain liaison with air force and naval police, aid the civil police. Finally, they carryout ceremonial functions all across the nation.

The corps has played an outstanding part in all operations against Pakistan. In 1971, in addition to the operational role with other fighting formations, in east Pakistan (now Bangladesh) the corps was given the gigantic task of guarding approximately 90,000 prisoners of war. The resources of the corps were stretched to the maximum, but it again came out with flying colours.

Outside the normal activities on 24 April 1982, corps of military police was presented colours by the then president of India Shri Neelam Sanjeeva Reddy in recognition of its dedication and distinguished services to the nation. The motorcycle display team, 'Shwet Ashwa' created a world record on 22 September 1995 and entered its name in the Guinness book of world records, when it put a pyramid of 133 persons on 11 motorcycles which traversed a distance of 350 meters, at Bangalore.

MP personnel have been part of UN mission contingents at Congo,

---

68 https://www.defencedirecteducation.com/cmp-corps-of-military-police/

Somalia, Rwanda, and Sierra Leone. Presently they are deployed at UNFIL, Lebanon and UNDOF, GOLAN heights

Regardless of their drift away from British MPs they still retain one tradition and that is of the Royal Military Police red beret. The term 'red berets' is synonymous with the personnel of the elite Corps of Military Police (CMP), since all ranks of this Corps adorn the exclusive red berets along with white belts to distinguish themselves from other Corps of Army. The role of this Corps is primarily to assist Army formations in maintaining a high standard of discipline of its troops, prevent breaches of various rules and regulations and to assist in the preservation of high moral of all ranks of the formation.

The Corps of Military Police has become the first in the Indian Army to recruit women in its rank and file. The training of the first batch of 99 Women Military Police commenced in January 2020. From basic military training to advanced provost training, the women will be trained for a span of 61 weeks at the Corps of Military Police Centre and School, Bengaluru, qualifying around early 2021.

The women soldiers will follow the same terms and conditions as their male counterparts. After training, the female military police force will perform duties akin to what the male military personnel performs. Besides being employed on mandatory operational and peacetime duties, the women's military police would be extremely beneficial for investigating gender-specific crimes. Identifiable by their red berets, white lanyards, and belts, black brassards with MP printed in red, the Corps of Military Police performs a variety of duties. From specific duties like handling Prisoners of War (POW), controlling stragglers and refugees during the war, assisting other regiments, provision of close protection to the Chief of Army Staff to general policing, investigation and maintenance of law and order, the police force is responsible for a wide range of tasks.[69]

69 https://www.theweek.in/news/india/2019/11/01/indian-army-to-have-first-woman-soldier-by-2021.html

Sri Lanka Army's Corps of Military Police

MPs have been heavily involved in the fight against Tamil Tigers over many years and are a highly trained professional element of the armed forces.

It was Napoleon who said that for an Army to function effectively there ought to be a Military Police Force which should monitor and inculcate discipline in the Army. In other words, the bedrock of an Army is the Military Police Force which is ensure the maintenance of a very high standard of efficiency. It is no exaggeration to say that if the Army could the compared to a fabric, the golden thread that runs through it is the discipline inculcated and maintained by the Military Police Force. The was precisely why the Sri Lankan Military Police Force was setup way back in 1949. The first Army commander of the Ceylon Army having realised the significance of that Napoleonic observation raised Ceylon Military Police Force with the Motto *'Example Decemuse'* ('By example shall we lead'), at the beginning there were 10 Military Policemen who comprised the nucleus of the Military Police, which was then known as number one provost company was commanded by the officer commanding Major ERP de Silva stationed at Echelon Square, Colombo.

In order to cater to the constant growth of the Army Military Police, it was gradually increased, and Provost Sections were formed in accordance with the tactical requirements in the Island under the existing command in the Sri Lanka Army. From the year 1949 to 1974 Military Police were like Nomads, shifting their headquarters to various environs until in 1975 when they established a permanent home in Narahenpita.

In 1983 the Tamil Organization called LTTE resorted to terrorism war against prevailed government. Therefore, the government had to be vigilant on North and East. In spite of that the Army had to be increased a hundred-fold and divisions were formed to eradicate tiger menace. Hence a requirement for the Sri Lanka Corps of Military Police to be increased to maintain law and order in the Army. A third Sri Lanka Corps of Military Police unit was inaugurated on 2nd of March 1991 to provide exclusive service to the then 3 Division at Pallekele, Kandy. Each of these three units had a strength of 35 Officers and 946 other ranks. Special Investigation Unit (SIU) came into existence to the July 1997. A further increase in February 2001, saw the 4th unit in order to cater to operational requirements of headquarters in Jaffna. With the intention of producing well-disciplined soldiers of a high standard Military personality, the School of Military Police (SMP) was established on 17th of February 2001 at Giritale. The military police family increased with the introduction of the 5th regiment in December 2009 at Kilinochchi.

The rapid growth in the strength of the Military Police paved the way to the opening of the Sri Lanka Corps of Military Police regimental headquarters on 18th April 1990 in order to provide better administrative services for the Officers and other ranks of this expanding regiment.

Many of Officers and other ranks have sacrificed their lives in the defence of the motherland. To remember them, a war hero monument has been declared open on 16th May 2004 at the 2nd Sri Lanka Corps of Military Police Giritale.

Sri Lanka army's Corps of Military Police which provide the Provost Service is an all-corps specialists unit whose role is to police the army in peace and war. This role is summarized as follows. Tactical police support to the army in all phases of operations. Law enforcement and crime prevention within the army in peace and war periods. Provision of provosts to military formations for the purpose of policing and maintaining high standard of discipline in the army.

The current tasks of the MPs are supervising all Military troops and routes by providing points men, conduct patrols, signage of routes, control of critical points. Secondly Prisoner of War tasks such as Administration, control and supervision of war camps Enforcement of punishments awarded to prisoners of war. Ensuring compliance with Geneva conventions. MPs also assist in the movement of the country's refugees by maintenance of records of the stragglers, recommending routes for movement of refugees.

Assist in the establishment of refugee collecting posts. Check on possible enemy infiltration through refugees. maintenance of road safety Control of access to places and events. Close protection of important or vulnerable people. Crowd control.

During wartime this also includes the enforce orders on camouflage, concealment, and night light restrictions. Interestingly, two unusual tasks that appear are: military execution when called upon, to assist in carrying out the sentence of death and the prevention of contracting venereal disease by military personnel!

Of course, in peacetime the Military Police provide many functions, during the Tsunami disaster the groups of Officers and soldiers of Provost Corps were deployed in Tsunami affected areas to look after the welfare of the Tsunami affected people.

The introduction of the Sri Lanka Army Women's Corps gave necessity to maintain the discipline of the women soldiers, and the Provost Section of MP Women was established in 1983. Since 1994 Sri Lankan Army has had the opportunity to participate on UN Missions. Since that time over 950 Military Police have been deployed to the Democratic Republic of Haiti and 150 MPs have rotated to Lebanon twice a year since 1995.[70]

The Colonel Commandant, Sri Lanka Corps of Military Police (SLCMP) Maj Gen LPR Premalal USP made his maiden official visit to 7th Sri Lanka Corps of Military Police on 18 August 2020. As at present following units and establishment come under the Sri Lanka Corps of Military Police (SLCMP) the 1st Regt SLCMP to the 7th Regt SLCMP inclusive, plus the Special Investigation Unit and School of Military Police.

Today 117 Officers and 2802 other ranks of Military Police are deployed under existing various Military Command in the country in the order to maintain law and order.

---

70 https://alt.army.lk/slcmp/

PART THREE

MILITARY POLICE AND CIVILIAN POLICE COMBINED ROLE

Some Military Police units traditionally found in old European countries such as the French Gendarmerie the Spanish Civil Guard Service, Dutch Marechaussee and the Italian Carabinieri have dual roles that of both a Civilian Police force but still retaining a military function in War as Military Police. The French National Gendarmerie is the heir to the *Maréchaussée* the oldest police force in France, dating back to the Middle Ages.

Netherlands Royal Marechaussee

Dutch MPs are a Para-military force used in both civilian and military roles.

The Royal Marechaussee serves as a police force for the Royal Netherlands Navy, the Royal Netherlands Army, and the Royal Netherlands Air Force. Consequently, Marechaussee brigades or posts are based wherever there are barracks, on or near military air bases and naval ports or with units of the Dutch armed forces serving abroad. in addition, the Marechaussee acts as a police force for all foreign armed forces stationed in the Netherlands, as well as guarding any international military headquarters.

The Dutch Royal Military Police (*Koninklijke Marechaussee* or KMar) is a police organisation with military status and wide-ranging responsibilities. These extend from protecting the country's national borders, to guarding royal palaces and the Dutch Prime Minister's residence. An elite force of specially trained and selected military personnel, the KMar acts as bodyguard for Dutch VIPs as well as a type of police SWAT team. Policing civilian airports is another of the force's vital and highly visible responsibilities and includes Schiphol International Airport, located near Amsterdam. People who like to travel in the Netherlands are often first in contact with the military police, both at airports and seaports and on trains and on the roads. The Royal Military Police are in many ways the first visible organization seen by the public in Holland. When a person begins their holiday flighting into Holland the boarding check and arrivals often begin with passport control by the military police.

Historically the establishment of the Marechaussee came about with the Decree of the Sovereign King William I of the Netherlands, dated 26 October 1814 of which the first article states:

"A Marechaussee Corps will be established to maintain law and order, to

Members of the Royal Netherlands Marechaussee serving with the European Gendarmerie Force in Afghanistan (ISAF / Police Operational Mentoring Liaison Team

ensure the due administration of the law and to guard the safety of the frontiers and highways of the Kingdom".

The word *Koninklijke* is of Saxon origin and *Marechaussee* seems to derive from an old French name given to an ancient court of justice in Paris, 1370, called the '*Tribunal of Constables and Marshals of France*'. These constables and marshals were to become members of the Gendarmerie which served as a model for the police forces of both Belgium and Holland.

In the Netherlands the term *Marechaussee* was first used in a Decree of the States of the Batavian Republic of 4 February 1803. This decree was never implemented, but in 1805 a Company of Gendarmerie was set up. Since then there have been many reorganizations, increases and reductions in strength and of changes in authority and responsibility. Despite this the mission of the Marechaussee remained by and large the same until 1918; police duties on behalf of the armed forces on one hand and service in a State Police role on the other.

French Gendarmerie

There are several European and South American Countries that traditionally use Military Police in both Civil and Military functions. Likewise, countries such as Mexico and Columbia who are fighting drug cartels and terrorism on its home sole use Military Police units to aid civil authorities on a daily basis. Whilst in Brazil MPs are the only uniformed police authority with a daily civilian function. In the case of several European Countries Military Police have evolved since their initial establishment of purely as Military units to encompass civilian law enforcement, they still however supply units to the Military in time of war.

The National Gendarmerie (*Gendarmerie nationale* is one of two national police forces in France apart from its civilian function the Gendarmerie fulfils a range of military and defence missions.

Historically the Provost, French *Prévôt*, in France, was described as an inferior royal judge under the ancient regime, who during the later Middle Ages, often served as an administrator of a region. The position appears to date from the 11th century, when the king sought a means to render justice within their realm and to subject their vassals to royal control. The provosts performed a variety of functions including taxes and fine collection. They served as military commanders for the district and sat as lower-court judges. By the 13th century they were under the control of the bailiffs, and after 1493 the provosts were paid by the crown as salaried officials.

A painting from a medieval book called the Hermit and the Provost. Miniature, fourteenth century, Paris. Photo: courtesy of Bibliotheque nationale de France, Paris.

Today the Provost Gendarmerie are the military police for overseas deployments. Whilst the functions of military police for the army on French soil are fulfilled by units of the Mobile Gendarmerie. Air Gendarmerie – military police for the French Air Force tasks include crash scene investigations involving French military aircraft under the dual subordination of the National Gendarmerie and the Air Force. The Maritime Gendarmerie operate the military police for the Navy and coast guard under the dual subordination of the National Gendarmerie and the Navy.

The (French) National Gendarmerie has a Canine unit called the National Centre for Canine Section of the gendarmerie (CNICG) it was established in December 1945 and is located in Gramat. The gendarmerie operates approximately 41 groups of dog teams totalling 645 dogs. The French Foreign Legion operates its own *Police Militaire.* The PM's role in the Legion has been clarified and codified by an instruction since June 2011. Officially called *Patrouille de la Légion étranger* (PLE) or Foreign Legion Patrol, its missions are to assist and protect servicemen serving as foreigners in their travels inside the garrison city. Enforce general discipline rules for legionnaires in uniform when they are in town off duty and participate in the protection of military installations. It's generally a temporary assignment, and if anything, more serious than a bar brawl happens, the matter will be transferred to the *gendarmerie* which will handle the case.

Italy

The *Arma dei Carabinieri* (Carabinieri Corps) polices both the military and civilian populations. The corps Carabinieri was instituted under the Royal Patents in1814 as part of the army. In 2000 its statue was changed to include all the armed forces (Army, Navy, Air Force) The Carabinieri perform all Military Police and security duties for the Ministry of Defence, within Italy and abroad. In the Second World War they fought in their function as Military Police against the allied forces and against Yugoslav Partisans. In recent years Carabinieri units have been dispatched on peacekeeping missions, including Kosovo, Afghanistan, and Iraq.

Since the middle of the nineteenth century the Carabinieri Force has been involved in numerous overseas peacekeeping operations assisting in the reconstruction of the forces of law and order. Over the past ten years mission include (United Nations Operation in San Salvador), MINUGUA (United Nations Verification Mission in Guatemala), UNTAC (United Nations Transitional Authority in Cambodia), TIPH (Temporary International Presence in Hebron), UNIFIL mission in Lebanon (United Nations Interim Force in Lebanon), ONUMOZ (United Nations Operation in Mozambique), INTERFET (International Force in Eastern Timor) and ISAF mission (International Security and Assistance Force).

NATO Missions: IFOR mission (Implementation Force), MSU (Multinational Specialized Unit), SFOR (Stabilization Force), KFOR, UNMIK mission (United Nations Mission in Kosovo).

Spain

Each branch of the Army, Navy and Air Force has its own military police (*Policia Militar*, *Policia Naval* and *Policia Aerea* respectively). They are only recognized as constabularies with jurisdiction over military installations and military personnel. They have no jurisdiction over civilians off of military installations. They are also in charge of the security of military installations, play a role as bodyguards of generals, admirals and other relevant military personnel, and provide security services to military transports and police military personnel abroad.

The Civil Guard is a military unit with similar police missions to the French Gendarmerie, the Italian Carabinieri, The Spanish police is essentially composed of three forces: the Guardia Civil, the Policia Nacional and the Policia Local. To all intents and purposes, the Guardia Civil is a conventional police force who operate in exactly the same way as the police of any other modern European country. They have the resources, powers and facilities of a normal police force and are generally admired within Spain for their high level of discipline and professionalism.

Whilst they are a military force (with military ranks) in peacetime they act under the civil authority and have no extraordinary powers.[71]

A Spanish military police officer guides Vili, an explosives detection dog, around a vehicle to practice explosives detection at Besmaya Range Complex, Iraq, Dec. 12, 2016. The Spanish military police use dogs as an additional defence against potential threats at BRC, one of four Combined Joint Task Force - Operation Inherent Resolve building partner capacity locations dedicated to training Iraqi security forces. Combined Joint Task Force-Operation Inherent Resolve is the global Coalition to defeat ISIL in Iraq and Syria. Photo by Sgt. Josephine Carlson, U.S. Army.

71 https://www.spanishsolutions.net/blog/miscellaneous/police-in-spain-the-different-types-of-spanish-police-2/

FASCINATION

During both WWI and WWII posters were produced to recruit military police, they still do today. Vehicle salesmen also got into the act advertising the virtues of cars and motorcycles used by MPs. There has always been a public fascination with police and crime, ranging from novels, TV such as *The Last Post,* which is a tale of the Royal Military Police, set in 1965 at the height of insurgency against British occupation in Aden. Movies have been produced showing off their exploits such as Jack Reacher a fictional Military Police character. Even science fiction has both direct and indirect versions of the military police. The Jedi Knight of Star Wars fame is called a galactic peacekeeper overseeing military forces the storm troopers themselves military police clones. MPs even appear as children's toys. When I was a boy, you could get Action Man as a Royal MP Red Cap (16" toy), today they have been upgraded to collectable figurines.

EXCELLENT PROMOTION PROSPECTS FOR
SMART MEN
21-45
HEIGHT - 5'7
Corps of
MILITARY POLICE
Civilians should apply at any Army Recruiting Centre Now
Soldiers should apply through their C.O.

MILITARY POLICE
US ARMY
19
CLASSIC CAR
57
MILITARY POLICE
FOR LAW ENFORCEMENT
AND
EMERGENCY USE
REGISTERED TRADEMARK

MP
MILITARY POLICE

MILITARY POLICE
MP

1ST
NCO Royal Military Police 1999
PA

ACTION
MAN
ROYAL
MILITARY
POLICEMAN

MILITARY MINIATURES
1/35 SCALE BRITISH BSA M20 MOTORCYCLE w/MILITARY POLICE SET
TAMIYA
イギリス軍用オートバイ
BSA M20 MPセット
Pont l'Eveque

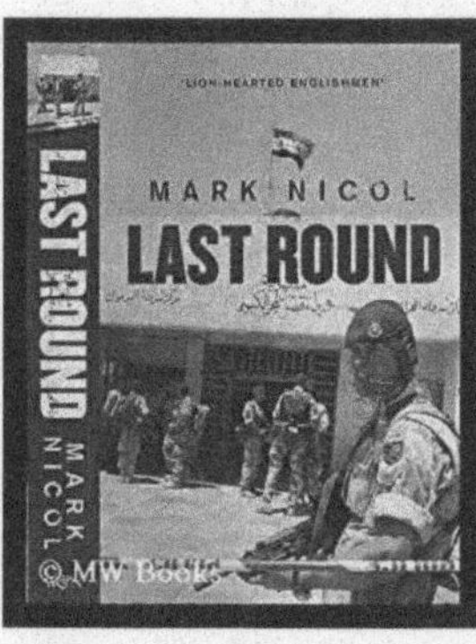
'LION-HEARTED ENGLISHMEN'
MARK NICOL
LAST ROUND
LAST ROUND
MARK NICOL
© MW Books

THE BERET BRASSARD AND BADGES

Military police in many countries can be identified by their Red Beret. It is said that the familiar red cap was designed by the wife of a Provost Marshal serving with the unit during the Egyptian campaign in 1882. Another theory was that it was descended from a red scarf tied around the right shoulder used during the Napoleonic Campaigns to identify one another.

The earliest U.S. Army Military Police Brassard was comprised of the outline of the initials 'MP' in white on a blue denim brassard. Although I can find no information to confirm exactly when this particular style of MP Brassard was adopted, it was likely sometime between 1907 and 1912. Sometime between 1914 and 1916, the Army adopted a slightly different style of MP Brassard.

The new brassard was made from blue wool and featured the initials 'MP' in solid white. The earliest mention of the white on blue MP Brassard turned up in 1914 edition of the field service regulations that had been corrected in 1916:

Officers and enlisted men, when actually performing the duty of military police, will wear a blue brassard on the left arm, halfway between the elbow and shoulder, bearing the letters 'MP' in white.[72]

The white on blue brassard was the primary style of MP Brassard worn in the U.S. during the Great War. It was also worn alongside the red on black British style MP Brassard in France. Note the drastic difference in the appearance of the two brassards in the period photographs. The brassard on the left is believed to be French made, while the right-hand brassard, as well as the one shown in the inset, are both thought to be of the 'regulation' style.

USMC MP Brassards

It's not entirely clear what colour MP Brassards were worn in the Marine Corps during WW I. At top is a black on red brassard that is attributed to a Marine from the V Marine Brigade. The centre brassard, also black on red, is a printed French made MP Brassard. It's possible that this type of black on red MP Brassard was made specifically for the USMC to wear in France. The bottom brassard was listed on a militaria vendor's website as being a WW I Marine MP Brassard. I have no evidence proving whether it is of WW I vintage or if it is not. However, brassards similar to this were worn post WW I by the USMC. The photo on the right shows a V Marine Regiment MP wearing the red on black British style MP Brassard. Note that this MP has pinned '13 M' for the 13th Marine Regiment, using French made brass letters and numbers on the front of his campaign hat.

Traditionally the colour of the Military Police has been red. This is usually via a red beret being worn by numerous of the world's MPs from the United Kingdom to Russia.

---

72 Army Field Service Regulations U.S. Army, 1914, corrected to December 20, 1916, page 164

The RMP were known as the 'Redcaps' which denoted the red 'slip on' hat cover which RMP qualified personnel wore over the issue khaki peak cap that all personnel of the British Army are issued. Supposedly the 'red' colour was chosen by the wife of the Provost Major in 1885 and another suggestion cites an Indian Military Police unit which had worn a red turban during the Indian Mutiny. Many Air Force and Naval military police units however retain their universal beret colour of Blue and Dark blue respectively.

COVID-19

Coronavirus disease (COVID-19) has influenced almost every sphere of our everyday life, starting from individual protection, through considerable modification of the extent and way of tasks execution, including

Plans are in place for the extensive domestic deployment of British soldiers, military police are reportedly 'stepping up' their training for public order roles, which will include 'guarding' hospitals and supermarkets. Thirty-eight military liaison officers will coordinate with local councils over the deployment and use of military forces while the Royal Military Police will work with local police forces and prison officers.

The US federal government has been slow to confront the COVID-19 pandemic, but the US military will assume a much larger role as the virus and its impact spreads. The National Guard will likely contribute tens of thousands of troops to the response, but specialty units from active duty and reserve military police units will also play a role. The vast majority of the approximately 440,000 National Guard troops across the country hold a full-time civilian job while also serving part-time as members of the National Guard.[73]

---

73 The United States National Guard is a reserve military force that augments an active-duty force of approximately 1.3 million personnel. The National Guard is composed

Soldier with the 289th Military Police Company, 4th Battalion, 3rd U.S. Infantry Regiment (The Old Guard), scans a Common Access Card, on Joint Base Myer-Henderson Hall, Va., April 9, 2020. Photo by Sgt. Nicholas T. Holmes courtesy U.S. Army.

In the United States during major natural or man-made disasters Presidents have turned to the National Guard to booster resources during civil unrest and during recent Covid-virus emergencies President Trump has called on the military to back up the police. What better units than the Military Police of the National Guard. Trained soldiers but with the advantage of specialist training in law enforcement, many of the MPs in the National Guard work in the civilian law enforcement area. When George Floyd died at the hands of a white police officer, the Pentagon called out the Military Police from Minneapolis.[74]

The US National Guard MPs have been used in high profile occasions patrolling for looters in recent hurricane disaster sites. Operation Garden Plot is a general US Army and National Guard plan to respond to major domestic Civil disturbances within the USA. It provides Federal military and law enforcement assistance to local governments during times of major civil disturbances.75 Garden Plot was last activated to provide military assistance following the September 11th attacks on the United States.

The Pentagon also activated it to restore order during the 1992 LA Riots and again in 2020 Black Lives Matter protests.

On December 10, 2008, the Californian Highway Patrol announced its officers, along with San Bernardino County Sheriffs Dept deputies and

---

of reservists and airmen assigned in each state and all four US territories, for a total of 54 separate organizations.

74 73CBS News May 30 2020

75 The US Military are limited to the Posse Comitatus Act a US Federal law that was passed in 1878, its intent was to limit the powers of local governments and law enforcement agencies from using federal military personnel to enforce the laws of the land. Contrary to popular belief, the Act does not prohibit members of the Army from exercising powers that maintain 'Law and Order', it simply requires that any orders to do so must originate with the United States Constitution or Act of Congress.

US Marine Corps Military Police, would jointly staff some sobriety and driver's license checkpoints. However, the Marines at the checkpoints are not arresting individuals or enforcing any laws, which would be a violation of the Posse Comitatus Act. A spokesperson said that the Marines were present to observe the checkpoint to learn how to conduct checkpoints on base, to help combat the problem of Marines driving under the influence. The Marines at a recent checkpoint learned techniques to conduct sobriety checkpoints and field sobriety tests.

On March 10, 2009, active-duty Army military police troops from Fort Rucker were deployed to Alabama in response to a murder spree. Samson officials confirmed that the soldiers assisted in traffic control and securing the crime scene.

The statute only addresses the US Army and the US Air Force. It does not refer to, and thus does not implicitly apply to nor restrict units of the National Guard under federal authority from acting in a law enforcement capacity within the United States. Under Homeland Security restructuring, it has been suggested that security missions should be provided by the National Guard Bureau based on the long-standing Garden Plot model in which National Guard MP units are trained and equipped to support civil authorities in crowd control and civil disturbance missions.

Army Reserve Military Police in fact are much sort after during conflicts, such are the skills necessary to become an MP it takes many months of training compared to an Infantryman. Therefore, reserve MP units and individuals within them are seen frequently deployed in current conflicts and NATO operations. This achieved as many MP Reserve formation possess a large percentage of Civilian Police Officers in their ranks whose skills are already present.

It's not just the army that have been called upon to assist during Covid-19, the USAF has a long history of supporting local police. Often due the isolation of many Air Bases, they are the only backup to local law enforcement officers.

The 10th Security Forces Squadron here shares jurisdiction of the U.S. Air Force Academy with the El Paso County Sheriff's Office, they also have an agreement with the Colorado State Patrol to provide assistance to incidents within the region. The squadron has an agreement with the Colorado Springs Police Department to provide military working dog support, and assist in large-scale events within the city, including the airport.

This ongoing partnership with local law enforcement agencies is one of the many ways the men and women of the 10th Security Forces Squadron team-up with their civilian counterparts to serve and protect their community, said 10th SFS commander Maj. Jose Lebron.

This squadron has a long history of partnership with the El Paso County Sheriff's Office, the Colorado Springs Police Department, and numerous other federal law enforcement agencies, including the Joint Terrorism Task Force.

CONCLUSION

Even when writing this book with the prior knowledge I had about the functions and roles of the Military Police, I was still amazed when it's all put out there, of what a truly elite force they are. I do not mean SAS status type when I use the word elite, but more its unique ability for adaption under adverse conditions, its high standards of physical and psychological endurance of its manpower. And above all the high quality of each member.

I believe future commanders must look at the Military Police function as an ideal format for the development of troops that will be deployed on peacekeeper or peace enforcement missions. They also have a vital role in domestic operations from anti-looting during civil unrest to anti-poaching tasks in the protection of wildlife.

Like the proverb a wolf in sheep's clothing, so too can this be related to the MP-Peacekeeper, protector, lawman-yet combat soldier. With all the attributes of all three.

They have had their unfair share of negativity towards them, usually from disgruntled servicemen who have broken the law or civilians ignorant of what they do. The movies usually portray them too as heavy-handed unsympathetic thugs, clearing bar of drunken soldiers 'just drunk having a friendly fight'.

There has been some criticism that MPs get a 'stripe' rank quite quickly. If you stand back and see the length and intensity of their training that is not so. One must also remember their role and functions they preform would normally require a junior none commissioned officer or higher in any other unit. The qualities of an MP of quick reaction, thinking on your feet, solving problems outside the box are those same requirements that Special Forces look for. There is no nice way of saying it to the Infantry, but as an ex-grunt myself I can do so. MPs have to be academically smarter than the norm. They frequently are relied upon by high-ranking officers for evaluations and opinions in areas such as a VIPs personnel safety or the best direction and route to undertake from point A to B. No other young soldier of a JNCO rank have such enormous responsibilities.

If I had to go to war again, I would be honoured to be in the company of these brave men and women of the Military Police Corps.

One common trend I have noticed during research of this book is MPs have become in recent times the first choice of many operations that require a professional force that can be trusted to act in a way that does not embarrass an administration. Namely they can act as soldiers with a policeman's ethics and code of conduct. In the Close Protection (CP) role (defined as the preventative and reactive measures taken by trained personnel to protect a person who is specifically or generally at threat from assassination, kidnapping, terrorism, or other illegal acts) it is the military police who have proven to be the world's best and most trusted bodyguards.

Perhaps it's their high level of training and professionalism or reputation that military police can be trusted by virtue of their creed.

People whom they face understand – maybe it's the term police in their name. That regardless of the guns, this force will do the right thing. They can impose justice with a sledgehammer but will ensure they are fair and even impartial when doing so.

With the recent surge in ex-soldiers training and directly participating in anti-poaching duties, many governments are now asking them to leave and, in some cases, throwing them out or cancelling contracts due to their heavy-handed and, in such cases, lethal prosecution of justice.

Soldiers after all are trained to kill, policeman only do so to protect themselves and others including felons they hunt. This attitude makes the military police soldier the ideal implement to train and supervise anti-poaching activities. They will bring the offenders to justice, which in turn enables investigations to seek the criminals up the chain of command. We must remember it's not the peasant poacher that received a few dollars for a Rhino horn that will stop poaching it's the syndicate that makes tens of thousands of dollars that are the criminals you want. Embedded MPs will not only train rangers like normal soldiers can, but they can educate, gather intelligence, and to help investigate who the real offenders are.

United Nations Peace keeping missions often require soldiers to remain impartial and not return fire. A discipline a trained law enforcement (peace officer) is best suited. I see a future where if countries who are increasingly involved in UN missions, may train Battalions of MPs, or convert and train existing units to carry out an MP role.

Finally, during these uncertain Covid-19 times military police are the ideal force to back up civilian law enforcement if required.

Military Police may have had a stop start history in regard to early establishment retainment and disbandment, but they are today an indispensable part of any military, no army can go to war without them.

BIBLIOGRAPHY

Military Police Operations, U.S. Department of the Army, U.S. Department of Defense, 291 pages 2014.

R. Bate, MP Australian Military Police, The First In South Vietnam May 1965, 2007. Robert E. Witter, *Chain Dogs: The German Army Military Police of World War II*

Pictorial Histories Publishing Co, 2015.

Gordon Williamson, *Kettenhund! The German Military Police in the Second World War*, font hill media, 2014

Chris Armold, Sky-Cops and Peacekeepers: Uniforms, Equipment and a History of the USAF Air Police and Security Police, 2000, Gallery Books.

Richard Keightley, *Deter suppress extract, Royal Military Police Close Protection the Authorised History*. Helion and Company, UK, 2014.

Military Police: Official Field Manual 3-39 Military Police Operations, CreateSpace Independent Publishing Platform, 2014.

Jack Turnbull & John Hamblett, *The Pegasus Patrol. The History of the 1st Airborne Division Provost Company Corps of Military Police 1942–1945*, Tommies Guides, 2009.

Wahlert, Glen, The Other Enemy, Australian Soldiers and the Military Police, 1999, 208 pages.

Military Police Operations, U.S. Department of the Army, U.S. Department of Defense, 291 pages 2014.

Jack Turnbull & John Hamblett, *The Pegasus Patrol, The History of the 1st Airborne Division Provost Company Corps of Military Police 1942–1945*, Tommies Guides, 2009.

Raymond Lamont-Brown, Kempeitai: Japan's Dreaded Military Police, 1998, Sutton Publishing; Illustrated edition

Maj. S. F. Crozier, *History of the corps of royal military police,* Naval and Military Press, 2014.

G. D. Sheffield, *The Redcaps: A History of the Royal Military Police and its Antecedents from the Middle Ages to the Gulf War*, Brassey's; 1st Edition, 1994.

Brian F. Samways, *By Example We Lead: Memories of a Military Policeman 1958 – 1980,* Forces & Corporate Publishing Ltd, 2014.

- Your brassard won't stop bullets.
- If it's stupid but works, it isn't stupid.
- Don't look conspicuous – it antagonizes officers.
- When in doubt, empty your shotgun.
- Never share a patrol car with anyone braver than you.
- Not wearing body armour attracts bullets and knives.
- 'Bullet proof' vests aren't.
- If your response goes well, you're at the wrong barracks.
- Your Patrol Supervisor will show up when you're doing something really stupid.
- The time it takes to respond to an emergency is inversely proportional to the importance of the call.
- The warrant you don't read is the one you'll serve at the wrong quarters.
- No matter how you write it, the Duty Room NCO will want it changed.
- If you charge in all alone, you'll be shot by your own officers.
- The diversion you're ignoring is the actual crime.
- The important things are always simple.
- The simple things are always hard.

  17. The easy ways are always blocked.
- The short cuts are always under construction by the base engineers.
- Anything you do can get you in trouble – including doing nothing.
- When you've secured a crime scene, don't forget to tell the officers.
- Using the siren and light to clear traffic – only attracts traffic.
- It only becomes a riot right after you show up.
- If you take out the newest patrol car, you'll have an accident.
- No streetwise unit ever passed inspection.
- No inspection-ready unit ever makes it on the streets.
- The thing you really need, will be left back at the MP Station.
- Radios will fail as soon as you desperately need back-up.
- Torch batteries always die, just when you really need light.

- Military working dogs attack anything that moves – including you.
- The helicopter will always be low on fuel, as soon as you need it.
- You'll find the suspect you want, when you're off-duty and unarmed.
- If you respond to more than your fair share of calls, you'll have more than your fair share of calls to respond to.
- The suspect will escape, just before you set up a good perimeter.
- The weight of the dead body you'll have to carry is proportional to the number of stairs you'll have to climb.
- Your weapon was made by the lowest bidder.
- You won't get called to a court martial – unless it's your day off.
- Empty guns – aren't.
- The alley you sprint down, is the wrong alley.
- Suspects always hide in the last place you look.
- There's no second place in a gunfight.
- Professional criminals are predictable, but the world is full of amateurs.
- Don't stand, if you can sit – don't sit, if you can lay down – if you can lay down, you might as well take a nap.
- The speed at which you respond to a fight call is inversely proportional to how long you have been an MP.
- High speed chases will always proceed from an area of light traffic to an area of extremely heavy traffic.
- If you have 'cleared' the rooms and met no resistance, you and your partner have probably kicked in the door of the wrong house.
- Domestic arguments will always migrate from an area of relatively few available weapons (living room) to an area with many available weapons (kitchen).
- Whatever you are about to do, if there is a good chance it will get you killed, you probably shouldn't do it.

What the report SAID	What the report MEANT
While on routine patrol…	I was in the car because the coffee shop was closed…
The motorist was operating his vehicle in a reckless manner.	I didn't like the car he was in, and he had a bumper sticker that said "Slow Down – Don't Feed the Pigs"…
The accident scene and the safety of the victims prevented this officer from doing traffic control.	It was raining and it was cold…
This officer went out-of-service to obtain intelligence information from a street informant.	It was too hot to ride in the car…
I observed the suspect acting in a suspicious manner…	The dirt bag looked at me when I passed by…
Knowing the suspect had a criminal history…	I arrested him once for public intoxication…
The informant is of known credibility and has provided reliable information in the past…	I've got two theft cases hanging over his head…
While being arrested, this subject resisted, being injured in the act…	He ripped my shirt and broke my new mirrored sunglasses…
The motorist was cited for multiple traffic violations…	I wrote one citation for each cuss word he used…
Upon announcing my title and purpose, I heard a voice from inside the house say "Come in" so this writer entered through the door…	The rock music was so loud they wouldn't have heard Patton's army, so I kicked in the door.
The members of the press at the scene were offered every courtesy within departmental policies…	I sent them to a non-existent address which I called the 'Command Post.'
I gave the motorist a verbal warning for speeding…	She was a good-looking blonde who owned a liquor store and who was free after my shift was over.
The Inspector appeared at the scene and took command…	I sent him to the same address as the reporters.

Further interview of the witness was impossible, due to conditions.	It was my bowling night...
The motorist eyes were bloodshot, he had slurred speech, was unsteady on his feet, and smelled strongly of an alcoholic beverage.	He was howling at the moon and trying to drive the car from the back seat, and had a loaded gun in his possession...
Using only enough force to restrain the subject...	I tried my hardest to break this a**hole's neck...
The defendant asked this officer's advice on how to act before the judge at his arraignment...	I told him he didn't have the balls to call the judge the same name he called me...

The Author

Nigel Allsopp has over 20 years of writing experience including an International best seller produced in English and Japanese. Three of his books have had multiple reprints due to demand. The book: *A centenary of war animals* is used as a reference at Museums and Military colleges. His book *K9COPS* has been used as a basis for TV documentaries. He has been published in numerous Law Enforcement journals throughout the world is a much sought-after speaker.

An operational Law Enforcement Officer with a career spanning 30 years, including Policing operations with the United Nations as Military Police Commander Mogadishu Somalia, Embassy Guard Commander in the former USSR. Service with both Military and Civilian Police departments in two countries. Most recently 18 years in the Queensland Police Service as General patrol officer, VIP Protection detail, and the last 10 years in the Bomb Squad as an explosive detection dog handler. Where he commanded multi-jurisdictional high-risk search teams for both G20 Summit and Commonwealth Games. He has a master's degree and currently teaches law to recruits at the Queensland Police Academy. A veteran soldier and Law Enforcement Officer writing on a subject he knows well.

Abbreviations

Provost	Military Police
PM	Provost Marshal
MP	Military Police
SP	Service Police
SF	Security Forces
RP	Regimental Police
ADJ	Adjutant
Cpl	Corporal – Rank
Sgt	Sergeant – Rank
CO	Commanding Officer
EDD	Explosive Detection Dog
NDD	Narcotic Detection Dog
MWD	Military Working Dog
PO	Petty Officer – Navy Rank
Bn	Battalion
Regt	Regiment
Abn	Airborne

First published in 2022 by New Holland Publishers
Sydney

Level 1, 178 Fox Valley Road, Wahroonga, NSW 2076, Australia

newhollandpublishers.com

A record of this book is held at the National Library of Australia.

ISBN 9781760795078

Managing Director: Fiona Schultz
Designer: Andrew Davies
Production Director: Arlene Gippert
Printed in Australia by IVE Group

10 9 8 7 6 5 4 3 2 1

Keep up with New Holland Publishers:

NewHollandPublishers

@newhollandpublishers